Literary TOUR OF IRELAND

Formerly editor of Bord Fáilte's internationally acclaimed *Ireland of the Welcomes*, Elizabeth Healy is an expert on Ireland with a deep love of her subject. She has toured in many parts of the world including the United States, Europe, the Middle East and through the Himalayas, developing along the way a strong instinct for the traveller's needs. Originally from Cork, she now lives in Monkstown, Co. Dublin, and works as a freelance journalist.

*Photograph: Enigmatic symbols at Lough Crew
(see page 188)*

Literary TOUR OF IRELAND

ELIZABETH HEALY

WOLFHOUND PRESS

First paperback edition published 2001

First published 1995 by
WOLFHOUND PRESS Ltd
68 Mountjoy Square
Dublin 1

The author and publsihers have made every reasonable effort to contact the
copyright holders of material reprodcued in this book. If any involuntary
infringement of copyright has occurred, sincere apologies are offered and the
owners of such copyright are requested to contact the publishers.

British Library Cataloguing-in-Publication Data
A catalogue record for this book is available from the British Library

ISBN 0 86327 446 3 hardback
ISBN 0 86327 731 4 paperback

Cover design: Terry Foley
Cover photgraphs: Bord Fáilte, Jan de Fouw
Typesetting and layout: Wolfhound Press, based on a design by Jan de Fouw
Maps: Eilis Ryan
Printed in Spain by Graphycems

CONTENTS

INTRODUCTION

Working on this book has given me the opportunity — call it excuse — to do what I most enjoy, which is travelling around the country exploring its odd corners. Such explorations are always a joy. This time it has been doubly enriching. Reading the works and lives of the writers has sent me to new places and given an extra layer of significance to those already familiar. Exploring the places has sent me back to the books, the contents of which have by the same process acquired a more intimate resonance.

The age-old Irish preoccupation with the sense of place gave rise to a whole genre of Gaelic literature, the Dinnsheanchas, devoted exclusively to place-lore. That sense has permeated Irish and Anglo-Irish literature down to the present day. It is interesting to see that, even in these days of an oyster-sized world, that consciousness is still evident in the torrents of new writing emanating over the last couple of decades.

Yeats, in his introduction to Lady Gregory's collection of hero-tales *Cúchulainn of Muirthemne*, wrote 'When I was a child I had only to climb the hill behind the house to see long, blue, ragged hills flowing along the southern horizon. What beauty was lost to me, what depth of emotion is still perhaps lacking in me, because nobody told me ... that Cruachan of the Enchantments lay behind those long, blue, ragged hills.' And he stated his purpose of writing in such a way as to 'make every lake or mountain a man can see from his own door an excitement in his imagination.'

It is hoped that this guide will help to capture some of that sense of excitement and even wonder. It is intended as a practical travel guide to some of the places with which poets and novelists have been associated, and some which have given rise to legends. It is planned as a series of tours; each one touches on at least one other at some point, to give flexibility.

It is a personal tour, rather than a definitive one, and few writers born after the mid-forties are included. They await another book, by another pen. On the other hand, some poets of purely local recognition are included. After all, it was Paddy Flynn, a 'little bright-eyed man who lived in a leaky one-room cabin' that inspired the young Yeats with his stories. Could we have a Yeats if we had no Paddy Flynns?

The routes can be followed comfortably from the series of four Ordnance Survey Quarter Inch holiday maps of Ireland which are currently available — except for the final chapter, exploring Anna Livia, which needs the Half Inch sheet no. 16. Detailed directions occur in the text only where a particular item is difficult to locate.

Acknowledgements

I would like to thank Mary O'Sullivan, who helped find reference material and wrote some of the entries; Kathleen Kelleher, who also plied me with books and, bless her, walked the entire Dublin Section to check it out; Shona Kendrick, who with great good-will drove me around various locations in County Down. Joris Minne of the Northern Ireland Tourist Board was generous in his support and assistance, as were James Larkin and Donal Guilfoyle of Bord Fáilte, The Irish Tourist Board, the staff of its Photographic Section, and Dr Peter Harbison and Letitia Pollard of its journal *Ireland of the Welcomes*. Christopher Moriarty and Gerard O'Flaherty guided my footsteps through the hither-and-thitherings of Anna Livia Plurabelle. Aoife Kerrigan offered some useful advice with regard to the Northern poets. Dr Maurice Harmon with great kindness took time to read the manuscript and offer most useful comments and suggestions. Lastly, of course, the publisher Seamus Cashman of Wolfhound Press, who started me on this course; Frances Power, who assisted with picture research, and, by no means least, Jan de Fouw, who not only designed the book but provided many of the illustrations.

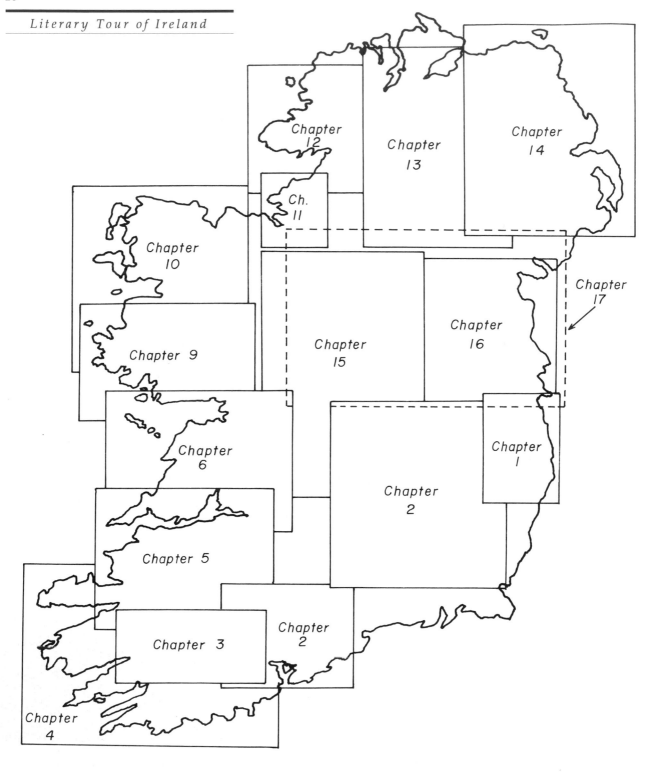

1. WICKLOW

Hills and Glens, and Counting Queens

Stand in Dublin city, near Merrion Square or St Stephen's Green, and look southwards. Seeming to rise from the city's streets, the hills rise in green-blue waves to a flowing horizon. Roads up and over these hills lead to a different world from that in which you stand; they lead into the fastnesses of the **Wicklow** mountains, 400 square miles of sprawling upland and deep softly-folding valleys, furred with woods and threaded with streams and cascades. Above all into a deep silence, not the silence of desolation, but the bird-speckled, water-sprinkled, wind-stirred silence of peace.

These were the roads that drew John Millington Synge into the heart of the moorland he loved.

You could follow him along one of those snaking upwards roads from Rathfarnham, the **Military Road** (built to help the military penetrate the strongholds of the O'Tooles and O'Byrnes after the Rising of 1798) and across **Featherbed** Mountain, passing the gaunt granite bulk of **Glencree** Reformatory. This was originally a barracks associated with the Military Road, before it was given over to 'reforming' recalcitrant youths through the disciplines of thinning cabbage plants in the snow or digging ditches, and still later was used as a Reconciliation Centre. Here the twin Loughs Bray are cradled in a dark and awesome coombe high over the Glencree valley, and you can stop for your picnic behind the isolated cottage where Synge often stayed on his wanderings. Follow the little track behind the cottage to the lake edge: it is a place of powerful atmosphere and great beauty, though the sun does not linger there for long. The second lake is enfolded away at a higher point. To see it one must either follow a rough track through the heather to the western ridge, or follow the road. Up now, higher still and higher, until you are looking down at both lakes, darkly brooding, and the long sweep of wooded valley framed at the end, as if deliberately designed by some great architect, by the cone of the **Sugarloaf Mountain**. A little further on a small heap of boulders on each side of the road marks a place of rare significance. It is **Liffey Head Bridge**, birthplace of the volatile, ever-changing She, the River Liffey, James Joyce's Anna Livia Plurabelle.

John Millington Synge (1871-1909)

Still south I went and west and south again,
Through Wicklow from the morning till the
    night,
And far from cities, and the sites of men,
Lived with the sunshine and the moon's
    delight.

I knew the stars, the flowers, and the birds,
The grey and wintry sides of many glens,
And did but half remember human words,
In converse with the mountains, moors, and
    fens.   ('Prelude')

Cottage at Glencree. Synge often stayed here when it was 'Mrs McGuirk's Tea House'

Seven dog-days we let pass
Naming Queens in Glenmacnass ...
Etain, Helen, Maeve, and Fand,
Golden Deirdre's tender hand ...
Yet these are rotten, so you're the Queen
Of all are living, or have been.

('Queens' by J.M. Synge)

LAURENCE STERNE

Annamoe Village, according to local folk-history, is the place where Laurence Sterne almost lost his life by falling into a mill-race. It was about the only way he made his mark in Ireland: he spent only his earliest years here, with his father who was an officer in the British Army. Sterne's most famous book, the extravaganza *Tristram Shandy*, was violently condemned as immoral and unliterary by critics such as Samuel Johnson and even Goldsmith!

These roads, and the ones beyond, are where Synge loved to roam. His solitary rambling induced in him, in his own words, 'a passionate and receptive mood like that of early man'. The most familiar image is of him in rough tweeds sitting amid the bracken with his pointer Ben, pipe in his mouth. He often had a bicycle along, and would dismount to talk to the occasional passerby, tramp or farmer, and gather their gossip and their wisdom. Through these meetings he could write with such passionate understanding plays like *The Well of the Saints*, where the wise old couple found their blindness a better way of seeing than the common sight the crochety saint offered: it was better to be able to sit 'hearing a soft wind turning round the little leaves of the spring and feeling the sun, and we not tormenting our souls with the sight of the grey days, and the holy men, and the dirty feet is trampling the world.'

You come eventually to **The Sally Gap**, not a gap at all but a crossroads in the wilderness, in the nothingness of bog and heather, and not called for a lass either, but for the salleys (*saileach*: willows) that once grew there. Whether you continue southwards, which is straight ahead, or turn to the left, you end up in **Laragh**.

The southward route carves a twisted path through wide moorland to **Glenmacnass**, where a waterfall marks the head of the glen.

The eastward route is the more spectacular. It skirts the great valley of **Luggala**, whose lake is sometimes called Lough Tay. It is a heart-stopping moment when that view opens: the great plunge downwards to the dark lake waters, near where stands a hunting-lodge built by a Guinness, and a river winding its way along the soft valley floor to meet the larger expanse of Lough Dan, with mountains rearing all around. This road arrives eventually on the Dublin-Glendalough road. Turn right and continue through the village of Roundwood. After another three miles, just before the road turns sharply right to cross a bridge into the village of **Annamoe**, a by-road forks left. Follow it a short distance, then take the next right turn. Very soon you will arrive at the high stone gates of Castle Kevin, where Synge spent many summers. Returning to the road you have just come from, turn right. In half a mile you come to Tomrilands Farm, the second-last house on the left before **Tomrilands Crossroads**. (Travellers should note that both of these are private homes, and their privacy should be respected.) It was here that Synge began to evolve the characteristic language of his plays, which is a kind of coloured composite of different dialects:

When I was writing *The Shadow of the Glen*, some years ago, I got more aid than any learning could have given me, from a chink in the floor of the old Wicklow house where I was staying, that let me hear what was being said by the servant girls in the kitchen....In Ireland, for a few years more, we have a popular imagination that is fiery and magnificent, and tender; so that those of us who wish to write start with a chance that is not given to writers in places where the springtime of the local life has been forgotten, and the harvest is a memory only, and the straw has been turned into bricks. (Preface to *The Playboy of the Western World*).

From Annamoe the road leads to **Laragh** and the hallowed valley of **Glendalough**, the Valley of Two Lakes, one-time city of Saint Kevin.

The finger of a round tower pointing towards heaven heralds your arrival at the central nexus of the scattered ruins of what was once a famous monastery, university and place of pilgrimage. Over a thousand years ago the saintly Kevin took himself off to this almost inaccessible valley, hidden between deep folds of the mountain, to escape from the world and live the life of an anchorite. A cave in the cliff-face above the Upper Lake is traditionally pointed out as Saint Kevin's Bed — not an ideal place indeed for a good night's sleep, but saints aren't like the rest of us, and Kevin's purpose was to mortify the flesh as a means to finding the path to heaven. However, man — even

Castle Kevin

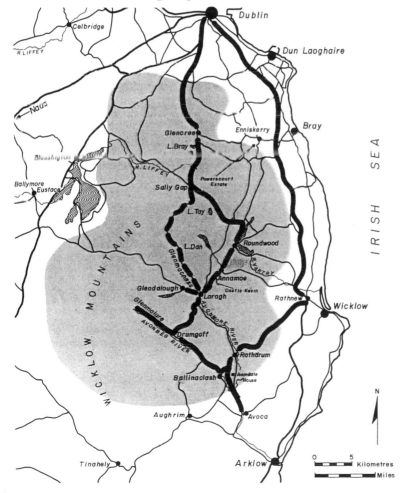

saints — may propose but God disposes. Word of his piety got around and disciples began to gather. Gradually the hermitage became a small monastery, then a larger one as numbers increased. Eventually the settlement became a renowned institution, a university where students gathered not only from Ireland but from all over Europe. The remnants of churches and other buildings from that time are scattered around the two lakes: the old gateway is just beside the Grand Hotel.

Tourists have visited Glendalough ever since Victorian times, and many celebrities have recorded their visits. An elderly Sir Walter Scott managed the popular feat of climbing up the cliff-face and into Saint Kevin's Bed; so did Lady Morgan of the famous Dublin salons. The Rev Caesar Otway, Protestant missioner and controversialist, guru to Carleton, scratched his name where he judged Kevin's shoulder would have lain. Even without the entertainment of such gymnastics, Glendalough is a singularly beautiful place in which to spend a day wandering among oak woods and lakeside paths, imagining the sound of the bell rung from the topmost window of the tower, calling all to prayer, in peace — or in worse times sounding a warning of less

Opposite page: The round tower at Glendalough

The Glendalough Saint

Like all the early Irish saints, Kevin had a reputation for remarkable asceticism. But great piety is an uncomfortable virtue when observed by those who do not possess it. Kevin became the subject of a ribald nineteenth-century street ballad, based on the legend of his rejection of a maiden named Kathleen.

At Glendalough lived a great saint
Who was famous for deeds of austerity
His manners was curious and quaint
For on girls he looked with asperity.
He was fond of readin' a book
When he got one quite to his wishes,
But was fonder of castin' a hook
And spent many a day anglin' for fishes,
Right foldidle doldidle dol,
Right foldidle doldidle addy,
Right foldidle doldidle dol,
Right foldidle doldidle addy.

But as he was fishin' one day
A catchin' some kind of a trout, sir,
Young Kathleen was walkin' that way,
Just to see what the saint was about, sir,
'You're a mighty fine fisher,' says Kate,
'Tis yourself is the boy that can hook them
But when you have caught them so nate,
Don't you want some young woman to cook them'
Right foldidle doldidle dol, etc.

'Be gone out of that,' said the saint,
'For I am a man of great piety,
Me character I wouldn't taint
By keeping such class of society.'
But Kathleeeen wasn't goin' to give in
For when he got home to his rockery
He found her sittin' therein,
A-polishing up of her crockery.
Right foldidle doldidle dol, etc,

He gave the poor creature a shake,
Oh! I wish that the peelers had caught him;
He threw her right into the lake,
And of course she sank down to the bottom.
It is rumoured from that very day,
Kathleen's ghost can be seen on the river;
And the saint never raised up his hand,
For he died of the right kind of fever.
Right foldidle doldidle dol, etc.

welcome visitors than those of today.

Return to Laragh and, continuing southwards, very shortly a right turn takes you over another high-flying mountain road to drop steeply down to **Drumgoff** in remote **Glenmalure**. The sight of an abandoned military barracks reminds us that this is a continuation of the Military Road. So does a huge boulder just a little way along towards the head of the glen, on the right hand side of the road. On one side is inscribed, — in Irish: 'Michael Dwyer and his men had their headquarters in this glen 1798 AD' — to rout them was, after all, the *raison d' être* of the road in the first place. The other side states, again in Irish: 'The Glen in which Fiach O'Byrne defeated the English 1580 AD'. Two claims to history, two centuries apart: how little things change. The road didn't exist in 1580, so it is little wonder that the Queen's troops were scattered and destroyed among the bogs and rocks which were home territory to the clans. Eleven years later a princeling of Donegal, Red Hugh O'Donnell, escaped from his imprisonment in Dublin Castle on a bitter Christmas night, and crossed the mountains in a snow blizzard to reach safe-keeping here with O'Byrne's people.

This is the remote fastness that Synge had in mind when he wrote *The Shadow of the Glen*. The cold and loveless home of Nora was at the extreme far end of the valley. To it comes a penniless tramp who woos her away from her tyrannical husband with bright words and visions, and persuades her to go with him, to leave behind the prison of the glen for the freedom of the open road. 'I'm thinking it's myself will be wheezing that time with lying down under the Heavens when the night is cold, but you've a fine bit of talk, stranger, and it's with yourself I'll go.' They flee together over the head of the valley, across **Table Mountain** and towards a richer life. 'The only truth we know,' Synge says elsewhere, 'is that we are a flood of magnificent life, the fruit of some frenzy of the earth.'

The cottage that Synge had in mind for Nora's home is no more. But in another far up the glen, and reached only by a ford over the tumbling Avonbeg river, Iseult MacBride and Francis Stuart spent some of their early young married life, and not too happily it seems, so that Maud Gonne (Iseult's mother) called on W.B. Yeats to try to mediate between them; he of all people, who himself had proposed to, and been rejected by, both women!

The Aran Islands in the west, rather than Wicklow, gave Synge the inspiration for his most famous play, *The Playboy of the Western World*: it was based on a tale that he or Yeats, or both, heard told by one of the islanders. When it was produced at the Abbey Theatre in Dublin, it scandalised the audience, and there were riots in the theatre.

The story is that of a lad who turns up in a remote Mayo shebeen, and is treated as a great hero when he confesses that he has 'kilt his

Cottage in Glenmalure

da'. When his da, with bandaged head, turns up vowing vengeance, all turn against the young 'hero', his beloved Pegeen Mike summing up a feeling with which many Irish people can identify today: 'there's a great gap between a gallous story and a dirty deed'. The idea of 'a drift of chosen females, standing in their shifts itself', in that tender decade of 1907 was enough to scandalise and enrage the Dublin audience. And where was the Irishman who would murder his own father? The newspapers savaged both the man and the play, the *Freeman's Journal* going so far as to sympathise with Miss Allgood at having to say a word that it was sure she would blush to utter even in the privacy of her bedroom.

Synge was born in 1871 at No. 2 Newtown Villas off Braemor Road in Dublin, a substantial semi-detached house at Rathfarnham, close to the Dublin mountains. He came from a long line of Church of Ireland dignitaries, but J.M. followed his own solitary road. The man who scandalised a nation, and caused riots that were reported around the English-speaking world, could describe himself as 'existing merely in his perception of the waves and of the crying birds and the smell of seaweed.'

Going east from Drumgoff and the hotel, we come via **Ballinaclash** to **Avoca** and the meeting-place of the Avonmore and Avonbeg. 'There is not in the wide world a valley so sweet / As the vale in whose bosom

Thomas Moore (1779-1852)

Evelyn Waugh in Glenmalure

Evelyn Waugh as a young man, on one of his occasional visits to Ireland, spent nine days at the Glenmalure hotel in 1924, which he describes as 'the least amusing part of our wanderings' — he and his companion had set out from London with only £10 between them.

'The hotel was uncomfortable; Terence had decamped to Lundy with Alastair's money, and all the time we were suffering from acute financial embarrassments; the hills which delighted Alastair's heart did not excite me over-much. We had an awful fear on the first night that we had come to a Temperance Hotel. All the ash-trays and things advertised mineral waters, and a pot of tea was brought to us at dinner. We found, however, that at great expense we could obtain a ghastly sort of ale, very fizzy and tasting strongly of baking powder, or a spirituous liquor — a mixture of bad rum, bad gin, and bad vodka called whisky — or, of course, the ubiquitous Bass... We walked a lot at Glenmalure and telegraphed for money a good deal which eventually arrived. The day I enjoyed most was when we walked to Glendaloch and saw the seven churches and lay in St Kevin's Bed... On the whole I did not enjoy Glen-malure. One thing of profit happened. We buried my stick in a peat bog to see if it would colour it and it turned quite black.'

Despite his lack of enthusiasm on that occasion, much later in his life he and his wife looked at various properties with the idea of acquiring a home in Ireland, but without success. He wrote to Nancy Mitford in May 1952:

'Among the countless blessings I thank God for, my failure to find a house in Ireland comes first. Unless one is mad or fox hunting there is nothing to draw one. The houses, except for half a dozen famous ones, are very shoddy in building and they none of them have servants' bedrooms because at the time they were built Irish servants slept on the kitchen floor. The peasants are malevolent. All their smiles are false as Hell. Their priests are very suitable for them but not for foreigners. No coal at all. Awful incompetence everywhere. No native capable of doing the simplest job properly.'

All in all, the only thing he appears ever to have enjoyed in Ireland was Jammet's Restaurant in Dublin!

(The Diaries of Evelyn Waugh)

Avondale House

the bright waters meet,' sang Thomas Moore of this place, quietly tucked away between rocky wooded hills. Sadly, it has been over-discovered and over-signposted, and the tree under which he is supposed to have sat in peaceful contemplation is now a dead skeleton. But Tom Moore, in spite of the patriotic sentiment of so many of his lyrics, belongs to Dublin's drawing-rooms rather than to Wicklow's fastnesses, and we'll meet up with him later. Let us spare a thought, however, for Parnell, 'the Chief', the Uncrowned King, whose political fate split Ireland down the middle. **Avondale**, between Avoca and Rathdrum, was his home. It is now owned by Coillte, the State Forestry body and the house is open to the public. The great appeal of Avondale, however, is not so much the house, but the grounds. The land sweeps down in terraces to the river, and everywhere there are trees, ranks and terraces of them, avenues and lines, exotic and commonplace, planted in turn first by Samuel Hayes who built the house in 1779, then by a couple of generations of Parnells, then by the State.

A sheep-farmer who lives nearby talked to me once about Parnell. He quoted Aristotle, to the effect that tragedy had to be brought about by a weakness *within* the hero. 'And so it was with him. Kitty O'Shea was his weakness, and his downfall. He was naive in ways, really. There he was, standing on the edge of a trapdoor, and all someone had to do was to pull the rope.' This referred to the famous scandal that had blackened Parnell's reputation and hounded him out of Irish politics and, no doubt, contributed to his early death in 1891. My companion spoke of how astute Parnell was in politics, winning so much with the Land Acts, but how naive in human affairs. 'But, then, what could you expect of a boy that was left in that great place all by himself when his father died? His mother off in Paris, seeking distraction. In the end his heart was broken. And when he was dying, he made no fight for it.' And we had a moment's silence, thinking of James Joyce's Mr Casey, at that famous Christmas dinner, his head in his hands, weeping, 'Poor Parnell! ... My dead king!'

The shortest road back to Dublin is by the hilly town of **Rathdrum**. If it is autumn, however, the beechwoods will be aflame along the road between Rathdrum and Laragh, and no one should miss that drive. Be generous, and allow another day for a visit to the **Powerscourt** estate and its wonderful gardens, at **Enniskerry**, and the spectacular waterfall, which has a separate entrance.

The Synge family, left to right, Samuel, Annie, Mrs Synge, Robert, John, Edward

J.M. Synge with his pointer, Ben

2. KILKENNY TO CORK
Kings and Commons

The route from Dublin to Cork — though indeed there is no good reason to think one has to start from Dublin — offers two alternatives: through Cashel, or through Kilkenny. As it is a difficult choice, one could, at a pinch, do both if one had both the time and the courage for a maze of minor roads between the two. We recommend this.

About forty miles south of Dublin (twenty miles south of Naas) the Kilkenny road passes through the adjoining villages of **Timolin** and **Moone**. Immediately off the main street — which is in fact the main road — a laneway leads 100 yards to the remnants of a very old monastery. Within the enclosure stands the most appealing of all the Irish High Crosses, carved from stone almost a thousand years ago, and still standing here to charm us and stop us awhile from our business, for reflection.

The Cross of Moone is unusually tall, 17 feet, and slender. The scenes it depicts manage to be both naive and sophisticated and humorous at the same time: Adam and Eve, Daniel in the Lions' Den, the Flight into Egypt, the twelve Apostles and others. Moone was one of the early monasteries of what is sometimes called the Celtic Church, whose Golden Age was the seventh to the eleventh centuries.

Kilkenny is a splendid and dignified city, with a splendid and dignified past. Several of its abbeys and churches date back to medieval times. Kilkenny Castle, bits of which go back to the thirteenth century, has a commanding presence. It bears all the proud and lordly airs of the Norman chieftains who ruled this territory for centuries; it now belongs to the plain people of Kilkenny through a generous gesture by the Marquess of Ormond. Across the river from it can be seen Kilkenny College, of which one Robert Langrishe wrote:

> Here Berkeley, Congreve, Swift in days of yore
> Lisped the first accents of their classic lore;
> Here Bushe, here Flood were born — here Grattan planned
> In early youth the welfare of the land.

The Banim brothers were born there, Michael in 1796, and the better-known John two years later. They were the first novelists to emerge from a middle-class Catholic background, so their perception was unique for their time. Their home district, and the ways of its people, feature largely in their stories. As brothers they were very close. They wrote under the pen-name 'the O'Hara Brothers' and academics still argue about the level of their respective contributions to the output which amounted to twenty-four volumes. *Crohoore of the Billhook, The Boyne Water* and *The Croppy Boy*, probably their best-known works, range over the whole gamut of life as experienced in Ireland, from the cabins of the peasantry, the world of superstition and the supernatural, to the effects of political violence. *The Nowlans*, the story of a 'spoiled priest' who went to live — in squalor as it turned out — with a Protestant woman, was an entirely new kind of Irish novel, approaching a subject hitherto taboo.

Nowadays Kilkenny is particularly noted for its quality craft goods, the Castle Gallery's art collection, and its Arts Festival in September. Callan, 10 miles (16km) to the south, is the location of the confrontation between a priest and his bishop upon which Thomas Kilroy's *The Big Chapel* is based.

Instead of turning west for Cashel at the first opportunity, it is worth making a loop further south by **Clonmel**, for two objectives. One is for **Mullinahone**, reached on a by-road to the right about two miles after Callan. This attractive village was the home of Charles J. Kickham, nineteenth-century novelist, poet and revolutionary. His *Knocknagow*,

Michael Banim (1796-1874)
John Banim (1798-1842)

Charles J. Kickham (1828-1882)

Above: Kilkenny Castle
Below: The Rock of Cashel

Opposite: The Cross of Moone

Frank O'Connor's translation remains the best of several of the poem 'Cill Cais' or, in English, 'Kilcash'.

What shall we do for timber?
  The last of the woods is down.
Kilcash and the house of its glory
  And the bell of the house are gone,
The spot where that lady waited
  Who shamed all women for grace
When earls came sailing to greet her
  And Mass was said in the place.

My grief and my affliction
  Your gates are taken away,
Your avenue needs attention,
  Goats in the garden stray.
The courtyard's filled with water
  And the great earls where are they?
The earls, the lady, the people
  Beaten into the clay.

I beseech of Mary and Jesus
  That the great come home again
With long dances danced in the garden,
  Fiddle music and mirth among men,
That Kilcash the home of our fathers
  Be lifted on high again,
And from that to the deluge of waters
  In bounty and peace remain.

Loud above the grassland,
In Cashel of the towers,
We heard with the yellow candles
The chanting of the hours,
White clergy saying High Mass,
A fasting crowd at prayer,
A choir that sang before them;
And in stained glass the holy day
Was sainted as we passed
Beyond that chancel where the dragons
Are carved upon the arch ....
  ('Pilgrimage' by Austin Clarke)

a short novel about rural life, was for decades the most widely read book in Ireland.

The second objective is **Kilcash**. Continuing southwards for about ten miles, a small road to the right (westwards) leads to a ruined Butler castle that does not look dramatic, but in fact carries an immense significance in the folk-memory. Once, every Irish child learned its name and associations in their schooldays and most Irish adults could until recently still recite the lines of verse in Irish written by an anonymous hand sometime in the eighteenth century, beginning:

Cad a dhéanfaimid feasta gan adhmad?
  Tá deireadh na gcoillte ar lár;
níl trácht ar Chill Chais ná ar a teaghlach
  is ní bainfear a cling go bráth.
An áit úd a gcónaíodh an deighbhean
  fuair gradam is meidhir thar mhnáibh,
bhíodh iarlaí ag tarraingt tar toinn ann
  is an t-aifreann binn á rá ...

Aicim ar Mhuire is ar Íosa
  go dtaga sí arís chúghainn slán,
go mbeidh rincí fada ag gabháil timpeall,
  ceol veidhlín is tinte cnámh;
go dtógtar an baile seo ár sinsear
  Cill Chais bhreá arís go hard,
is go bráth nó go dtiocfaidh an díle
  ná feictear é arís ar lár.

This lament for a lost world would have been written at about the same time as the roof was stripped from Cashel's Cathedral. **The Rock of Cashel**, in County Tipperary, is Ireland's greatest landmark, dominating the plains. It bears on its summit a dramatic collection of medieval monuments, castle and fortress, chapel and cathedral, round tower and high cross. It also bears an immense weight of civil and ecclesiastical history. It was the seat of the Munster kings from the fourth to the eleventh centuries, when Muircheartaigh O'Brien handed it over to the church. The lovely Cormac's Chapel was built in 1134: the cathedral came later, squeezed in between the chapel and the round tower, which accounts for some of its odd corners. The Earl of Kildare burned down the Cathedral because, he explained to Henry VII, he thought the archbishop was inside. It was finally abandoned and deroofed by Archbishop Price, who said he found the Sabbath climb up the Rock too much of an effort. Price, incidentally, was the man with whom, at an earlier stage, Jonathan Swift had tried to arrange a match for his 'friend' Vanessa, but she politely declined. Perhaps she had some sense, after all.

Moone and the Little Monasteries

We would probably know little or nothing of the ancient literature of Ireland, the mythology and the great epics, stories of Cúchulainn and the Fianna, were it not for the early monasteries, places such as Moone in County Kilkenny, which was founded by the great Saint Colmcille (whom we shall meet again in Derry).

The clerics introduced writing to Ireland in the wake of Saint Patrick, and from that point on the Irish were 'mad for books.' The power of books and learning was praised in poetry; the saints and the chieftains were eager to possess books, and in at least one instance a major battle was fought about one, Colmcille's own book, *The Cathach*.

Major monasteries such as Armagh, Derry, Bangor and Clonmacnois, and the one here at Moone, had scriptoria where gospel books were written and illuminated, philosophical and grammatical treatises were analysed, law tracts were codified and old tales were recorded. The famous Book of Kells was the product of such an endeavour.

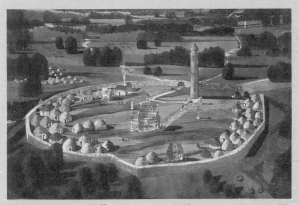

The monastery at Kells — a reconstruction

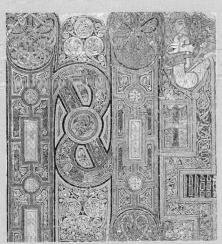

'If you take the trouble to look very closely, and penetrate with your eyes to the secrets of the artistry, you will notice such intricacies, so delicate and subtle, so close together and well-knit, so involved and bound together, and so fresh still in their colourings, that you will not hesitate to declare that all these things must have been the result of the work, not of men, but of angels.' — Comment by Giraldus Cambrensis, 1185

Pictures of the scribes emerge from old Irish poems (particularly captured in Frank O'Connor's collection *The Little Monasteries*) sitting under the trees, in the scriptoria or in isolated huts, praising their lot: 'A cuckoo sings to me — goodly utterance — in a grey cloak from bush fortresses. The Lord's indeed good to me. Well do I write beneath a forest of woodland.'

Uniquely, the Irish scribes, labouring over their usually Latin texts, were given to noting down in the margins some passing thoughts of their own in Irish, and a very human picture emerges. A delightful poem of one cleric, comparing his own chasing of words with the chase of his cat, Pangur Bán, for mice, turns up as such a marginal distraction. Another is moved to note his pleasure at sitting in the open over his lined book, listening to the blackbird and the cuckoo. Some complain: 'My chest is killing me,' moans one. 'New vellum, bad ink — O I say no more,' grumbles another. A manuscript of a later date tetchily remarks, 'It is a gossiping and disparaging lot the scholars are.' One marginal note in the great law-tract, the Seanchas Már, reads 'One thousand three hundred and fifty years until tonight since Jesus Christ, Amen, was born, and in the second year after the coming of the Plague into Ireland that was written. And I myself am full twenty one years old ... and let every one who shall read this utter a prayer of mercy for my soul.' The death of this young scribe is recorded only nine years later, when he is described as 'the choice of the brehons of Ireland.'

William Trevor (1928-   )

But **Cork** is our objective, and Cork, never noted for its modesty, certainly thinks of itself as just as literary a place as Dublin and with good reason. Sean Dunne's engrossing *Cork Anthology*, published in 1993 by Cork University Press, adequately demonstrates that fact.

The River Lee flows through the city in two main channels so that you find yourself constantly crossing bridges — it gives the city part of its charm. As the hilly streets go up and down, so do the voices of the citizens — the sing-song Cork accent is the object of affectionate mockery by others less blessed. Read Daniel Corkery's *The Threshold of Quiet* or some of his short stories for a flavour of Cork and its racy idiom. To William Trevor, as a child living in rural Skibbereen, Cork seemed the ultimate in elegance:

Twice a year perhaps, on Saturday afternoons, there was going to Cork to the pictures ... No experience in my whole childhood, and no memory, has remained as deeply etched as these escapes to the paradise that was Cork. Nothing was more lovely or more wondrous than Cork itself, with its magnificent array of cinemas, the Pavilion, the Savoy, the Palace, the Ritz, the Lee, and the Hadji Bey's Turkish Delight factory. Tea in the Pavilion or the

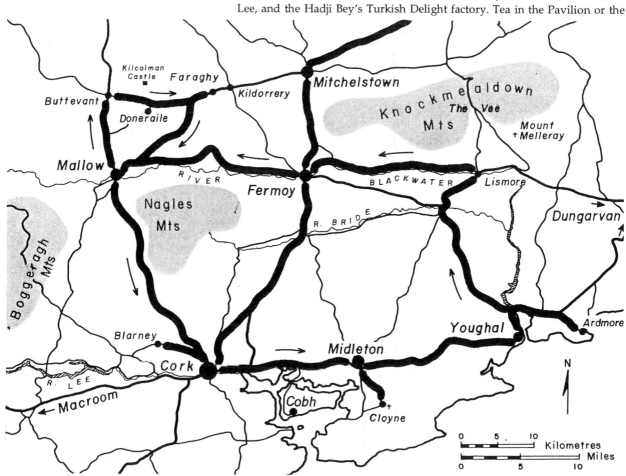

Savoy, the waitresses with silver-plated tea-pots and buttered bread and cakes, and other people eating fried eggs with rashers and chipped potatoes at half-past four in the afternoon. The sheer sophistication of the Pavilion or the Savoy could never be adequately conveyed to a friend in Skibbereen who had not had the good fortune to experience it. The gentleman's lavatory in the Victoria Hotel had to be seen to be believed, the Munster Arcade left you gasping. For ever and for ever you could sit in the middle stalls of the Pavilion watching Claudette Colbert, or Spencer Tracy as a priest, and the earthquake in San Francisco. And for ever afterwards you could sit while a green-clad waitress carried the silver-plated tea-pot to you, with cakes and buttered bread. All around you was the clatter of life and of the city, and men of the world conversing and girls' laughter tinkling. Happiness was everywhere.

(*Excursions in the Real World*)

But some people had other kinds of memories.

My memories begin in Blarney Street, which we called Blarney Lane because it follows the track of an old lane from Cork to Blarney. It begins at the foot of Shandon Street, near the river-bank, in sordidness, and ascends the hill to something like squalor.

Frank O'Connor's mother — Mary Teresa (Minnie) O'Donovan

Frank O'Connor (1903-1966)

The memory is that of Frank O'Connor, born Michael O'Donovan, from his autobiography *An Only Child*. The squalor he describes exists no longer, of course, but it's not difficult to visualise the older look of the street, along which a small boy is helped home, drunk and sick, by his sober and apprehensive father, the boy having been despatched to prevent the Da getting drunk after a funeral, but having, out of boredom, sneaked mouthfuls of the Da's porter. Anyone setting out on foot to find the birthplace should be warned: Blarney Street is the longest street in Cork, it's all uphill and the house, No. 251, is near the top. The original house is gone, replaced by one just a little larger, so that the plaque on the pavement marking the spot is at No. 248.

When O'Connor (born in 1903) was about five years old his father got lonely for his own home territory, so the family moved to Harrington Square, above St Luke's Cross, between Ballyhooley Road and the Old Youghal Road (all of about a mile and a half away) where poor young Michael had to tolerate his hated grandmother at closer quarters. One of his stories, 'First Confession', has the small boy explaining to the priest how he had planned to kill the grandmother with a hatchet, and to cut her up with a knife and take away the pieces and bury them. 'I could get an orange box for threepence and make a cart to take them away.' And coming home sucking bulls' eyes from the priest, to his sister's fury. His drunken and alcoholic father played the big drum in the Blackpool Brass and Reed Band, and the activities of that group gave him material and to spare for stories.

His description of the dignified ritual between old Dan Bride and the police sergeant in 'The Majesty of the Law' is typical of his sureness

Frank O'Connor, his wife Harriet and daughter Hallie-Óg in Cluny, France in 1959

Frank O'Connor speaking at the Yeats Summer School in the 1960s.

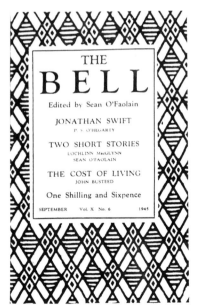

THE
BELL

Edited by Sean O'Faolain

JONATHAN SWIFT
P S O'HEGARTY

TWO SHORT STORIES
LOCHLINN McGLYNN
SEAN O'FAOLAIN

THE COST OF LIVING
JOHN BUSTEED

One Shilling and Sixpence

SEPTEMBER   Vol. X No. 6   1945

Sean O'Faolain (1900-1991)

and delicacy of touch, and his understanding of how people relate in small communities. Dan has refused to pay a fine he incurred for striking a neighbour. The sergeant calls to the house to serve a warrant for his arrest. Dan makes him welcome: they sit at the fire, chat, share a mug of tea and a drop of poteen. It is only as he is leaving that the sergeant stops, half turns back.

'They gave me the warrant,' the sergeant said at last, in a tone which dissociated him from all connection with the document.

'Ay, begod!' said Dan, without interest.

'So whenever 'twould be convenient to you —'

'Well, now you mention it,' said Dan, by way of throwing out a suggestion for debate, 'I could go with you now.'

'Oh, tut, tut!' protested the sergeant with a wave of his hand, dismissing the idea as the tone required.

'Or I could go to-morrow,' added Dan, warming up to the issue.

'Just as you like now,' replied the sergeant, scaling up his voice accordingly.

'But as a matter of fact,' said the old man emphatically, 'the day that would be most convenient to me would be Friday after dinner, seeing that I have some messages to do in town, and I wouldn't have me jaunt for nothing.'

'Friday will do grand,' said the sergeant with relief that this delicate matter was now practically disposed of. 'You could just walk in yourself and tell them I told you.'

O'Connor was a master of the short story, as was his friend and contemporary Sean O'Faolain. They were among the first of the 'moderns,' the first to turn away from what they saw as the Celtic Twilight romanticism of Yeats to model themselves on the Russian short story writers. O'Connor introduced Ibsen and Chekhov to the Cork stage, and the level of his achievement may be judged by the fact that he earned the comment that 'he would go down in posterity at the head of the Pagan Dublin Muses.' In spite of his struggle to break away from what he regarded as the domination of the past, his translations of poems from the Irish opened doors of perception for many who would not otherwise have encountered their archaic beauty.

Sean O'Faolain was born in 1900 at No. 15 **Half Moon Street**, in a milieu he describes as 'shabby-genteel at the lowest possible social level.' The family moved to No. 5 shortly after. The little street is beside the Crawford Art Gallery, which is beside the Cork Opera House. No. 5 was the corner house, now Matthews' sports shop. Bruce Matthews, the proprietor, is the third generation of his family in business on the spot. Bruce's father remembered the family living upstairs. They kept lodgers, who included players from the Opera House, and the young boy was awed and excited by the passage of kings and sages through the house. There were also the chorus girls, and Bruce's father remembers O'Faolain's mother sitting on the stairs at night, firmly separating

Photo by poet Richard Murphy of Sean O'Faolain in 1956.

the girls from their escorts. O'Faolain himself describes her as a sorrowfully pious, self-driving woman, burdened with anxieties. The father, a constable in the Royal Irish Constabulary, was fiercely loyal to the British empire, a background which didn't stop his son's later involvement in the nationalist movement. Like O'Connor, O'Faolain learned Irish and began to move among Irish-speakers 'so that,' he said, 'the language acted both as a matrix to the tissues of our political faith and as its sign and password.' Many of his stories relate to the political, social and cultural state of Ireland during the first half of this century. His founding, with Peadar O'Donnell, of the pioneering liberal literary journal *The Bell* in 1940 created a platform for an inspiring group of young writers. Disillusioned with the Ireland he saw emerging when the fighting was all over, he determined to live abroad, but found eventually that he had to return. 'We belonged to an old, small, intimate and much-trodden country, where every field, every path, every ruin had its memories, where every last corner had its story.' (*Vive Moi*)

O'Connor and O'Faolain may have international reputations, but most beloved of Corkonians is 'Father Prout,' really the Rev Father Sylvester Mahony, and his somewhat tongue-in-cheek celebration of the Bells of Shandon (which visitors are invited to play). Anybody you ask will recite for you a couple of verses!

Father Prout (Rev. Sylvester Mahony 1804-1866)

I've heard bells tolling	With cymbals glorious,	But thy sounds were sweeter	Oh! the bells of Shandon
Old 'Adrian's Mole' in	Swinging uproarious	Than the dome of Peter	Sound far more grand on
Their thunder rolling	In the gorgeous turrets	Flings o'er the Tiber,	The pleasant waters
From the Vatican,	Of Notre Dame;	Pealing solemnly.	Of the river Lee.

...when my heart was as light as the wild
  winds that blow
Down the Mardyke through each elm
  [*pronounced ell-um*] tree
Where I sported and played, 'neath each
  green leafy shade,
On the banks of my own lovely Lee.

Richard Alfred Milliken (1767-1815)

You won't be let go, either, without hearing at least one verse of the Cork anthem, 'On the Banks of my Own Lovely Lee' — (frequently referred to as 'De Banks').

Anyone making the obligatory 5-mile detour to **Blarney** (by far the best way to go, Padraic Colum assures us, is via Blarney Street) to indulge in the ritual of kissing the Blarney Stone, which is set into the battlements of the fifteenth-century castle tower, might well be subjected to the more obviously satirical 'Groves of Blarney' of R.A. Milliken:

There's statues gracing	Bold Neptune, Plutarch,
This noble place in —	And Nicodemus,
All heathen gods	All standing naked
And nymphs so fair;	In the open air!

Against that bit of oul' nonsense, set Theo Dorgan's 'Nocturne for Blackpool':

Theo Dorgan (1953-   )

... The bells of Shandon jolt like electricity through lovers
In a cold-water flat beneath the attic of a house in Hatton's Alley,
The ghost of Frank O'Connor smiles on Fever Hospital Steps
As Mon boys go by, arguing about first pints of stout and Che Guevara.

The unicorns of legend are the donkeys of childhood, nobody
Knows that better than we know it ourselves, but we know also that
Dolphins are coursing through the blue air outside our windows
And the sparking stars are oxygen, bubbling to the moon ...

('Nocturne for Blackpool')

At the east side of Cork harbour is Cloyne, where the philosopher George Berkeley reigned as Bishop from 1734 to his death in 1753. He propounded the theory that nothing exists except in its perception and advocated the drinking of tap-water as the panacea for all ills. He failed in an attempt to establish a university in the Bermudas 'for the civilisation of America' partly with money bequeathed to him by Jonathan Swift's 'Vanessa'. There is a fine alabaster effigy of the Bishop in the small Cathedral, where he is buried. The Round Tower may be visited.

Further east is **Youghal**, an old walled seaport town. It had the distinction, if one might call it that in the light of history, of having as Governor Sir Walter Raleigh in the 1580s. His home there, Myrtle Grove, is occasionally opened to the public. There has always been a strong tradition that as well as being the first in Ireland to smoke

Sir Walter Raleigh (1552-1618)

Above: Robert Gibbings' illustration from Lovely is the Lee

tobacco, his other introduction from the colonies was the potato, which was first planted in his garden. Tradition, however, and historians do not always see eye to eye.

A little way on is **Ardmore**, where one might manage to locate the Mass Rock that Molly Keane remembers in the Introduction to her *Ireland* anthology:

Molly Keane (1910-   )

> Tucked into sheer cliffs, it seems that you almost have to step off the edge of the world to reach it. It is strangely hidden from land or sea; visible only to a seagull's eye or God's eye. A huge sheet of limestone edged with lichens and, at the appropriate season, with sea pink and rock-rose. I am told it is now a trysting place for lovers. However, when it comes to my inward eye, I see it in its previous incarnation, with bedraggled figures slowly gathering on the horizon and disappearing over the cliff-face to worship in this beautiful but dangerous place.

Back inland, the lovely Blackwater valley leads to **Lismore** (County Waterford), with its stunningly romantic castle of the Dukes of Devonshire. Here in a modest stone-built home an extraordinary woman works away quietly. Dervla Murphy nursed her totally incapacitated mother for twenty years, then mounted her bicycle and cycled to India. It was 1963, the worst winter in living memory, and her account of the six-month journey is told in her first book *Full Tilt*. Since then, usually alone but twice accompanied by her daughter (who was five years old for the first trip) she has travelled in the most remote regions of the earth, usually on foot, occasionally on a bicycle or mule and with the very minimum of resources. Her journals have been written in the most severe circumstances, by candlelight in a tent in Peru, by smoking oil-lamp in freezing Himalayan shelters.

Dervla Murphy (1930-   )

Dervla Murphy

Left: Myrtle Grove, Youghal, home of Sir Walter Raleigh

Edmund Spenser (c.1552-1599)

Bind up the locks the which hang scattered
  light,
And in his waters, which your mirror make,
Behold your faces as the christall bright,
That when you come whereas my love doth
  lie,
No blemish she may spie. ('Epithalamion')

Her books and her remarkable adventures relate to remote and exotic lands and peoples, but she can write as movingly about her own place:

Directly opposite my gatepost a mountain pass forms the letter V against the sky; this route across the Knockmealdowns is named, with un-Irish prosaicness, the **Vee**. Wolves were hunted hereabouts less than 300 years ago and not much more than one hundred years ago peasants were evicted from their homes near the river and forced to settle on these barren moors. In 1832 other settlers arrived, when a band of Cistercian monks received from Sir Richard Keane of Cappoquin a tract of wild land some six miles east of the Vee. Soon that land had been tamed and now the grey Abbey of **Mount Melleray** stands solitary and conspicuous against a background of blue hills — an echo of those ancient monasteries which once made known, throughout civilised Europe, the name of Lismore.

And she goes on:

I thank providence every day that I was born and reared in the Blackwater Valley...There is a sense in which everybody owns their birthplace, and all the land around it that can be covered in a long day's tramp — the natural, immemorial limit to the territory of a human being. Or is it that the place owns the person, exacting a special, subtle loyalty, a primitive devotion that antedates by tens of thousands of years the less spontaneous emotion of patriotism? (*Ireland of the Welcomes*)

While Raleigh was sitting at his casement window in Youghal, writing letters to Queen Elizabeth and indulging in the quaint habit he had acquired in the New World of rolling up dried leaves, putting them in his mouth and setting fire to them, Edmund Spenser, Clerk to the Council of Munster and Sheriff of Cork, was reposing in his castle at **Kilcolman**, away up in north Cork near **Buttevant**, writing elegant verse. Though his estates once encompassed three thousand acres of land confiscated from the native owners and tenants under the Elizabethan Plantation of Munster, there is little standing now of Kilcolman Castle but an ivy-clad shell. It is signposted about two miles (3 km) out the **Mitchelstown** road from Buttevant, located within a network of little roads fringed with a froth of Queen Ann's Lace in early summer. It is hardly worthwhile to search it out: it is practically invisible and inaccessible within an area which is preserved as a nature reserve. One wonders whether the ancestors of the whooper swans which gather there in winter came to grace His Lordship's view four centuries ago.

When bringing his new bride (the golden-haired Elizabeth Boyle from Kilcoran near Youghal) to Kilcolman, he bade the 'Nymphes of Mulla' (the Awbeg river) to create perfection for her delight.

Spenser's use of English was most elegant. He considered it 'unnatural that any people should have another language more than their own.' He found it 'very inconvenient and the cause of more evils' that some of his English compatriots had begun to use Irish and take up other local ways. However, whilst not appreciating 'the wylde Irishe', he did appreciate the landscape of north Cork wherein lay his territories, which consoled him when Her Majesty didn't seem interested in bringing him back to England to high office:

> I from thenceforth have learn'd to love more deare
> This lowly quiet life which I inherit here.

He prized the woods too, and names the trees at length, their character and their uses.

He writes too of lazy days here 'among the cooly shade of the green alders' taking his ease with Sir Walter Raleigh and Sir Philip Sydney, three gentlemen pursuing the cultivated art of moral versifying. But this aesthete who penned *The Faerie Queene* and many lovely sonnets here is not remembered kindly. His memory is not that of a gentle and romantic dreamer, but as a man whose barbarous views on the treatment of the Irish shocked even his own caste. Inevitably, perhaps, the castle was burned, the land laid waste, in a fierce act of revenge by those hiding in what woods had not been felled.

Kerryman Brendan Kennelly, in his long nightmare sequence in *Cromwell* where Bufún (the fool, rogue, poet) pursues a dialogue with Oliver Cromwell, has Spenser grumbling:

> 'I am master of the chivalric idiom' Spenser said
> As he sipped a jug of buttermilk
> And ate a quaite of griddle bread.
> 'I'm worried, though, about the actual bulk
> Of *The Faerie Queene*. She's growing out
> Of all proportions, in different directions.
> Am I losing control? Am I buggering it
> All up? Ruining my best intentions?
> As relief from my Queene, I write sonnets
> But even these little things get out of hand
> Now and then, giving me a nightmare head.
> Trouble is, sonnets are genetic epics.
> Something in them wants to grow out of bounds.
> I'm up to my bollox in sonnets' Spenser said. ('Master')

Spenser's estate was later acquired by the St Legers, who built **Doneraile Court**, a fine mansion which itself fell on hard times. The State took over the demesne, which is now an admirable public park, and the house is being gradually restored. Elizabeth Bowen describes it in its prime: 'A lyrical place ... Carriage-drives loop about, there are bamboo groves, a soporific lime walk, a clotted lily pond.'

Elizabeth Bowen could appreciate such a place. Her own home, **Bowenscourt**, was at **Farrahy**, only about 8 miles (12 km) to the east, close to **Kildorrery**. 'A high bare Italianate house,' as she describes it

The Laurell, meed of mightie Conquerours
And Poets sage, the Firre that weepeth still,
And Eugh obedient to the benders will,
The Birth for shaftes, the Sallow for the mill,
The Mirrhe sweete bleeding in the bitter
  wound,
The warlike Beech, the Ash for nothing ill,
The fruitful Olive, and the Platane round,
The carver Holme, the Maple seldom
  inward sound .... (*The Faerie Queene*)

Elizabeth Bowen (1900-1973)

FARAHY CHURCH

On summer Sunday mornings at Farahy church we had, in those days of King Edward, quite a parade — the little Olivers from Rockmills, the little Galeses from the other side of Kildorrery, myself and the little Johnsons from Lisnagorneen. The sun winked in through the trees and the south windows on the pewfuls of little girls in white muslin dresses and starched white muslin hats, and of little boys in sailor suits. Parents, grandmothers ... visitors, governesses, Protestant farmers and, packed at the back, the Protestant servants of all households, composed the rest of the congregation; the organ was played either by Mrs Oliver or by Mrs Gates, and we all sang loud confident Protestant hymns.' *(Bowen's Court)*

The little church is in need of repair and restoration. Contributions are welcomed.

herself. 'It was intended to form a complete square, but the north-east corner is missing. Indoors, the plan is simple; the rooms are large, lofty and few. The house stands three stories high, with, below, a basement sunk in an area. Outside the front door a terrace, supported on an unseen arch, bridges the area; from this terrace the steps descended to the gravel sweep.' Gone now, pulled down for the value of the roof lead, as happened to a tragic number of beautiful houses in this century.

Like so many of her background, she had an intense love of the land, and in many ways a great understanding of it. Their sense of conflicting loyalties is put exactly in her preface to *The Last September*. With the people of her caste, she points out, 'inherited loyalty to England — where their sons went to school, in whose wars their sons were killed, and to whom they owed in the first place their land and power — pulled them one way; their own latent blood-and-bone "Irishness," the other.' Her description of 'The Last Garden Party' of their disintegrating world is particularly poignant, even if comic in ways. It took place at **Mitchelstown Castle** shortly after the outbreak of war had been announced:

That afternoon we walked up the Castle avenue, greeted by the gusty sound of a band. The hosts of the party...were not young, and, owing to the extreme draughtiness everywhere, they received their guests indoors, at the far end of Big George's gallery. In virtue of this being a garden party, and of the fact that it was not actually raining, pressure was put on the guests to proceed outside — people only covertly made incursions into the chain of brocade saloons. Wind raced round the Castle terraces, naked under the Galtees; grit blew into the ices; the band clung with some trouble to its exposed place. The tremendous news certainly made that party, which might have been rather flat. Almost everyone said they wondered if they really ought to have come, but they *had* come — rightly: this was a time to gather. This was an assemblage of Anglo-Irish people from all over north-east County Cork, from the counties of Limerick, Waterford, Tipperary. For miles round, each isolated big house had disgorged its talkers, this first day of the war. The tension of months, of years — outlying tension of Europe, inner tension of Ireland — broke in a spate of words. Braced against the gale from the mountains, licking dust from their lips, these were the unmartialled loyalists of the South. Not a family had not put out, like Bowen's Court, its generations of military brothers — tablets in Protestant churches recorded deaths in remote battles; swords hung in halls. If the Anglo-Irish live on and for a myth, for that myth they constantly shed their blood. So, on this August 1914 day of grandeur and gravity, the Ascendancy rallied, renewed itself...

It was an afternoon when the simplest person begins to anticipate memory — this Mitchelstown garden party, it was agreed, would remain in every one's memory as historic. It was, also, a more final scene than we knew. Ten years hence, it was all to seem like a dream — and the castle itself would be a few bleached stumps on the plateau. *(Bowen's Court)*

Elizabeth Bowen died in England, but with others of her family she is buried in the little churchyard at Farrahy. Her grave is just in front of the main door. A commemorative plaque in the porch reads:

> She left in her writings
> a proof of her genius,
> a reflection of her personality and
> a history of her home.

A key to the little church can be had from Molly O'Brien at her home just across the street. A gentle and charming lady now in her eighties, she went to work in Bowenscourt at the age of fifteen in the 1920s, first as a parlourmaid, then as cook. She will tell you what a happy place it was with such a joyful atmosphere, always full of people, and that Elizabeth Bowen herself was 'a lovely person with a smile for everybody.' After she (Bowen) inherited the place from her father in the 1930s, she had the entire house, which was quite run-down, renovated, doubtless spending more than she could afford in the process. The house was sold in 1959 and pulled down stone by stone. It is best not to look now for even where it stood, back from the church: it is too depressing, with nettles flourishing where over sixty acres of woods were felled.

Bowen's world is that of the Anglo-Irish, of the Big House, that of the Protestant descendants of the English colonists granted large tracts of confiscated land after the Elizabethan conquest. It was a world which was orderly and apparently serene. We must return to Cork and take the road westwards toward **Macroom** to encounter the other side of the equation.

EDITOR'S NOTE:
The key is now available from Mrs Brenda Hennessy, who lives nearby.

Robert Gibbings' illustration from the title page of Lovely is the Lee *(1945)*

Billy Roche
Colm Tóibín
See *Crossing the Millennium*, page 259

Kilcrea Abbey, Co Cork, where Art Ó Laoghaire is buried.

3. WEST CORK AND KILLARNEY
The Hidden Ireland
and the Horns of Elfland

Kilcrea Abbey is 12 miles west of Cork on the south side of the River Lee. In the south-east corner of the nave, a tomb-slab reads:

Lo Arthur Leary
Genrous Handsome Brave
Slain in his Bloom
Lies in this humble grave.

The epitaph is, surprisingly, in English; the story of Arthur Leary, more properly Art Ó Laoghaire, is a very Irish one.

The village of **Carriganimma** is on the road leading northwards through the hills from Macroom towards **Millstreet**. It was here one May morning in 1773 that dashing young Art Ó Laoghaire, at the time a Captain in the Austrian Hussars, was murdered, apparently in a fracas arising out of his refusal to sell his splendid bay mare for £5 (Catholics were forbidden by the Penal Laws from owning a horse of more than that value). His death gave rise to one of the most famous poems in the Irish language, a passionate outpouring of grief by his wife, Eileen Dubh (dark) O'Connell. Her 'Lament for Art Ó Laoghaire' is in the great tradition of the Gaelic keen, or lament for the dead, and the extraordinary intensity of language and emotion, the hypnotic beat as of fists on the heart, cannot be properly rendered in translation:

Eileen Dubh O'Connell (born c.1743)

Mo ghrá go daingean tu!
Lá dá bhfaca thu
Ag ceann tí an mhargaidh,
Thug mo shúil aire dhuit,
Thug mo chroí taitneamh duit,
D'éalaíos óm charaid leat
I bhfad ó bhaile leat ...

My love forever!
The day I first saw you
At the end of the market-house,
My eye observed you,
My heart approved you,
I fled from my father with you,
Far from my home with you ...

Mo chara go daingean tu!
Is cuimhin lem aigne
An lá breá earraigh úd,
Gur bhreá thíodh hata dhuit

My friend forever!
My mind remembers
That fine spring day
How well your hat suited you,

Faoi bhanda óir tarraingthe,
Claíomh cinn airgid
Lámh dheas chalma —
Rompsáil bhagarthach —
Fír-chritheagla
Ar námhaid chealgach —
Tú i gcóir chun falaracht
Is each caol ceannann fút.
D'umhlaídís Sasanaigh
Síos go talamh duit,
Is ní ar mhaithe leat
Ach le haon-chorp eagla
Cé gur leo a cailleadh tú,
A mhuirnín mh'anama ...

Mo chara thu go daingean!
Is níor chreideas riamh dod mharbh
Gur tháinig chugham do chapall
Is a srianta léi go talamh,
Is fuil do chroí ar a leacain
Siar go t'iallait ghreanta
Mar a mbítheá id shuí 's id sheasamh.
Thugas léim go tairsigh,
An dara léim go geata,
An tríú léim ar do chapall.

Do bhuaileas go luath mo bhasa
Is do bhaineas as na reathaibh
Chomh maith is bhí sé agam,
Go bhfuaras romham tu marbh
Cois toirín ísil aitinn,
Gan Pápa gan easpag,
Gan cléireach gan sagart
Do léifeadh ort an tsailm,
Ach seanbhean chríonna chaite
Do leath ort binn dá fallaing —
Do chuid fola leat 'na sraithibh;
Is níor fhanas le hí ghlanadh
Ach í ól suas lem basaibh.

Bright gold-banded,
Sword silver-hilted —
Right hand steady —
Threatening aspect —
Trembling terror
On treacherous enemy —
You poised for a canter
On your slender bay horse.
The Saxons bowed to you,
Down to the ground to you,
Not for love of you
But for deadly fear of you,
Though you lost your life to them,
Oh my soul's darling ....

My friend you were forever!
I knew nothing of your murder
Till your horse came to the stable
With the reins beneath her trailing,
And your heart's blood on her shoulders
Staining the tooled saddle
Where you used to sit and stand.
My first leap reached the threshold,
My second reached the gateway,
My third leap reached the saddle.

I struck my hands together
And I made the bay horse gallop
As fast as I was able,
Till I found you dead before me
Beside a little furze-bush.
Without Pope or bishop,
Without priest or cleric
To read the death-psalms for you,
But a spent old woman only
Who spread her cloak to shroud you —
Your heart's blood was still flowing;
I did not stay to wipe it
But filled my hands and drank it.

(Trans. Eilís Dillon)

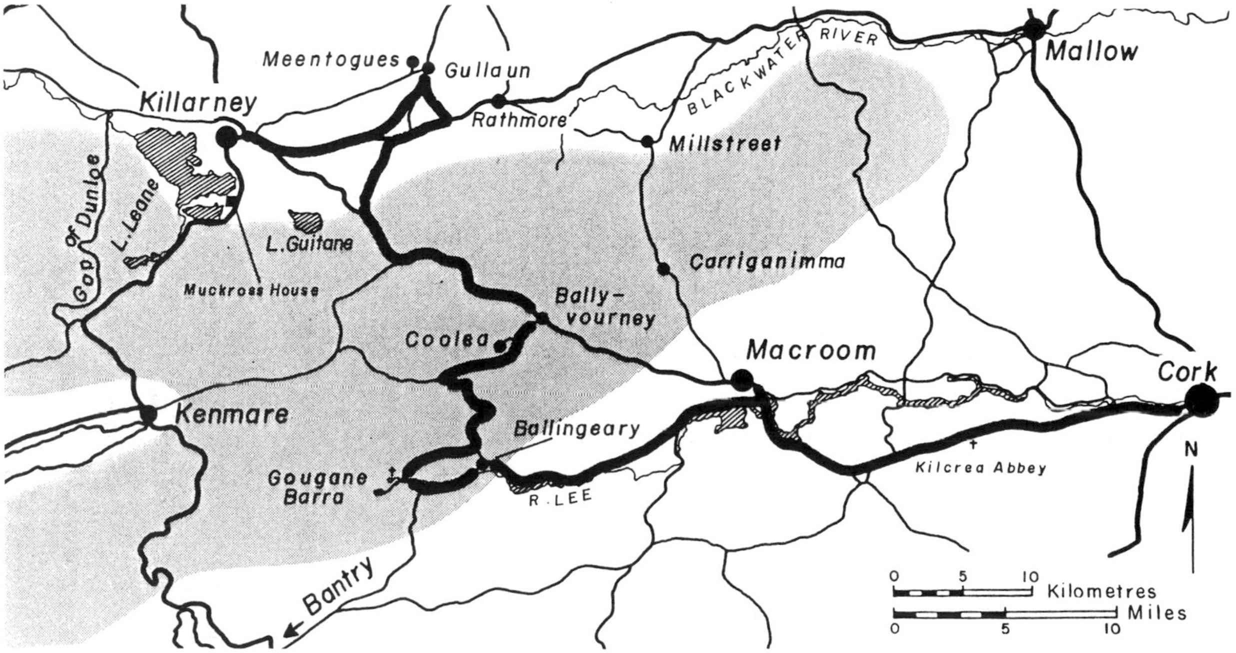

It goes on in this agonised fashion for many verses, sometimes entering into dialogue with Art's sister who accused her of absenting herself from the wake. She defends herself:

Neighbours, don't listen
To such lying tales!
Is there a woman in Ireland,
Who, at each day's end,
Stretched at his side,
Who bore his three children,
Would not lose her mind
After Art O'Leary, who
Lies spent here with me
Since yesterday morning ... ·

A dhaoine ná n-aeistigh,
'Bhfuil aon bhean in Eirinn,
Ó luí na gréine
A shínfeadh a taobh leis,
Do bhéarfadh trí lao dho,
Ná raghadh le craobhacha
I ndiaidh Airt Uí Laoghaire
Atá anso traochta
Ó mhaidin inné agam?

Raleigh House, near Macroom, where Art O'Laoghaire and Eileen Dubh lived their short married life.

Lest anyone should think that Eileen Dubh's distraught act of drinking blood from her hands is a melodramatic invention, Edmund Spenser tells of witnessing the execution of Murrough O'Brien in 1570 and his foster mother drinking of the blood from the severed head.

The O'Laoghaires and the O'Connells were among a small number of Catholic families who had managed to hold on to their land and some of their wealth into the oppressive eighteenth century. Eileen was one of the O'Connells of **Derrynane** in Kerry, and an aunt of Daniel O'Connell, 'the Liberator'. She seems to have married the hot-blooded young hussar against her family's wishes. Their first meeting was at the market-house at Macroom. The O'Laoghaires lived at **Raleigh House,** to the left of the Killarney road just outside Macroom.

Even two centuries after that, almost into our own time, the last flicker of the old Gaelic ways had not yet been quite extinguished. Continuing westwards, not on the high road to Killarney but by the more southerly one towards **Bantry**, you'll hear fragments of the older tongue. Seventeen miles after Macroom a small road to the right leads to Gougane Barra.

Gougane Barra is one of the places Eileen Dubh mentions, along with **Ballingeary** and **Millstreet** and **Grenagh**, and is the entry to a territory where an older way of life can be encountered.

There is a green island in lone Gougane Barra,
Whence Allua of songs rushes forth like an arrow;
In deep Valley Desmond a thousand wild fountains
Come down to that lake, from their home in the mountains.

Thus wrote J.J. Callanan about the year 1800. To Eileen Dubh it was 'Gougane of the Saints.' To Saint Finbarr, founder of Cork City, it was the place of his island hermitage. And to us it is, added to these things, the place of The Tailor.

'A star danced and under that was I born.' That is his epitaph, carved on the stone that marks his lakeside grave. Tim Buckley and

Drawing by Jack B. Yeats for the 1940 Cuala Press handcoloured edition of Frank O'Connor's translation of 'A Lament for Art O'Leary'

Eric Cross (1903-1980)

his wife, Ansty, lived in the third house (now painted golden yellow) on the left of the small road leading to the lake. The house has been altered and extended in the years between. Around that fireside gathered friends and neighbours, poets and scholars, musicians and storytellers, for talk and merriment. The Tailor was a genuine *seanchaí* (storyteller) of the traditional kind, with a keen intelligence and sharp wit. Let Frank O'Connor, one of his many friends, describe him:

The Tailor, when I knew him first, was over eighty, a crippled little Kerryman with soft, round, rosy cheeks exactly like a baby's and two brilliant, mischievous baby eyes. His eyes were the first thing that attracted you. He had no teeth, and he spoke very fast from far back in his throat, and talk and laughter mixed and bubbled like water and wind in a pipe.'(*My Father's Son*)

Apart from the simple household goods, one cow was the extent of the Tailor's possessions. But his hearth was the merriest, and the least conscious of lack, in all of Ireland. A gentle northerner named Eric Cross who was a 'regular' made a book, *The Tailor and Ansty*, out of those evenings, and it is a joy to read.

The Tailor's explanation to a few of his more innocent neighbours as to how his friend, sculptor Seamus Murphy, was going to make him a new head — a 'busht' as he called it, is typical: 'Yerra, man alive. It's easy enough. You stick your head into a pot of stirabout and when it is cold you pull out your head and melt the metal and pour it into the hole your head made. Then you eat up the stirabout and you find your new head inside the pot.' And wife Ansty's reaction when the 'busht' arrives: 'Look at him, will you? Look at my ould shtal (stallion) ... my ould devil of the two heads and the one he has already is no use by him. It's another bottom he needs for the one he has he's nearly worn out, sitting on it in the corner all day long, and shmoking and planning lies.' ('The Tailor's "busht"')

But this was the 1940s, and the puritanical leaders of the nation couldn't stomach the earthy wisdom of the Tailor, any more than they could the novels of the foremost Irish writers of the time. The book was banned; the Tailor was forced by the local priest to burn his copy in his own hearth, and the heart of the place was lost. We leave the last words to Frank O'Connor, after one of those magic evenings:

Late that night as we stumbled out along the little causeway from the cabin to the road one of the old men slapped me vigorously on the shoulder and roared: 'Well, thanks be to the Almighty God, Frinshias, we had wan grand dirty night.' I admit that at the time I was a little surprised, but, remembering it afterwards, I felt that to thank God for a good uproariously bawdy party was the very hallmark of a deeply religious mind. I don't know, but I commend the idea to moralists. (*Leinster, Munster & Connacht*)

Gougane Barra from Lovely is the Lee *by Robert Gibbings (1889-1958), author and engraver*

Seamus Murphy, another Corkman, the creator of the Tailor's

'busht,' was nearly as good a talker as the Tailor himself. A fine stonecarver and sculptor, he wrote an autobiography which he called *Stone Mad*, fascinating not only for the anecdotes, but for the portrait it drew of the life of those craftsmen and their pride in their skills.

For Frank O'Connor, as a lonely child in the back streets of Cork but with an imagination wide open and waiting to be fuelled, and for O'Faolain also, the gateway to the intellect, and to the riches of literature, both Irish and English, was opened by schoolteacher Daniel Corkery. Up to the day the new assistant came to take over the class, O'Connor hated school with a great loathing — 'I would cheerfully have risked an eternity of hell sooner than spend a day in that school.' But Corkery changed all that. O'Connor describes him as 'a small man with a lame leg who trailed slowly and painfully about the classrooms, though whenever he wanted to, he seemed to glide round on skates and had a violent temper that sent the blood rushing to his head. In spite of his affliction, he was like that, light and spare and clean. He had a small, round head, and a round face with a baby complexion on which a small dark moustache and the shadow of a beard looked as inappropriate as they would have done on a small boy.' (*An Only Child*). This baby-faced half-cripple was the man whom many regard as the real father of the Irish short story. The collection *A Munster Twilight* influenced many who came after him. His views on literature and politics are, inevitably, under question today, but there is no denying the value of the excitement and hunger for knowledge he stirred in the minds of his young charges.

Corkery believed that, whatever the quality of the writings of Anglo-Irish writers such as Maria Edgeworth and William E.H. Lecky, it was a serious misjudgement to regard these as Ireland's literary giants of the period, because the riches of the Gaelic culture were not taken into account, being totally unknown or disregarded. Corkery's work *The Hidden Ireland* is a study of the poetry and culture of Irish-speaking Munster as it survived during the period of the Penal Laws — what he called 'the riches of that starving people', and 'of that land, so dark, so scorned, yet so secretly romantic to those who know it.'

The Penal Laws, however patchily implemented, helped to maintain the populace in a state of abject poverty and powerlessness, denying them church, language, education or recourse to law. Corkery looks under the apparent degradation to reveal the still-living remnants of an ancient high culture. The best place to look for some of the finest poetry from this period is in *An Duanaire 1600-1900: Poems of the Dispossessed*, first published in 1981 by Dolmen Press. The poet Thomas Kinsella is one of Ireland's major literary figures. It was he, in collaboration with Seán Ó Tuama, also a poet, and Professor of Irish at University College Cork, who compiled this most important work, as

Daniel Corkery (1878-1964)

> The Gaelic culture ran underground, with its ceaseless poetry of lament. (Gaelic was spoken in the kitchens and fields and in untouched country the settlers did not know). It has taken the decline of the Anglo-Irish to open to them the poetry of regret: only dispossessed people know their land in the dark.
>
> Elizabeth Bowen, *Bowen's Court*

Thomas Kinsella (1928-   )

SEÁN Ó RIADA

Seán Ó Riada came to live in Cúil Aodha in 1964, and by doing so had a profound effect on the soul of Ireland. Musician extraordinary, he almost single-handedly rescued Irish traditional music from neglect and impoverishment, and renewed a great heritage. His modest home in the remote mountainous backwater became such a meeting-place of distinguished minds and personalities that it was likened to Camelot.

He was an errant, erratic genius. His personal output was relatively small, though his theme music for the film *Mise Éire* (I am Ireland) made him famous overnight. His most lasting work was in gathering together a group of traditional musicians, whom he called the Ceoltóirí Chualann and with whom he retrieved the nobility of the heritage. After Ó Riada's death this group evolved into the widely-acclaimed musical innovators The Chieftains.

Ó Riada inspired intense personal devotion and loyalty, and several poetic tributes, including John Montague's 'The Lure':

Again, that note! A weaving
melancholy, like a bird crossing
moorland;
   pale ice on a corrie
opening inward, soundless harp-
strings of rain...
   That point
where folk and art meet, murmurs
Herr Doktor as
   the wail of tin
whistle climbs against fiddle and
the *bodhrán* begins —
    lost cry
of the yellow bittern!

His untimely death in 1971, at the age of 40, was an occasion of national mourning.

The Ó Riada Mass is sung in Cúil Aodha every Sunday morning by the all-male choir that Sean founded, led by his son Peadar on the church organ.

a kind of repossession of a whole body of literature almost unknown to English speakers. The poems are given in the original Irish, set against Kinsella's own translations. The Introduction outlines the evolution of Irish poetic forms, and the poets' function and status after the collapse of the Gaelic order in the seventeenth century.

In the early eighteenth century with English forcibly replacing Irish for all formal occasions and, as pointed out by Lecky the historian, the phrase 'common enemy' being the habitual term by which the unrepresentative Irish Parliament described the great majority of the Irish people, encounters with the law became such a regular part of life that legal terms such as 'Whereas' became a feature of Munster poetry. This was usually in satirical mode, as in O'Rathaille's poem about a priest's stolen cock, which opens with:

Opposite: Séan Ó Riada (1931–1971) playing the bodhrán

WHEREAS the learned Aonghus,
a holy Christian priest,
came before me today
to state his case ...

WHEREAS Aonghus fáithcliste,
sagart cráifeach críostaiteach,
do theacht inniu im láthairse
le gearán cáis is firinne: ...

and concludes:

WHERESOEVER hiding place
Ye find the greedy-gut
Bring him here on a rope
Till I hang him like a blackguard.

WHERESOEVER cuainseachán
ina bhfaighidh sibh an tórpachán
tugaidh chúghamsa é ar ruainseachán
go gcrochad é mar dhreoileacán

Fuaifidh mé mo bhéal le sring fhite
's ní luaifead réad dá bpléid bhig sprionlaithe,
ach fuagraim tréad an chaolraigh chuimsithe
's a bhfuath, a Dhé, tar éis mo mhuintire.

Even the Church bowed to the civil authority. Half a century earlier, when word went out that the Irish chapterhouses had decreed that the clergy were forbidden to make any more songs or verses, the fury of one Dominican priest, Pádraigín Haicéad, who was also a poet, comes bursting explosively through his 'act of submission':

I will sew up my lips with plaited cross-stitching
and not speak of their niggardly pettiness,
but I denounce this pack and their censoring
and their hate, O God, for my fellow-countrymen.

(trans. Michael Hartnett)

In the great bardic schools of old, scholars came to learn history and genealogies, and lay for seven years in darkness perfecting their complex verse-making art, in order to earn high caste, power and riches by their poems (the worst thing that could happen to you was to have a poet write a lampoon about you: it was nearly as bad as the curse of a saint, you had no life thereafter). These schools died in their old form about the middle of the seventeenth century, and were gradually replaced by gatherings which the participants called Cúirteanna Filíochta or Courts of Poetry, where verses were exchanged, recited and judged by their peers.

Corkery, talking about an old illiterate woman he met in Kerry in 1915 who broke into a classic Irish Aisling (or Dream) poem for him, but amusingly changed some of the allusions to more contemporary events, says:

In the Munster of the eighteenth century, there can scarcely have been a single peasant's hut which did not shelter beneath its thatch either such an old woman as this, or an old man of like temper — Gaels who would have thousands upon thousands of lines of well-wrought verse laid up within their memories. Illiterates, yet learned in literature, they were critics who appraised the poems as was right, that is, as lyric poetry, and not as anything else. They gave them welcome rather for the art that was in them than for the tidings. One such poem they put against another, testing both, comparing this poet's opening with that other's, or matching this description (always elaborate) of the flowing locks of the *Spéir-bhean* (the Vision) with that other's painting of them, or evaluating this song's close by the aid of the remembered cadences of a hundred others. (*The Hidden Ireland*)

If in the beginning they were convened for serious study and scholarship, the 'Courts' gradually became gatherings for merriment and rivalry. Instead of being held in someone's house, they were likely to take place in a hostelry. Something resembling those old Courts of Poetry survives into our own day (usually held on a day shortly after Christmas) in the Irish-speaking village of **Cúil Aodha** (or **Coolea** as it is often written in English, and pronounced kool- *ay)* on the borders of Cork and Kerry.

Two major figures of this 'Hidden Ireland' emerged in the area of **Slieve Luachra**, which is just to the north of Cúil Aodha and Rathmore by a tangle of twisty roads between rocky hillsides. They were Aogán Ó Rathaille, towards the end of the seventeenth century and, shortly after his death in 1729, Eoghan Rua Ó Súilleabháin (1748-1784). Separated by three-quarters of a century, they were at opposite poles of style and temperament, alike only in their genius.

Ó Rathaille, born at **Scrahanaveale** (*Screathán an Mhíl*, the Riverside place of the Honey), near the village of **Gullaun,** just north of the Killarney-Rathmore road, was almost the last *file* of the old school, an austere man full of professional pride and arrogance, and bitterly conscious of his loss of dignity and traditional status. In his time the MacCarthys, hereditary rulers of this territory, had been supplanted by the Brownes and, though they were sympathetic and reasonable landlords, and generous in their improvements to their estates, and though they extended their patronage to him, his heart was with the dispossessed MacCarthys.

The Irish held on to their hope of a reversion of fortunes long after the time that good sense would have shown the cause to be hopeless. As an expression of this hope, the 'Aisling' came into being, a form of poetry in which a beautiful young woman — a *spéir-bhean*, a 'sky-woman' or vision — appears to the poet in a dream, and speaks of the lover who will come over the sea to rescue her. The vision is, of course, Ireland herself, and the lover the Stuart prince. Ó Rathaille's Aisling, 'Gile na Gile', is regarded as the most perfect and most exquisite poem of this form ever written, a masterpiece of sibilance and alliteration, almost impossible to translate. Frank O'Connor's version perhaps comes as near as the English language can manage.

Aogán Ó Rathaille (c.1675-1729)

Brightness of brightness lonely met me where I wandered,
Crystal of crystal only by her eyes were splendid,
Sweetness of sweetness lightly in her speech she squandered,
Rose-red and lily-glow brightly in her cheeks contended.

Ringlet on ringlet flowed tress on tress of yellow flaming
Hair, and swept the dew that glowed on the grass in showers
  behind her,
Vesture her breast bore, mirror-bright, oh, mirror-shaming
That her fairy northern land yielded her from birth to bind them.

There she told me, told me as one that might in loving languish,
Told me of his coming, he for whom the crown was wreathed,
Told me of their ruin who banished him to utter anguish,
More too she told me I dare not in my song have breathed.

Gile na gile do chonnarc ar slí in uaigneas,
criostal an chriostail a goirmroisc rinn-uaine
binneas an bhinnis a friotal nár chríonghruama,
deirge is finne do fionnadh 'na gríosghruannaibh.

Caise na caise i ngach ribe dá bui-chuachaibh,
bhaineas an cruinneac den rinneac le rinnscuabadh,
iorra ba ghlaine ná gloine ar a broinn bhuacaigh,
do gineadh ar ghineamhain di-se san tír uachtraigh.

Fios fiosach dom d'inis, is ise go fíor-uaigneach,
fios filleadh don duine don ionad ba rí-dhualgas,
fios milleadh na droinge chuir eisean ar rinnruagairt,
's fios eile ná cuirfead im laoithibh le fíor-uamhan.

Leimhe na leimhe dom druidim 'na cruinntuairim,
im chime ag an gcime do snaidhmeadh go fíorchrua mé;
ar ghoirm Mhic Mhuire dom fhortacht, do bhíog uaimse,
is d'imigh an bhruinneal 'na luisne go bruín Luachra.

Rithim le rith mire im rithibh go croí-luaimneach,
trí imeallaibh corraigh, trí mhongaibh, trí shlímruaitigh;
don tinne-bhrugh tigim — ní thuigim cén tslí fuaras —
go hionad na n-ionad do cumadh le draíocht dhruaga.

Brisid fá scige go scigeamhail buíon ghruagach
is foireann de bhruinnealaibh sioscaithe dlaoi-chuachach;
i ngeimhealaibh geimheal me cuirid gan puinn suaimhnis,
's mo bhruinneal ar broinnibh ag broinnire broinnstuacach.

D'iniseas di-se, san bhfriotal dob fhíor uaimse,
nár chuibhe di snaidhmeadh le slibire slímbhuartha
's an duine ba ghile ar shliocht chine Scoit trí huaire
ag feitheamh ar ise bheith aige mar chaoin-nuachar.

Ar chloistin mo ghutha di goileann go fíor-uaibhreach
is sileadh ag an bhfliche go life as a gríosghruannaibh;
cuireann liom giolla dom choimirc ón mbruín uaithi —
's í gile na gile do chonnarc ar slí in uaigneas.

Frenzy of frenzy 'twas that her beauty did not numb me,
That I neared the royal serf, the vassal queen that held me vassal,
Then I called on Mary's Son to shield me, she started from me
And she fled, the lady, a lightning flash to Luachra Castle.

Fleetly too, I fled in wild flight with body trembling
Over reefs of rock and sand, bog and shining plain and
   strand, sure
That my feet would find a path to that place of sad assembling
House of houses reared of old in cold dry druid grandeur.

There a throng of wild creatures mocked me with elfin laughter
And a group of mild maidens, tall with twining silken tresses,
Bound in bitter bonds they laid me there, and a moment after,
See my lady laughing share a pot-bellied clown's caresses.

Truth of truth I told her in grief that it shamed her,
To see her with a sleek foreign mercenary lover
When the highest peak of Scotland's race already thrice
   had named her
And waited in longing for his exile to be over.

When she heard me speak, she wept, but she wept for pride,
And tears flowed down in streams from cheeks so bright
   and comely,
She sent a watchman with me to lead me to the mountainside,
Brightness of brightness who met me walking lonely.

(*trans. Frank O'Connor*)

After his old patron Sir Nicholas Browne died, Ó Rathaille came to his English-educated son, Sir Valentine, expecting due favours. His disappointment provoked one of his most bitter — though still elegantly-wrought — lamentations. The poet used to be maintained in style by princes and chiefs; now he had to beg small favours from an upstart:

Caiseal gan cliar, fiailteach ná macraí ar dtúis
is beanna-bhruig Bhrain ciarthuilte,
   'mhadraíbh úisc,
Ealla gan triar triaithe de mhacaibh rí
   Mumhan
fá deara dhom triall riamh ort,
   a Vailintín Brún.

That royal Cashel is bare of house and guest
That Brian's turreted home is the otter's nest,
That the kings of the land have neither land nor crown
Has made me a beggar before you, Valentine Brown.

(*trans. Frank O'Connor*)

At the end of his life, an impoverished tenant, only his pride upheld him. The last we know of this lone remnant of a line of high caste comes from a note among the accounts of the Kenmare estate: 'Allowed Egan O'Rahilly when his only cow was appraised last winter, 1726...for composing songs for Master Thomas Browne and the rest of his Lordship's children as per song appears on voucher — at John Riordan's prayer and request: £1-10-0. August 1727.' A great poet is reduced to composing songs for children, for a pittance. But, near death, he refuses to beg any more: he will go to join his family's ancestral patrons:

Now I shall cease, death comes, and I must not delay	Stadfadsa feasta — is gar dom éag gan mhoill
By Laune and Laine and Lee, diminished of their pride,	ó treascradh dragain Leamhan, Léin is Laoi;
I shall go after the heroes, ay, into the clay —	rachad 'na bhfasc le searc na laoch don chill,
My fathers followed theirs before Christ was crucified.	na flatha fá raibh mo shean roimh éag do Chríost.
(trans. Frank O'Connor)	('Cabhair ní Ghairfead' / 'No Help I'll Call')

Eoghan Rua Ó Súilleabháin was born some twenty years after Ó Rathaille's death, at Meentogues, just about a mile from Ó Rathaille's birthplace, and one wonders what muse resides in that remote place to produce two such geniuses, though the contrast in their lifestyles shows how much life had changed in the interim. To quote Corkery: 'Ó Rathaille is a tragic figure, mournful, proud; Eoghan Ruadh's life was even more tragic, but then he was a wastrel with a loud laugh.' Ó Rathaille remembered past glories in want and poverty, clinging with the last ounce of his strength to his shredded dignity; Ó Súilleabháin was the rakish adventurer and womaniser who never knew anything but direst poverty and never had much company but that it was as poor as himself.

Eoghan Rua wrote in both English and Irish. Even today, in the Irish-speaking districts of Munster, you may hear some of his verses from a farmer or publican, and hear tales of his exploits as if he were around yesterday. That wastrel wrote, among much else, nineteen *Aislinge*, each of them full of the most beautiful lyric quality: and, to quote Thomas Kinsella, 'of astonishing technical virtuosity.' One time the Vision came to him in a wood:

Eoghan Rua Ó Súilleabháin (1748-1784)

Ridged thick, plaited yellow, and golden,	Ba trinseach tiubh buí-chasta ar órdhath
Tumbling down to her shoes was her hair;	a dlaoi-fholt go bróig leis an mbé,
Eyebrows unflawed and like amber,	a braoithe gan teimheal is mar an ómra
Her eye a death-lure to the brave;	a claonroisc do bheo-ghoin gach laoch;
Sweet, fluent, delicious, melodious,	ba bhinn blasta fírmhilis ceolmhar
Her voice with *sídhe*-harps would compare;	mar shí-chruit gach nóta óna béal,
Smooth breasts, white as chalk, fully rounded,	's ba mhín cailce a cí' cruinne i gcóir chirt
Defiled by no human, I'd swear. (trans. Gabriel Fitzmaurice)	dar linne nár leonadh le haon.
	('Ceo Draíochta')

Eoghan of the Sweet Mouth arrived in the world at a time when the poets had to find other ways of making a living. He was sometimes a class of hedge schoolmaster, did a few years in the English army or navy, possibly having been press-ganged, and spent a fair bit of his time as a spailpín, a wandering farm labourer. One of his best poems is 'A Chara mo Chléibh' ('Friend of my Breast') written to a friend asking him, in mock-heroic style, to put a handle on his spade, symbol of his servitude and his means of sustenance:

A chara mo chléibh 's a Shéamais ghreannmhair ghráigh
d'fhuil Ghearaltaigh Ghréagaigh éachtaigh armnirt áigh,
maide glan réidh i ngléas bíodh agat dom rámhainn
's mar bharra ar an scléip cuir léi go greanta bacán ...

Make me a handle as straight as the mast of a ship,
Seamus you clever man, witty and bountiful,
Sprung through the Geraldine lords from the kings of Greece,
And fix the treadle and send it back to me soon ...

And he tells how he will charm and distract the foreman with tales of the Trojan wars and Alexander the mighty, and at the end of the day spend his pay —

Mar is fear tú mar mé do chéas an seana-thart lá,
racham araon faoi scléip go tabhairne an stáid;
is rabairneach ghlaofam *ale* is dramanna ar clár,
is taisce go héag ní dhéan d'aon leathphingin pá.

For you're a man like myself with an antique thirst,
So need I say how we'll give the story an end?
We'll shout and rattle our cans the livelong night
Till there isn't as much as the price of a pint to spend.

(*Trans. Frank O'Connor*)

Seafraidh O'Donoghue (1620-1678)
Pierce Ferriter (1600-1653)

Memorial in Killarney to 'The Four Kerry Poets'

In **Killarney** town a *Spéir-bhean*, a Sky-Woman in stone, the work of Seamus Murphy (though not at all one of his best pieces) commemorates 'the Four Kerry Poets' — the two poets of Sliabh Luachra, along with Seafraidh (Geoffrey) O'Donoghue of the Glens and Pierce Ferriter of **Dingle**. Ferriter was a chieftain of Norman origin who ruled in the Dingle peninsula and wrote courtly love-poetry in Irish. He joined the rebellion of 1641 and was hanged for it here in Killarney, on this very spot, which is Gallows Hill. O'Donoghue was involved in the same battle, but somehow managed to save his neck. The O'Donoghues lived at **Glenflesk**. T. J. Barrington, who chronicled the County so thoroughly in his definitive book *Discovering Kerry*, remarks that the O'Donoghues lived wildly in wild places. Seafraidh's parties at Glenflesk castle were as famous as his poetry, and remembered as long. He managed to live on until 1678.

They all lie together now, presumably peacefully, poet and patron, hereditary chief and Norman or English supplanter, in **Muckross Abbey** or nearby **Killegy**. After Ferriter was hanged that October morning in 1653, some other, nameless poet wrote a sweet Aisling for him: 'I saw a vision on the morning of the bright day...'

To the Browns, and to the Herberts, were granted, under the Elizabethan settlement, great tracts of land which included the **Lakes of Killarney**. Even from those times it has been one of the world's best-loved beauty spots. Largely through the generosity of a twentieth-century generation of Herberts, most of that territory has become the property of the State and comprises the bulk of the Killarney National Park. Poets and writers have for generations been inspired by the beauty of the surrounding mountains, lakes, romantic ruins and waterfalls, all brightened even further nowadays in spring by the vivid cloaks of pink rhododendron that fringe the roads and clothe the mountainsides. Beautiful as the rhododendron is, it has become an ecological problem, and intensive efforts have to be deployed to control its virility.

'The King of France might lay out another Versailles, but ... with all his revenues he could not lay out another Muckross,' wrote Bishop Berkeley. 'What is to be said about Turk Lake?' wrote Thackeray in 1843. 'When there, we agreed that it was more beautiful than the large lake, of which it is not one-fourth the size; then, when we came back, we said, "No, the large lake is the most beautiful." And so, at every point we stopped at, we determined that that particular spot was the prettiest in the whole lake.' 'When we consider ... the character of the islands, the singular circumstance of the arbutus, and the uncommon echoes, it will appear, upon the whole, to be in reality superior to all comparison,' said Arthur Young in 1780.

More interesting, perhaps, is an entry in the *Annals of Innisfallen* dated 1180 which says that, because the abbey of Innisfallen was regarded as a secure sanctuary, 'the treasure and the most valuable effects of the whole country were deposited in the hands of its clergy; notwithstanding which, we find the abbey was plundered in this year by Maolduin, son of Daniel O'Donoghue. Many of the clergy were slain.'

In Killarney there is no shortage of aids to discovering and enjoying nature's lavish endowments. There is the folk museum, Muckross House, with its colourful gardens. There are islands, and waterfalls, and picturesque ruins. Red deer roam the mountains as they have since time immemorial, and the ghost of O'Donoghue of the Glens rides the lake by night on his white charger. Dion Boucicault chose the Lower Lake as the setting of his melodrama *The Colleen Bawn*. What matter that the event that inspired the story, the foul murder of an innocent lass, took place on the Shannon estuary; here you will be shown 'the very rock' from which the poor girl was hurled, and the cottage of Danny Mann, the boatman who murdered her for his villainous master.

When you decide to move on, leaving cataracts and rhododendrons and lakes and mountains and woods and deer herds, you might hear the bugle note from the **Gap of Dunloe**, echoing the words of Tennyson, after his visit there in 1848:

> The splendour falls on castle walls
>   And snowy summits old in story,
> The long light shakes across the lakes,
>   And the wild cataract leaps in glory.
> Blow, bugle, blow, set the wild echoes flying,
>   Blow, bugle; answer, echoes, dying, dying, dying. ('Blow, bugle blow')

Tennyson was in Killarney on the invitation of Aubrey de Vere of **Curraghchase**, Co. Limerick — the second invitation, as it happened. On the first occasion, six years earlier, Tennyson and de Vere managed

Bewilderhin the tourists. (A scene at the gap of Dunloe, Killarney.) The various solicitations with which we were beset, to taste the 'Mountain Dew', to hear the 'Wonderous Echoes,' to buy bog oak, and arbutus ornaments, or to invest in 'The Photographs' of 'The Colleen Bawn' or 'The Colleen Das' composed a scene neither to be described nor forgotten. Vide — Diary of a Bewildered Tourist
   (Postcard, c.1900 by Lawrence, Dublin)

Dion Boucicault (1820-1890)

Aubrey de Vere (age 20) (1814-1902)

to miss each other in London when starting out, so Tennyson ended up wandering around disconsolately by himself, at a time when he was in a state of personal and financial distress. This time he was looking for inspiration for his Arthurian cycle, and agreed to come to Ireland where, de Vere assured him, the seascape was wilder, bigger and better. The great man agreed to come under four conditions:

— there was to be no mention of the Irish distress

— he was to be permitted to breakfast late

— he would spend half of each day entirely devoted to writing

— he must be allowed to smoke in the house.

All was agreed to. William Allingham, who was an intimate and an admirer of Tennyson all his life, records his visit: 'On his way home he stopped by the lake of Killarney and there heard a bugler playing by a ruined castle, the echoes continuing until he had heard nine of them, the last "like a chant of angels in the sky," which later became "the horns of Elfland faintly blowing".'

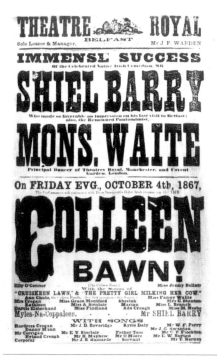

Below: The Colleen Bawn (1911)

(Above) A winged horse guards the lake at Powersourt Gardens near Enniskerry, Co Wicklow. (Right) Glendalough, the 'Valley of the Two Lakes'. Sir Walter Scott, in spite of his lameness, managed the popular feat of crawling into the cave in the cliff-face known as St Kevin's Bed, in 1825.
(Below) Lough Dan, seen on the road from Sally Gap to Roundwood.

(Above) Glenmalure where, writes J.M. Synge, 'after a stormy night's rain the whole valley is filled with a riot of waterfalls.' It is the setting for 'The Shadow of the Glen'.

(Right) Two sides of a boulder in Glenmalure record, in Irish, two battles in the valley, one in 1580, the other in 1798. At that date Wicklow was described as 'a wilderness as impenetrable as the jungles of the Amazon'. (Saunders Newsletter)

(Below) Kilcash, a house of the Butlers. Built in the sixteenth century, it was dismantled and its great woods felled in the eighteenth century, circumstances that gave rise to an anonymous lament beautifully translated by Frank O'Connor.

Shandon Church, with its golden fish weathervane, stands overlooking Cork city.
   'Tis the bells of Shandon
   That sound so grand on
   The pleasant waters of the river Lee,'
sang Frances Sylvester Mahony, alias 'Father Prout'.

The Rock of Cashel, Co. Tipperary. To Aubrey de Vere
it was 'Royal and saintly Cashel.'

(Left) Ross Castle, Killarney, was built in the sixteenth century by O'Dònoghue Mór, one of whose descendants was Seafraidh O'Donoghue of the Glens, one of the Four Kerry Poets commemorated at Gallows Hill in the town.

(Below) Gougane Barra: Watercolour by George Petrie. The valley was the home of Eric Cross's 'Tailor and Anstey', and the setting for Sean O'Faolain's story 'The Silence of the Valley'.

(Above) The Blasket Islands. They look like mere rocks in the western ocean, but the inhabitants of the largest island produced a sizeable body of literature in Irish around the turn of the century.

(Right) Portrait of Mrs Windham Quin of Adare, painted in the 1750s by Stephen Slaughter. Seán Ó Tuama addressed her, in verse, as 'The Dame of the Slender Wattle'.

Coumeenduff, the Black Valley near Killarney, lit by a rainbow. It is scarcely surprising that this wild and lovely territory produced 'a power o' poets'.

"It's the pleasure and diversion of the world you'll hear and see in them Magic Glasses." The Magic Glasses, by Geo. Fitzmaurice.

(Above) 'The Magic Glasses'. Detail dedicated to George Fitzmaurice from the Geneva Window by Harry Clarke. Commissioned by the government as a gift for the League of Nations, it was hastily 'abandoned' on sight of its perhaps 'too virile' Playboy and its virtually naked ladies! A major literary icon by a great artist, it is now owned by the Wolfsonian Foundation, Miami. It features excerpts from fifteen writers: Pearse, Lady Gregory, Shaw, Synge, O'Sullivan, Stephens, O'Casey, Robinson, Yeats, O'Flaherty, AE, Colum, Fitzmaurice, O'Kelly and Joyce.

(Below) 'The Way the Fairies Went' points the way to James Scanlan's sculpture park at the village of Sneem on the Ring of Kerry.

4. KERRY and a touch of CARBERY
'A Power o' Poets'

West of Killarney a wilder Kerry sprawls to the Atlantic in three peninsulas, strange and wonderful territories where the latter-day incursions of summer migrant holiday-makers barely dent the sense of the present being a very thin layer over endless ages of time piled upon time. Puck Fair in **Killorglin**, at which a wild mountain puck goat is crowned and garlanded and hoisted aloft on a platform to reign over three days of post-harvest trading and boisterous drunken merry-making, needs no interpretation of its age-old fertility message.

As you travel down the **Dingle Peninsula**, you travel on roads that thread their way between visible remains of the dwellings, the stockades, the tombs and the lignums of a race or races long vanished.

Stories of these people are still told: legend, myth and pseudo-history intertwined. You can climb, if you have the legs for it, to the summit of **Caherconree** and find there the stone enclosure of Cúroí MacDaire's mist-enshrouded fortress. Half god and half mortal king of an ancient race, the Fir Bolg, he could take the shape of an animal at will, preferring the shape of a hound. He kidnapped Bláthnaid, mistress of the warrior Cúchulainn, and made her his wife. But as a pre-arranged signal Bláthnaid poured milk into the stream descending from the mountain when Cúroí was safely asleep and unarmed. Seeing the river run white, Cúchulainn took the fortress and killed Cúroí. Not far away, a fallen *gallán* in a field near **Camp** village, one of a number of pillar stones in the area, is called after Naoise, doomed lover of Deirdre of the Sorrows. Mad Sweeney, the cursed king (we'll meet him again in County Antrim) came to Gleann na nGealt, the Glen of the Madmen, to drink at the healing well and eat the cress it nourished; the road from Camp to Annascaul runs through the valley. The village of **Annascaul** itself is called after the maiden Skal, who was kidnapped by a giant and drowned herself in the lake before Cúchulainn could reach her.

Ventry strand, further west, was the scene of one of the earliest legendary invasions of Ireland when the Milesian Daire Donn, king of the World, landed to be defeated, in one version of the tale, by Finn MacCumhaill, but in an older and more interesting version by the

The Song of Amergin

I am a stag: of seven tines,
I am a flood: across a plain,
I am a wind: on a deep lake,
I am a tear: the Sun lets fall,
I am a hawk: above the cliff,
I am a thorn: beneath the nail,
I am a wonder: among flowers,
I am a wizard: who but I
Sets the cool head aflame with smoke?

I am a spear: that roars for blood,
I am a salmon: in a pool,
I am a lure: from paradise,
I am a hill: where poets walk,
I am a boar: ruthless and red,
I am a breaker: threatening doom,
I am a tide: that drags to death,
I am an infant: who but I
Peeps from the unhewn dolmen arch?

I am a womb: of every holt,
I am the blaze: on every hill,
I am the queen: of every hive,
I am the shield: for every head,
I am the tomb: of every hope.

(Robert Graves)

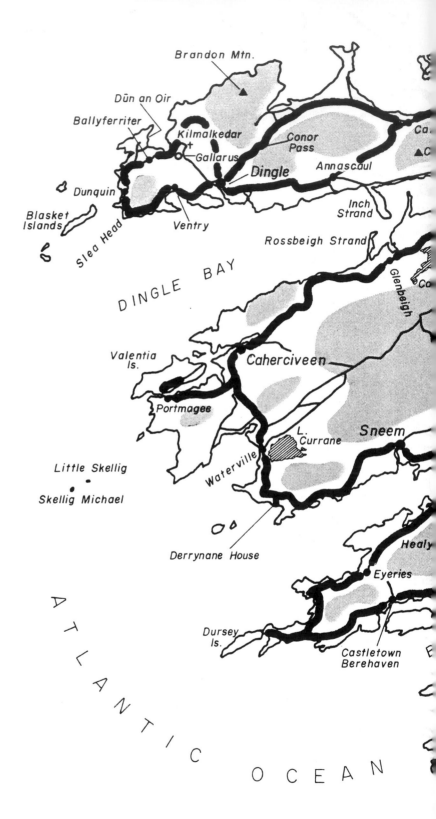

The Blasket Centre at Dún Chaoin (on the mainland) with a windswept Tomás Ó Criomhthain by sculptor Michael Quane.

Tomás Ó Criomhthain (1856-1937)
Muiris Ó Súileabháin (1904-1950)
Peig Sayers (1873-1958)

Robin Flower (1881-1946)

magical arts of the Tuatha de Danann, the people of Danu. (A matched pair of mountains just east of Killarney, each with a cairn on the summit, are named the **Paps of Danu**.) But the Milesians eventually forced a landing, and to this occasion is ascribed the most ancient poetic incantation known to the western world, the Song of Amergin, leaping straight out of the darkness of the creation myth. What has come down is in very archaic Gaelic, in an intricate half-rhyming form. Robert Graves has dealt with it extensively in *The White Goddess*, his poetical exposition on the origins of myth. His version is quoted on page 50 above.

The myth still doesn't let go its grip. **Kilvickadownig**, a ruined chamber tomb inland from Ventry, is said to be the grave of Daire Donn. It is close to the townland of **Caherbullig**, the holding of Bolg, god of lightning and tutelary god of the Fir Bolg.

From Ventry the road westward reaches a veritable crescendo of magnificence as it passes under the hillside crowded with ancient habitation sites, to round **Slea Head** in a grand flourish as the **Blasket Islands** break on the view. Beyond, there is nothing but the rough and rude Atlantic. This is the next parish to America.

The tail-end of the mountain ridge that runs the 30 miles down the peninsula emerges from under the sea as the **Great Blasket Island**, surrounded by smaller islands and a cluster of jagged rocks, monster's teeth. Until 1953 a small community shared these rocky sea-lashed perches on the ultimate edge of Europe with the seabirds: their elemental lifestyle has been recorded for us by a number of the islanders. *An tOileánach*, (*The Islandman*), by Tomás Ó Criomhthain, was the first and remains the most important of these accounts, and covers his life from earliest childhood memory, about 1860, to the mid-1920s. It was published in 1929.

Fiche Bliain ag Fás (*Twenty Years a-Growing*) by Muiris Ó Súileabháin followed in 1933 and *Peig*, the autobiography of Peig Sayers, came out in 1936. Poor Peig's recollections have suffered from having been prescribed reading for generations of bored schoolchildren. There were other fragments too, stories and poems. It is astonishing that despite their near-subsistence economy, the islanders were in the early years of this century literate in both English and Irish, and spared the time from their labours to write about their lives, or at least dictate their stories.

It was 'scholars' from outside who influenced the islanders to write those stories in their own language. Synge came in August 1905, the first of the literary visitors. His photos were probably the first ever taken on the island. Norwegian Carl Marstrander came in the summer of 1907 to learn Irish. The islanders called him 'An Lochlannach', the

Tomás Ó Criomhthain

Viking. They loved and admired him for his strength and his pole-vaulting prowess.

The Viking sent his student, Englishman Robin Flower to the island, and he became known affectionately there as 'Bláithín', the little blossom. His own book *The Western Island* offers a lovely insight into life on the island, and *The Irish Tradition* is a fine scholarly work. There were others too, but in the end it was a Killarney man, Brian Ó Ceallaigh, who persuaded Tomás Ó Criomhthain to write an account of his life, having lent him some of Maxim Gorky's works. Later came George Derwent Thomson. He it was who persuaded Muiris Ó Súile-abháin to join the Garda Síochána, the police force, instead of following a trail of island people to Springfield, Massachusetts.

Twenty Years a-Growing was introduced by E.M. Forster, who

Love poem by Pierce Ferriter
(trans. by the Earl of Longford)

I charge you, lady, young and fair,
Straightway to lay your arms aside.
Lay by your armour, would you dare
To spread the slaughter far and wide?

O lady, lay your armour by,
Conceal your curling hair also
For never was a man could fly
The coils that o'er your bosom flow.

And if you answer, lady fair,
That north or south you ne'er took life,
Your very eyes, your glance, your air,
Can murder without axe or knife.

And oh! if you but bare your knee
If you your soft hand's palm advance
You'll slaughter many a company.
What more is done with shield and lance?

Oh, hide your bosom limey white
Your naked side conceal from me.
Ah, show them not in all men's sight,
Your breasts more bright than flowering tree.

And if in you there's shame or fear
For all the murders you have done,
Let those bright eyes no more appear,
Those shining teeth be seen of none.

Lady, we tremble far and near!
Be with these conquests satisfied
And lest I perish, lady dear,
Oh, lay those arms of yours aside.

Top Right: Peig Sayers

described it as 'an account of neolithic civilisation from the inside' and as 'the egg of a sea-bird — lovely, perfect, and laid this very morning.'

At the turn of the century, the population of the islands — a few of the other rocks were inhabited too — was about 150. At the time of the final evacuation in 1953, there were only 20 souls left; for a while the island school catered for just one small boy.

A newspaper article at the time headlined a story about the boy, Gearóid Ó Catháin, as 'The Loneliest Boy in the World', but in a interview a few years ago he declared that in fact his memories are of unalloyed bliss. 'It was a tremendous childhood, like being in Disneyland. I felt I was as old as the people around me. There was no such thing as "go home and mind your own business." I was brought everywhere, hunting, fishing, rowing.' And the newspaper article had brought him gifts from all over the world.

A boat from **Dún Chaoin (Dunquin)** will take you to the Great Blasket. The island is four miles long, half a mile wide at its lowest and widest point, and nearly a thousand feet high along a knife-like backbone running away into the teeth of the south-western gales. After years of loneliness, when only the occasional fisherman or sheepherder visited the island, some life has returned to the Blasket; some of the old houses have been repaired and reroofed, families take up summer abode, and children once more run free among the rocks. At times a simple guesthouse offers bed and meals.

Strange as it may seem, even these fragments off the edge of real land had a landlord as far back as the Middle Ages. The chieftains were the Feiritéaraigh, or Ferriters, an important Anglo-Norman family who came as settlers in the thirteenth century. Back on the mainland, beyond Dún Chaoin and Ballyferriter, a small road leads to Ferriter's Cove and, standing guard over it on the hillside, is Ferriter's Castle.

One of this family was Pierce Ferriter, scholar and soldier, and one of the 'Four Kerry Poets' commemorated by the monument in Killarney. He is remembered with many romantic legends. As a chieftain of this West Kerry area he fought with the insurgents in the wars of 1641–53, and was captured and hanged at Gallows Hill in Killarney in 1653. Despite his Norman origins, he wrote in Irish rather than French or English, though his poems were straight out of the high European tradition of the *amour courtois*, here at the remote edge of Kerry:

Pierce Ferriter (1600-1653)

O Woman, shapely as the swan,
On your account I shall not die:
The men you've slain — a trivial clan —
were less than I.

I ask me shall I die for these —
For blossom teeth and scarlet lips —
And shall that delicate swan shape
Bring me eclipse?

Well shaped the breasts and smooth the skin,
The cheeks are fair, the tresses free —
And yet I shall not suffer death,
God over me!

Those even brows, that hair like gold,
Those languorous tones, that virgin way,
The flowing limbs, the rounded heel
Slight men betray!

Thy spirit keen through radiant mien,
Thy shining throat and smiling eye,
Thy little palm, thy side like foam —
I cannot die!

O Woman shapely as the swan,
In a cunning house hard reared was I:
O bosom white, O well-shaped palm,
I shall not die!   *(trans. Padraic Colum)*

Some at least of his love poems were addessed to Meg Russell, an English relative of Richard Boyle, Earl of Cork, and one wonders where and when he met her or caught sight of her, what the poems meant to her, if anything — did she even understand Irish?

Close to Ferriter's Cove lies **Dún an Óir**, Fort del Oro, the Fort of

Above poem trans. by Padraic Colum is attributed to Pierce Ferriter (possibly erroneously)

Gold: whichever language it is named in, it is now no more than a grassy knoll on a headland. Its associations are far from golden. One day in the year 1580 six hundred Spanish and Italian soldiers, who had come to aid the Irish in the Elizabethan war, surrendered 'at discretion' to a superior force. They were disarmed, and massacred. Helping Lord Grey in this nice act of war was the poet Edmund Spenser and, some historians say, Sir Walter Raleigh.

But gentler ghosts are more welcome here. Places of such scenic grandeur as this western peninsula always attracted those in search of solitude: hermits, monks, contemplatives. The earliest and most primitive church, **Gallarus Oratory**, which has the shape of an upturned boat, is close to **Smerwick Harbour**. Not far from it is **Kilmalkedar** church, of a later and possibly more relaxed date, with an alphabet stone and sundial. From it, faintly, can still be traced the Saint's Road disappearing upwards into the mists which usually shroud the summit of Brandon mountain.

Brandon, of course, is named for Saint Brendan — Brendan the Navigator. He was born near **Tralee** around the year 490, founded several monasteries, and is known to have visited the island of Iona, the Orkney and Shetland Islands, Britain and Brittany, before he died at a ripe old age. Based on stories and some fragmentary Latin accounts of some of his travels, there grew up a tale which medieval Europe took to its heart and translated into several languages. It told of a long and tortuous voyage undertaken by Brendan and his crew in search of the promised land of the blessed far to the west. Many of the episodes are clearly fantastical. Others, which seem fanciful on first reading, are open to interpretation: the sea of curdled milk for instance, and pillars of transparent crystal, the island of giants fighting with flames and burning rocks. Could these not be descriptions of an ice-pack, icebergs, and the volcanos of Iceland? An island on which they landed and attempted to camp submerged as soon as they lit a fire: it was a great whale. This episode is illustrated on several medieval maps. They visited an Island of Sheep and an Island of Birds — the Faroes and Hebrides? And in the story, the saint found land beyond a swirling fog which could be identified with the mists which frequent the Newfoundland coast.

The *Navigatio Sancti Brendani Abbatis* became one of the most famous and enduring stories of western Christendom. The possibility that Brendan actually reached America in his voyagings, a thousand years before Columbus, gained new currency in the 1970s when writer and intrepid traveller Tim Severin built a leather boat to the exact description of that in the old manuscripts, and sailed it to America. His voyage, like that of Brendan's, began at **Brandon Creek**, at the westerly foot of the mountain.

A fifteenth-century illustration — St Brendan and the whale island.

Tim Severin's famous Brendan Voyage in the 1970s.

It is worth climbing Brandon if you have the time and energy — and are sufficiently mountain-wise — for the glory of sea and landscape all around. (The ascent from the eastern side of the mountain is more spectacular, but more tricky in unpredictable weather). If your energy doesn't extend to such an undertaking, you could, at least, like J.M. Synge, climb **Sybil Head**:

I walked up this morning along the slope from the east to the top of Sybil Head, where one comes out suddenly on the brow of a cliff with a straight fall of many hundred feet into the sea. It is a place of indescribable grandeur, where one can see Carrantuohill and the Skelligs and Loop Head and the full sweep of the Atlantic, and, over all, the wonderfully tender and searching light that is seen only in Kerry ... One wonders in these places why anyone is left in Dublin, or London, or Paris, when it would be better, one would think, to live in a tent or hut with this magnificent sea and sky, and to breathe this wonderful air, which is like wine in one's teeth.

Wood cut for one of the 1,000 medieval versions of the Brendan voyage.

An even earlier voyage-tale than Brendan's, one which some relate also to Brandon mountain, is *The Voyage of Bran*. As everyone knows, Tír na nÓg, the Land of Youth, Hy Brasil, lies away to the magical west. As Bran sails outward, Manannán Mac Lir, god of the sea, travels over the sea in his chariot towards the mortal voyager: and again as everyone knows, things are different in the Otherworld: what is sea to one is land to the other. Manannán speaks:

> It seems to Bran a wondrous beauty
> in his curragh on a clear sea;
> while to me in my chariot from afar
> it is a flowery plain on which I ride.
>
> What is a clear sea
> For the prowed craft in which Bran is,
> is a Plain of Delights with profusion of flowers
> for me in my two-wheeled chariot ...

Speckled salmon leap from the womb
of the white sea on which you look;
they are calves, they are bright-coloured lambs,
at peace, without mutual hostility.   (*trans. Proinsias MacCana*)

In this enchanted territory such visions could well come to confuse even the modern traveller. When you leave, it might be as well to avoid the **Glen of the Madmen** between Annascaul and Camp, and make your journey instead over the wild grandeur of the **Conor Pass**.

The **Ring of Kerry** is the Grand Atlantic Route which encircles the Iveragh Peninsula. From Killarney back to Killarney is 120 miles, to be savoured slowly. Through Killorglin, then on through **Glenbeigh** to look down on the silver sprawl of **Rossbeigh** strand, and on to the busy untidy market town of Cahirciveen. Beyond Cahirciveen lies **Valentia Island**. From your 'Ring' road a smaller road leads to **Portmagee** where a bridge spans the gap between mainland and island. Cross over, and turn to the left. Then stop. Far off on the horizon you will see emerging from the sea, almost like a mirage, two rock pyramids. The smaller one, the **Little Skellig**, harbours a great colony of gannets that wheel and cry and plunge dizzily into the sea with

Beehive huts on the Skelligs — one of western Europe's strangest places

immense speed. The larger island is one of western Europe's strangest places. **Skellig Michael**, as it is known, 700 sheer sea-battered feet high, harbours on one of its twin peaks a nest, not just of sea-birds, though the comical puffins love this rock, but of drystone anchorite cells, along with an oratory, a tiny graveyard marked by a handful of crudely carved crosses, and the remnants of a few terraces once cultivated to grow a few handfuls of grain to help sustain life in this ultimate retreat from the world. Pilgrims came here well into the nineteenth century to make the ritual ascent of the second and even dizzier peak — a heart-stopping climb of sheer rock walls, through a narrow upward passage — the proverbial eye of a needle — to step at last and lean over nothingness to kiss a cross-marked slab. 'Skellig Michael,' said Shaw, 'is not after the fashion of this world.'

Coming back to earth, you might want to continue the journey around the Ring through airy **Waterville**, to pause at **Derrynane**, once the home of Daniel O'Connell, the great eighteenth century Liberator of Ireland's Catholic poor. Derrynane House, now a museum of sorts, was built in the late 1700s by Donal Mór O'Connell; it was the first slated house in Kerry. One of his children was Eileen Dubh, who eloped with dashing and reckless Art O'Laoghaire. His murder only a few years later led to her famous caoineadh, the anguished Keen for Art O'Leary, some of which is given in Chapter 3.

The O'Connells of Derrynane were one of a very few old Catholic Gaelic families that survived with some substance through the worst of the penal times, largely because of their remoteness. Their main business was that of 'export/import' — in other words smuggling, which was a major occupation and livelihood all along this largely inaccessible coast. 'Imports' consisted mainly of contraband such as brandy, cloths and tobacco. Exports included young men and women, on their way to the Continent for education, for holy orders and for service in armies overseas, all forbidden to Catholics by the Penal Laws. One of them later summed it up: their faith, their education, their wine and their clothing were equally contraband.

Of the numerous members of that extended family, the most illustrious was Daniel 'the Liberator', born in 1775 near **Cahirciveen** and inheriting Derrynane and its estate. As a lawyer he was totally committed to constitutional agitation; as an MP he and his supporters often held the balance of power. Under his influence many of the old restrictive laws were lifted, and Catholic Emancipation was achieved. Because he taught the common people, the poor and the landless their power in numbers, he became known as the King of the Beggars, which is the title of Sean O'Faolain's biography of this larger-than-life figure: his eloquence, wit, energy, ambiguity, slyness, legal genius, and appetite for life were legendary.

A visit to 'The Skellig Experience' Visitor Centre on Valentia Island, and the sea-trip around the two islands, is the recommended way nowadays to view this extraordinary place. The Visitor Centre is a good place too to find out about the remarkable richness of marine life out there, making it one of the finest diving areas in western Europe.

Literary Tour of Ireland

Alfred Perceval Graves (1846-1931)

Och! Father O'Flynn, you've the wonderful
  way wid you,
All the ould sinners are wishful to pray wid
  you,
All the young childer are wild for to play
  wid you
You've such a way wid you, Father avick!
Still for all you've so gentle a soul,
Gad, you've your flock in the grandest
  control,
Checking the crazy ones,
Coaxing on aisy ones,
Lifting the lazy ones on wid the stick.

Daphne du Maurier (1907-1989)

The Hag of Beara (trans. John Montague)

Ebb tide has come for me:
My life drifts downwards
Like a retreating sea
With no tidal turn.

I am the Hag of Beara,
Fine petticoats I used to wear,
Today, gaunt with poverty,
I hunt for rags to cover me ...

These arms, now bony, thin
And useless to younger men,
Once caressed with skill
The limbs of princes! ...

Sadly my body seeks to join
Them soon in their dark home —
When God wishes to claim it,
He can have back his deposit ...

Why should I care?
Many's the bright scarf
Adorned my hair in the days
When I drank with the gentry.

No storm has overthrown
The royal standing stone.
Every year the fertile plain
Bears its crop of yellow grain.

Sneem is a brightly-painted village with two village greens and a collection of sculptures including one called 'The Way the Fairies Went'. Alfred Perceval Graves is remembered here. Father of Robert Graves, author of *I Claudius* and *The White Goddess*, he was a distinguished and talented member of a distinguished and talented family. Their home was **Parknasilla**. Local priest Fr Michael Walsh was the model for a 'poem' of Alfred's which became a drawing-room favourite.

But then, Kerry always had, as one Kerryman put it to me, 'a power o' poets'. A tiny village like **Kilgarvan**, on the back road from Kenmare to Killarney, could find it proper to erect a plaque on the Community Centre wall to honour one of their number, Johnny Nora Aodha Ó Tuama, 'and all Kilgarvan's poets'. The fact that their fame had not spread through the English-speaking world made them no less honoured in their own territory. Denis O'Sullivan, the postmaster (for there is also a power of Denis O'Sullivans around), will be happy to talk to you, and recite you a few lines of Sean's, or some other local poet's — or, maybe, his own!

The southern peninsula, that of **Beara**, Kerry shares with Cork; the county border runs along the spine of mountains that marches along it from root to tip. All routes across and around it are spectacular; it is worth the time to take a kind of zig-zag course, **Kenmare** to **Glengarriff** over the 'tunnels' road, along the coast to **Adrigole**, then up over the ribbon-folded **Healy Pass** to **Lauragh**, and westwards as far as you are drawn towards the peninsula's tip — even onto **Dursey Island**, by the ramshackle cable car which conveys you creakingly over the rushing tide-race, accompanied maybe by a bicycle or two, a dog or even a cow. The shoulder of **Hungry Hill** rises towards the west beyond Adrigole village; Daphne du Maurier's book named for the hill and the five generations of a family who ran its copper mines, made a successful film in 1945 with Margaret Lockwood. It is claimed that, despite the explicit location, du Maurier never visited the place.

Timeless images still persist. The ancient fertility goddess is remembered here as An Cailleach Beara. The Hag of Beara, now in the form of an old crone, mourns her lost youth. In the Christianised version we know now, she apparently has taken the veil, but her mind wanders back to the delights of her young and pagan life.

But I, who feasted royally
By candlelight, now pray
In this darkened oratory.
Instead of heady mead

And wine, high on the bench
With kings, I sup whey
In a nest of hags:
God pity me!

Flood tide
And the ebb dwindling on the sand!
What the flood rides ashore
The ebb snatches from your hand.

That poem probably came into being over a thousand years ago. The earth-goddess vision still lives, evoked strongly in the poetry of Nuala Ní Dhomhnaill. Nuala lived some of her youth in Kerry — in the Dingle Gaeltacht — and finds expression in Irish for her powerful poems. Leading poets have tried their hands at translation. Her twentieth-century 'Cailleach' echoes the old one of Beara:

Nuala Ní Dhomhnaill (1952-   )

Taibhríodh dom gur mé an talamh,
   gur mé paróiste Fionntrá
   ar a fhaid is ar a leithead,
   soir, siar, faoi mar a shíneann sí.
Gurbh é grua na Maoilinne grua
   mo chinn agus Sliabh an Iolair
   mo chliathán aniar;

Once I dreamt I was the earth,
The parish of Ventry its length and breadth,
east and west, as far as it runs,
that the brow of the Maoileann
was my forehead, Mount Eagle
the swell of my flank ...
   (trans. John Montague)

Her daughter ran to her crying in fright:

'... Tuigeadh dom go raibh na cnoic ag bogadáil,
   gur fathach mná a bhí ag luascadh a cíocha,
   is go n-éireodh sí aniar agus mise d'íosfadh.'

'... I thought I saw the mountains heaving
like a giantess, with her breasts swaying,
about to loom over, and gobble me up.'

Her poetry has the fierce tenderness of Kerry's rocky acres. Journalist Kevin Myers has found in them 'ancient narratives and unseen and ceaselessly potent divinities infesting word, stream and field.' Her love poem 'Stronghold' or 'Dún' echoes in its intensity, and in some of its images, the 'Keen for Art O Laoghaire':

Id ghéaga daingne
   ní bhfaighidh mé bás choíche,
   ní thiocfaidh orm aon sceimhle,
   ní líonfaidh orm anbhá.
Ní chloisfidh mé
   ag gíoscán ins an oíche
   fearsaid na cairte fuafair'
   a ghluaiseann trí pháirc an áir ...
Coinnigh go daingean mé
   laistigh don gciorcal draíochta
   le teas do cholainne
   le teasargan do chabhaile.
Do chneas lem chneas
   do bhéal go dlúth lem béalaibh
   ní chluinfead na madraí allta
   ag uallfairt ar an má.

In your fortress arms
I will never die
I will fear no evil
Terror will not strike me
I will not hear
The creaking in the night
The loaded wheels
Moving through the battlefield ...
Hold me in your strong
Conjuring circle
With the heat of your body
The warmed, sound frame,
Your skin on my skin
Mouth on my mouth firmly
I will not hear the wolves
Howling on the plain.

Before leaving Beara, a visit to the garden glories of **Garinish Island** is a joy worth the price of tolerating the too-enthusiastic blandishments of the boatmen offering their services.

Drombeg stone circle

Somerville and Ross (1858-1949 and 1862-1915)

From **Bantry** one can take the coast road — The Carbery Coast — back to Cork; easily said, but this is no ordinary coast. **West Cork** is a world of its own. The route goes by **Ballydehob**, colourful hamlet on a hill, skirts **Roaring Water Bay** with Carbery's Hundred Isles, to **Skibbereen**, then on to **Clonakilty** and **Bandon**. Take it slowly.

The Bronze Age miners who hollowed out tunnels in Beara's Mount Gabriel left their ritual monuments scattered throughout this territory. Most remarkable are the stone circles — almost a hundred of them, ranging in size from the large coastal rings of up to seventeen stones, to the class of small five-stone circles of the hillsides. Two high portal stones open to the east, a recumbent stone points to the west, to the eye of the setting sun. They were not for burials: these people buried their dead in wedge-shaped tombs covered by a mound of earth. Nobody knows what spirits were called up here, or what propitiations were offered for weather or fecundity, but they have outlasted any other evidence of the human imprint in their four-thousand-year existence. Some of them are signposted; others you will come by accidentally as you wander by the laneways. Their life as gathering-places might be judged by the fact that the circle at **Drombeg**, east of **Glandore**, has by it a cooking pit which can hold up to seventy-five gallons of liquid.

A road southwards out of Skibbereen leads one into the fictional world of Skebawn, where the unfortunate 'Irish R.M.' (an Englishman, of course) tried to cope with the vagaries and antics of the locals. The Resident Magistrate (or R.M.) was a kind of cross between Chief Constable and local Sheriff, and the bafflement of an English gentleman meeting up with a very different way of looking at things created the humour for a television series that became immensely popular some years ago.

The Irish R.M., his friend Flurry Knox ('who looked like a stable boy among gentlemen, and a gentleman among stable boys'), Knox's indomitable grandmother, Lady Knox, all that grand cast of wise and zany characters, and the life of hunting, sailing and fishing, were a pretty true reflection of life in the there and then, but observed with an eye which had a grand sense of the absurd. They were the unlikely invention of two remarkable Victorian ladies from Castletownshend, cousins and close collaborators, Edith Œnone Somerville and Violet Martin, called 'Ross' because that was the name of her first home in County Galway.

Both Somerville and Ross were born in the middle of the last century. 'Ross' died in 1915; Edith Somerville lived on until 1949, maintaining a vigorous literary output to the end. The **Castletownshend** of their time has barely changed. It consists mainly of one steep street falling 'unhesitatingly as Niagara' towards a small harbour,

Somerville and Ross (Violet Martin, 'Ross', on right) about 1895.

interrupted half way by the Two Trees — two sycamores growing in the middle of the road and acting as a kind of central focus of the village. Apple trees show over high stone walls, and one can imagine ladies in long skirts playing tennis with large wooden rackets, frozen in time.

A handful of families have lived here for a couple of centuries, intermarrying and largely insulated from the outside world — the Townshends who gave the place its name, the Somervilles, the Coghills and the Chavasses. Their lives may be still, for all we know, taken up with hunting, boating and regattas, tennis parties and picnic excursions. A few outsiders have infiltrated to buy homes in the village but the old families are still firmly rooted. The Townshends still live at **Castle Townshend** at the bottom of Main Street next to the harbour (it is now a guesthouse); **Drishane**, Edith Somerville's home, is at the top of the hill near the entrance to the village. To her it was 'the most

Castletownshend

wonderful and splendid house in the world.'

The genius of Somerville and Ross was not limited to lively stories of romps and gleeful hunting escapades. *The Real Charlotte* is an unsentimental portrait of a jealous and ruthless woman, and *The Big House of Inver* chronicles the decline of an almost feudal lifestyle. The remarkable collaboration of the two women continued, according to Edith, even after Ross's death. Edith had been drawn somewhat to spiritualism by then, as were Yeats and AE, and anything she wrote thereafter was signed in their joint names.

They rest close together in the little churchyard of the Protestant church of St Barrahane at the bottom of the hill close to the sea, a cross for Ross, a plain stone for Somerville. Inside are three stained-glass windows by Harry Clarke, and a whole wall taken up by a detailed history of the Townshend family. It is a wonder of the stone-cutter's craft, but nobody seems to know who carved it.

On a hill nearby a line of three Standing Stones, called **The Three Fingers**, stands against the sky. 'They are sudden and strange, breath-taking in their unexpectedness,' wrote Edith. She and her brother one midsummer morning proved them to be aligned to the rising sun. Once there had been four Fingers. Someone removed the fourth to make a pretty feature for a rock garden.

If you are returning to Cork along the Bandon road, you will shortly find yourself in the countryside through which Alice Taylor danced so happily *To School through the Fields*. After Alice was heard in a radio interview one morning in May 1988 talking about growing up in Innishannon, there were queues outside every bookseller's shop by midday to buy her enchanting book.

Continuing towards Cork, a little before **Rosscarbery** are the ruins of **Derry House**, where Charlotte Payne Town-send (whether or not it had a 'h' in the middle was always a matter of argu-ment among various branches of the family) spent 'a perfectly hellish child-hood' before getting away to London to join the suffragette movement and, eventually, to marry George Bernard Shaw when they were both in their for-ties. When, some years later, they paid a visit to her old home, the relatives got into quite a state about it, terrified that they wouldn't be able to cope with his socialist opinions, his acerbic wit and vegetarian diet.

An illustration by Edith Somerville

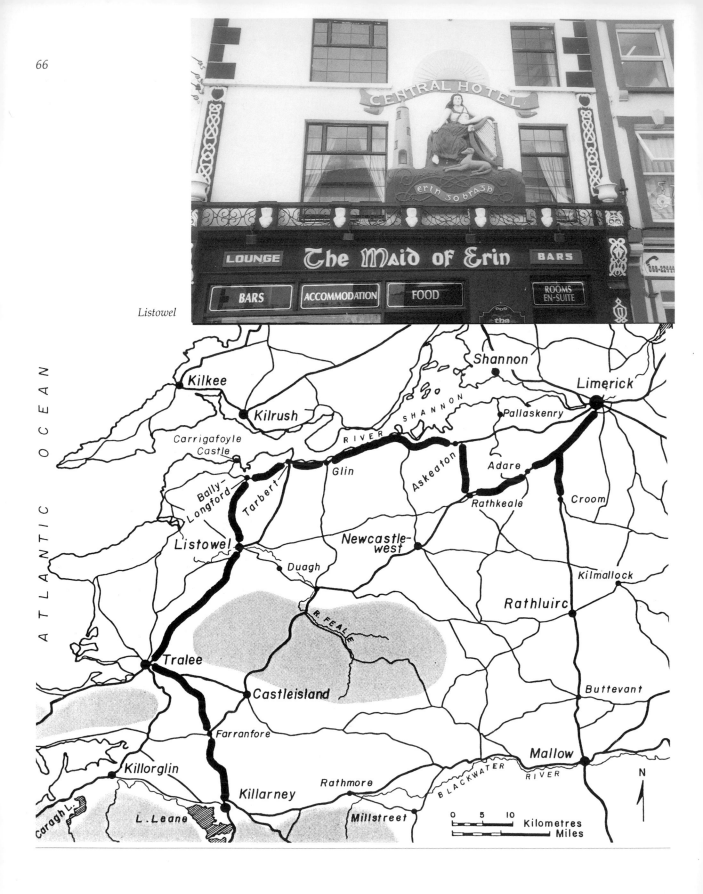

Listowel

5. KILLARNEY TO LIMERICK
Pubs, Roses and the Colleen Bawn

Our road from Killarney to Limerick is via Listowel and Tralee —
where they crown a Rose every year not with thorns but with the
warmest of compliments: 'The Rose of Tralee' is not only one of
Ireland's favourite songs but also the occasion for one of its best parties.

Listowel is home every summer to a Writers' Week of lectures
and workshops. And with good reason, because this small town
and district has produced more than its share of eminent storytellers
and dramatists. One of them was Bryan MacMahon, whom a couple
of generations of schoolboys were lucky enough to have had as
schoolmaster. This is what he had to say about his native town
(prefaced by a remark, mind you, that you can't believe a man's
oath when he talks about his native place):

Bryan MacMahon (1909–1998)

In Listowel we have a literary tradition nurtured by a rare bookseller called
Dan Flavin who corresponded with Axel Munthe when the young Swedish
doctor, then in Naples, had just written his first book, *Letters from a Mourning
City*.

Many years ago Dan sent to the Shakespeare Press in Paris for copies of the
first edition of Joyce's *Ulysses*; a copy of the massive uncut book he thrust into
my boyish hand and said: 'Read that and don't let anyone see it.'

The word Walpurgisnacht almost bowled me over. And, wheeoo! when I think
of my callow mind struggling with the enormities of Molly Bloom's soliloquy,
I feel suddenly assured that boys are tougher than the proverbial hames-strap.

Dan and a fine classical college named for the Archangel Michael, produced a
tribe of writers in our small community.

The 'tribe of writers', apart from MacMahon himself, includes
Maurice Walsh and John B. Keane. Walsh wrote a short story called
The Quiet Man. It was taken up by John Ford, expanded, inflated and
transformed into a multi-million dollar movie which created an image
of Ireland more potent and more enduring than the combined efforts
of the Tourist Board, the Board of Trade and even Eurovision. Ford
chose to shoot the film around Cong in County Mayo, which we will
reach eventually.

John B. Keane is a local publican. His pub is near the bottom of

Maurice Walsh (1879-1964)
John B Keane (1928-   )

John B. Keane

George Fitzmaurice (1877-1963)

George Fitzmaurice portrait by Harry Kernoff. See also colour pages for reproduction of the panel dedicated to him in Harry Clarke's Geneva window.

William Street and around the corner from where Bryan MacMahon lived in **Church Street**. John B. has spent many years serving pints and listening and exchanging gossip and stories with his customers. Out of these stories, and what his keen eye, ear, wisdom and wit gleaned in a lifetime of observing, he has fashioned a series of dramas that, earlier on, were regarded as wildly improbable, certainly over-melodramatic. The Abbey Theatre, true to form, rejected his first play, *Sive*, but it was taken up with more enthusiasm by the amateur dramatic movement. Gradually a more sophisticated world, with a more honest appraisal of current affairs, was forced to accept his contention that, far from exaggerating the foibles and passions of human nature, he had to understate to gain any acceptance at all. A story of Keane's, *The Field*, made another spectacular film — also shot in County Galway rather than Kerry. I should also mention that another memorable film, *Ryan's Daughter*, directed by David Lean, was shot mostly in the Dingle Peninsula.

Then there was George Fitzmaurice, strange, shy, reclusive but with a fantastic imagination. Micheál MacLiammóir described him as 'a kind of literary Rousseau de Douanier, who bridged the worlds of fantasy and reality in a manner that is only today (i.e. in 1949) beginning to find real appreciation.' He wrote some short stories which were published in *The Weekly Freeman*, but he was middle-aged, and still a lowly civil service clerk, before he wrote his wonderful fantasy plays, *The Enchanted Land*, the even stranger *The Dandy Dolls*, and *The Magic Glasses*. So innovative was the latter that when it was first produced at The Abbey Theatre, in August 1913, the critic Joseph Holloway wrote: '*The Magic Glasses* is the maddest of the Abbey madhouse farces yet presented. Nothing surprises an Abbey audience now — they expect everything and anything in the plays.' On the other hand, stained glass artist Harry Clarke regarded it so highly that he used it for a panel in his famous 'Geneva' window, illustrating the best Irish writing from 1900 to 1930. Strange creatures, Fitzmaurice's people. Half-real and half-bewitched, some of them gods of other elements, especially of the sea, others from more mysterious realms. What they have in common is that they all have the outward characteristics of ordinary peasants, and they all talk in explosive torrents in the language of his own north Kerry district, so highly idiomatic that it takes on a totally exotic quality, at times almost requiring an interpreter.

The Fitzmaurice family home was Doagh House at **Doagh**. When George's parson father died the family moved to **Kilcarabeg**, a mile upstream. Doagh is about four miles from Listowel on the Abbeyfeale Road. To visit the site, turn left at the crossroads in the middle of Doagh's one street onto a narrow leafy lane: a gate where the road turns sharply leads into the old estate grounds of Doagh House, or

Springmount, as they liked to call it. The Fitzmaurices are all gone from here now; the house as well. But unlike the story of Bowenscourt, the O'Connor family, who now own the land, having once been tenants of the Fitzmaurices, honour their predecessors. The oak avenue is still there, and the lime grove, and the O'Connors treasure some of the family papers.

George is remembered as a man who enjoyed his quiet pint in a pub, loved the music hall, and always kept his hat on. Shy and reserved at the best of times, he turned his back on the world after some unfavourable reviews, and became almost forgotten. He died, unnoticed, in a cold and bare back room at No. 3 Harcourt Street, Dublin. Beside the bed was found a pencilled note: 'Author is prepared to sell outright all rights in 14 plays dealing intimately with life in the Irish countryside. Most have already been either printed or published. Suitable on which to build musical, television etc. Pass to anyone interested.'

Some time after his death Michael O'Connor took a stone from the old house and, with publisher Liam Miller, had it inscribed and placed on his grave in Mount Jerome in Dublin.

Producer Hugh Hunt said in an interview: 'I came across the play (*The Dandy Dolls*) recently when the Fitzmaurice collection was sent me for review ... The power of its fantasy and its extraordinary imagery simply bowl you over. When the Abbey asked me do (Synge's) *The Well of the Saints* this summer, I decided I simply had to have *The Dandy Dolls* as the curtain-raiser. How Yeats and Lady Gregory could have turned it down I can't understand — unless perhaps it was too good.'

As you drive on towards the Shannon estuary, you might remember a bit of information from one of his plays, *The Green Stone*: 'There do be great tasby in mermaids in the month of June,' (meaning that they are high-spirited and frolicksome). It might be as well to know.

Who else in the magic circle of Listowel and its hinterland? Contemporary scholar-poet Brendan Kennelly, from the corner pub at **Ballylongford**, less than ten miles north near the Shannon. Professor of Modern Literature at Trinity College, Dublin, he is as prolific as he is engaging and popular of personality. Poetry, he has said, was a gift that took him unawares, and he accepted it with gratitude. A ribald Kerry humour emerges in his early poetry:

> I went to the town
> O' Lishtowel for a few drinks, and there
> I met a Knockanore woman with red hair
> And gamey eye. I made bold ... (*Moloney Up and At It*)

But later, in a different mood, he would meditate on the Famine:

> And yet upon the sandy Kerry shore

JAYMONY Then there's the three red glasses, and the three blue glasses that makes up the set.

QUILLE What's in the three red glasses?

JAYMONY Women. Full of the purtiest women was ever seen on the globe. It's myself got very fond of one of them, and maybe of two. And in the glass I could see myself and the one I was doting on, and we together for the six days of the week. Times we'd be talking and times there wouldn't be a word out of us at all, our two mouths in one kiss and we in a sort of a daze ...

MAINEEN [*rushing forward*] You shameless thing! Don't mind him, Mr Quille, it's ravelling he is in his immoral talk.

PADDEN Two months now since he was at church or chapel, and 'tis years since he seen a priest.

QUILLE [*rising and bending towards Maineen and Padden, who shrink back*] Them three blue glasses: in God's name what might be in them?

JAYMONY [*excitedly*] Ha! it's the rousing wonders is in them entirely. You'd see a dandy army in the grey of the night rising out of the dark glens, and the places where the herons do be screeching ...

(*The Magic Glasses* by George Fitzmaurice)

Brendan Kennelly (1936-   )

The woman once had danced at ebbing tide
Because she loved flute music — and still more
Because a lady wondered at the pride
Of one so humble. That was long before
The green plant withered by an evil chance;
When winds of hunger howled at every door
She heard the music dwindle and forgot the dance... ('My Dark Fathers')

Later still, in his long grim nightmare poem or, rather, sequence of poems *Cromwell*, the narrator Buffún, a kind of fool-rogue, a figure representing the Irish psyche or race-memory, holds dialogue with 'the Butcher'. In this sequence, all time merges, with profound and comic effect.

It was to a pub in Ballylongford that John Scanlan and his servant Stephen Sullivan came on a fateful day in July 1819, to buy some whiskey to screw up their courage for a foul deed. Scanlan was a handsome young man, full of charm and gallantry, the son of one of the leading families in the County. Sullivan, as well as being a servant, was also a close companion who shared in all Scanlan's sporting activities. The Scanlan home was Ballycahane Castle, near **Croom** (remnants of it still stand, incorporated into some farm buildings). Nearby lived a shoemaker, John Connery, and his niece Ellen Hanley. Ellen was not yet sixteen, but was already attracting notice for her beauty. She caught the eye of the dashing young Scanlan. She responded, and that was her undoing. He persuaded her to elope with him, and they went through a bogus marriage ceremony in Limerick — it is thought with Sullivan dressed as a priest. He took her to live at **Glin**, and presumably they were happy for a while. But it became clear to Scanlan that he couldn't hope to introduce the peasant girl, no matter how appealing, to his family and aristocratic friends. And there were better marriage prospects in the offing.

One day the three set out on some pretext for Kilrush on the north side of the Shannon, and a storm broke as they were making their way back. They took shelter for the night at **Carrigafoyle**, on the shore close to Ballylongford, with some others. In the morning the other passengers set off for Glin, leaving Ellen and her two men behind. That was the last time she was seen alive. When next she was seen, six weeks later, it was as a bloated corpse washed up on the shore of Moneypoint with a rope tied tightly around her neck.

The Knight of Glin, magistrate for Limerick, took charge of the case but Scanlan and Sullivan had disappeared by then. Scanlan was discovered some considerable time later in a loft over the Ballycahane stables. He was brought to trial and, though defended by Daniel O'Connell, probably the finest advocate in Ireland at the time, he was found guilty and hanged at Limerick on 16 March 1820.

I threw a party for Oliver Cromwell
at the Royal Yacht club in Dunleary.
He was boring the arse off me with all
His talk about that estate down in Kerry
Where he planned to fish the Cashen and
    Feale
Till the people would breathe his name in
    awe.
Bored to my bones, I introduced Cromwell
To the giant who was standing in the
    harbour,
Cooling off. The giant is not at home in
    crowds.
Today, as ever he was very peckish.
'Pleased to meet you, Oliver,' the giant said,
'it's not easy having one's head in the clouds
And one's belly yearning. What do you
    suggest?'
'For starters,' Cromwell smiled, 'try twenty-
    thousand dead.'

('Party')

Sullivan was tracked down some months later in Tralee jail, where he was serving a sentence for passing forged notes. A year after the murder, he was tried, found guilty, and hanged also, confessing from the gallows, 'I declare before Almighty God that I am guilty of the murder! But it was Mr Scanlan who put me up to it.'

As can be imagined, the event created a considerable stir at the time, both because of the girl's extreme youth and innocence, and because of the Scanlans' place in society. A young reporter named Gerald Griffin, who was living at **Pallaskenry** farther east along the Shannon at the time, covered the trial for the Limerick newspapers. A decade later Griffin's novel *The Collegians* appeared. Based on the murder and trial, it established Griffin's reputation as a writer. But he was the wrong kind of person to be immersing himself in such tragedies. A sad introverted man, he was plagued by poverty and ill-health. Few of his works are read today. He withdrew from the world into the Christian Brothers a year and a half before he died of typhoid fever, having burned most of his manuscripts.

Gerald Griffin (1803-1840)

In *The Collegians*, the action was moved to Killarney and the tall well-set Sullivan became Danny Mann, a hunchback. Dion Boucicault took Griffin's story and staged it as a play under the title *The Colleen Bawn*. It was a huge success and ran for months in London. Queen Victoria came to see it four times. One of the high points in the staging was Myles na Gopaleen, played by Boucicault himself, taking a dramatic dive into the 'lake' — a concoction of green-blue gauze supported by several small boys whose job it was to keep it flapping to look like angry waves. As if all that wasn't enough, *The Colleen Bawn* became *The Lily of Killarney* for Benedict's popular opera.

Dion Boucicault (1820-1890)

Further on towards Limerick, and south from **Askeaton**, you come to **Rathkeale**, where Sean O'Faolain's mother came from, and where he set his novel *A Nest of Simple Folk*. Here we have left County Kerry and crossed into County Limerick. On to **Adare**, 'the prettiest village in Ireland,' they say. There they are, the olde-world thatched cottages, the lichened medieval ruins, the great manor house of the Earls of Dunraven (now a hotel). When it was still the home of the Dunravens, a portrait of an earlier lady of the manor, one Mrs Windham Quin, hung there. A poet once kept her hens. He didn't like her imperious ways, nor the wattle, or birch, she carried around with her — she apparently wasn't beyond using it from time to time on lazy hen-keepers. He rewarded her with a poem. Here are the first and last verses, as translated by James Clarence Mangan:

Adare

The Dame of the Slender Wattle
Ochone! I never in all my dealings met with a man to snub me,
Books I have studied, however muddied a person *you* may dub me,
I never was tossed or knocked about — I never was forced to battle,

With the storms of life, till I herded your hens, O Dame of the Slender Wattle ...

O! I pray the Lord, whose powerful Word set the elements first in motion
And formed from nought the race of Man, with Heaven, and Earth, and Ocean,
To lift my spirit above this world, and all its clangour and brattle,
And give me a speedy release from you, O Dame of the Slender Wattle!

Seán Ó Tuama (1706-1775)

Andrias MacCraith (1708-c.1795)

In the 1970s some local writers decided to revive Féile na Maighe, the Poetry Court of Coshma, at Croom, with prizes for the best Limerick. It was won by an eminent bishop with the following entry:

The traditional poets of the Maigue
Knew nothing of White Horse or Haig
   But *Uisce beatha* Hot
   Distilled in a pot
Kept them merry, poetic and vague.
      (Bishop Wyse-Jackson)

Adare is on the Maigue River, and Seán Ó Tuama, sometime hen-keeper and author of that poetic bouquet, was one of the poets of **Coshma** (*Cois Maighe,* beside the Maigue River). In the eighteenth century a whole school of poets lived in the Maigue lands, and they held court in **Croom** 'of the Merriment'. Ó Tuama kept a tavern there, until he bankrupted himself through liberality. A fellow-poet was Andrias MacCraith: they both spent time as hedge-schoolmasters, teaching Irish, Latin, Greek, English and trigonometry. O'Tuama boasted — in verse, of course — about his good ale:

I sell the best brandy and sherry
To make my good customers merry,
But at times their finances
Run short, as it chances,
And then I feel very sad, very!

MacCraith replied:

O'Toomey! you boast yourself handy
At selling good ale and bright brandy,
   But the fact is your liquor
   Makes everyone sicker
I tell you that, I, your friend Andy.   *(trans. James Clarence Mangan)*

And so, in this playful cut-and-thrust, the *Limerick* was born.

Playful and high-spirited they could be, but when MacCraith was banished from Croom, probably for reasons to do with a woman, as he had a reputation in that direction, he wrote a most plaintive and mournful poem — a real song of exile, called 'Farewell to the Maigue'. In Irish it is taut, economical and intense. A literal translation gives:

One hundred and one farewells I send from this place
To Coshma of the berries, the boughs, the abundance,
The farms, the properties, the craftsmen, the crowds,
The poems, the stories and the cheerful heroes

Alas, my grief! I am in anguish,
With no belongings or supplies, company or money,
Without any enjoyment, valuables, or diversions
Since I was driven to this place of loneliness. *(trans. Diarmuid Breathnach)*

He was all of nine miles away from Croom!

You might like to drive a few miles northwards from here to **Curraghchase** Forest Park. Now a public pleasure ground, a caravan and camping site, it was until the 1940s the stately demesne of the de Veres, a family of compassionate Protestant landed gentry of whom two members, Sir Aubrey de Vere (1788-1846) and Aubrey Thomas de Vere (1814-1902) were poets and authors. The latter Aubrey is the one whose work is most familiar today: he said of his father, 'landscape gardening was one mode of expressing the poetry which was so deeply seated within him.'

Aubrey de Vere embraced both the Catholic faith and Irish native culture with enthusiasm. He retold the old epic tale, the Táin, as 'The Foray of Queen Maeve' and he reworked the Children of Lir and the confrontation of St Patrick and Oisín, last of the Fianna. He and his family did all they could to alleviate the effects of the Famine, seeing 'the whole food of the great mass of the country melt like snow before our eyes' as he wrote to a friend. His brother Stephen travelled with a party of emigrants to Canada, and by giving a full account of the hardships of the voyage, helped to bring about much-needed improvements.

The great house was burned in 1941. It is told that the Limerick City Fire Brigade somehow managed to lose their way and reached the house when it was already too late to save it. Gate lodges, used as stores, remain, and the fine specimen trees planted by the de Veres have been maintained and added to by the State.

At **Limerick City** the Shannon River becomes tidal and reaches in a wide estuary towards the sea. Strategically it was always important, so much so that a strong castle was built there as early as 1210 by the express orders of King John of England to guard his colony against the O'Briens and other native septs.

Limerick is the 'Mellick' of that formidable novelist Kate O'Brien who grew up in **Mulgrave Street** in a house called Boru House, one of solid red-brick respectability. Her novels probed the lives of the newly-emerged Catholic upper-middle class, the prosperous business and professional families; she was the first to address those women's issues which are so widely discussed nowadays. *Without my Cloak* is something of an Irish Forsythe Saga. Its main theme over a number of generations is the struggle of the individual, particularly of women, against the constraints of respectability, conformity and almost claustrophobic tribal loyalty.

Her life was nomadic, and intensely private, but of her native Limerick she could write:

The freest spirit must have some birthplace, some *locus standi* from which to view the world and some innate passion by which to judge it.

Aubrey Thomas de Vere (1814-1902)

Kate O'Brien (1897-1974)

Frank McCourt
See *Crossing the Millennium*, page 259

An early photograph of Kate O'Brien, 'a beauty with a flair for writing about her native Limerick'.

Modestly I say the same for my relationship with Limerick. It was there that I began to view the world and to develop the necessary passion by which to judge it. It was there indeed that I learnt the world, and I know that wherever I am it is still from Limerick that I look out and make my surmises. And, 'to possess without being possessed' — that may seem unfair, but it is the gift an exile can take from a known place, and more enriching, or so the recipient thinks, than the average portion of the stay at home.

The Limerick of Kate O'Brien's time (she died in 1974) was recognisably the one of her novels, narrow, sober, conventional, rigidly Catholic, unquestionably orthodox. The establishment in 1972 of the National Institute of Higher Education, now the University of Limerick, has changed that city utterly. It now resounds to the loud voices and laughter of irreverent jean-clad youth, the music of guitars and discos. **King John's Castle** has been largely restored and opened itself to visitors with an impressive historical exhibition, so that it once more plays a significant part in the life of the city. A new spirit is abroad which has brought in its train some of the common services and practical facilities which the city greatly lacked — pleasant cafés, decent restaurants, comfortable pubs, a fine concert hall. It has become a happy place.

Leaving Limerick you can head west towards Clare, or follow the route through the Midlands (Chapter 15).

Dion Boucicault

6. CLARE
The Fertile Rock

This small county is so rich in associations that it deserves a generous allowance of time. The spell of its unique landscape alone would be reason enough to linger, even without the resonance of singular minds.

On the road to Ennis, the massive bulk of **Bunratty Castle** rises like a great exclamation point tethered to the skyline. Whatever your views about medieval banquets and harping maidens, it would be a pity to deprive yourself of a visit. Bunratty is one of the finest fifteenth-century tower houses in Ireland, magnificently restored and containing a superb collection of late medieval furnishings and artefacts. Adjoining it, almost in the way that villages of old clustered around the feet of the lord's castle, is the Folk Village, a collection of farmhouses furnished in the style of the turn of the century or earlier, and a village street with shops and a schoolhouse. Cows are milked, pigs fed, peacocks wander down from the lawns of the Big House to forage with the humbler poultry, and the smell of baking mixes with the reek of turf smoke from the many hearths. Apart from being a pleasant indulgence in nostalgia, it is in fact a salutary immersion in a world that connects one with history and the lives of older generations, adding an extra layer of perception to much that has been written.

Ennis offers good rooms and sustenance, and the remains of a fine Norman abbey. But we hurry along, for there are treasures ahead. We permit a few pauses, though. At **Ennistymon**, for instance, to contemplate the destiny that took young Caitlin MacNamara from her family home, now the Falls Hotel, to become the wife of one of the most tempestuous poets of our times, the inspired but tragic Dylan Thomas of Wales. Though it seems they were well matched — the MacNamaras were a pretty tempestuous lot themselves. Father was known generally as 'Fireball' MacNamara, and of Caitlin it was said that with her the chance of a scene was like the smell of gunpowder to an old charger.

Taking the coast road, make a pause at **Liscannor** to visit one of the most poignant of Ireland's hundreds of folk shrines, the Holy Well of St Brigid, still venerated, still a place of pilgrimage on the last Sunday of July. The date is the traditional 'Garland Sunday' or Lughnasa, the feast of Lugh, celebrated since pre-Christian times. The votive offerings which line the entry passageway testify to faith and conviction. The mighty ramparts of the **Cliffs of Moher** attract hordes of awe-struck wanderers, so you may as well stop and have a dizzying look.

You are now entering one of Ireland's sweetest territories, the **Burren**. The word means a stony place. It's an understatement. The Burren looks as if it might be a barony of the moon. It extends over north Clare, covering an area of about one hundred square miles. It is composed entirely of naked limestone, ranged in terraces, and if first seen on a dull or misty day can seem as dreary a place as you could imagine. But on the first lifting of the light, its magic starts to reveal itself. It is a vast natural sculpture park, the limestone cracked and fissured in intricate patterns and fantastic shapes, with here and there a scattering of giant erratic boulders, all looking as if carefully arranged by a celestial hand. Light reflects from a thousand shades of grey, with blue and mauve and purple of rock alone. But there is more. In this

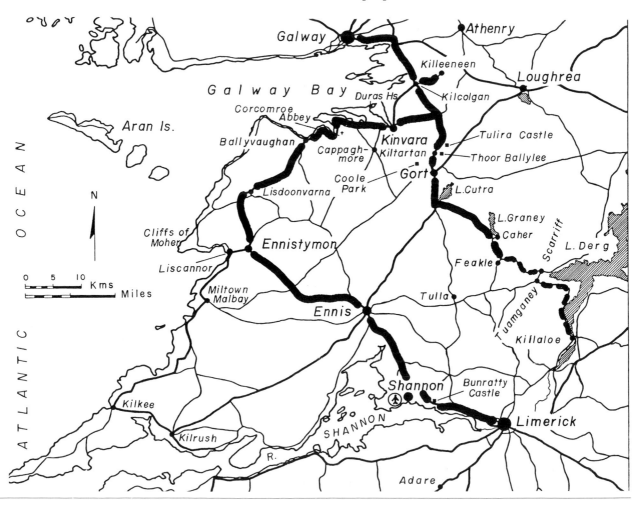

apparently totally sterile landscape, the fissures host a collection of rare and delicate blossoms, arctic and mediterranean types rubbing shoulders companionably here on the edge of the Atlantic. Old forts, abbeys and burial structures, often barely distinguishable among the stone, add another layer of fascination. The limestone filters rainwater off immediately into its elaborate cave labyrinths, and the combination of characteristics led to the most oft-quoted grumble attributed to one of Cromwell's generals, that the place had not enough water to drown a man, wood to burn him or tree on which to hang him.

As imagined by Emily Lawless it is of these stony acres that some of the soldiers of the Irish Brigade dream, between sleeping and waking on the night before the Battle of Fontenoy in 1745, when the Irish fought with the French and won great praise for their valour in the field:

> O little Corca Bascinn, the wild, the bleak, the fair!
> Oh little stony pastures, whose flowers are sweet, if rare!
> Oh rough and rude Atlantic, the thunderous, the wide,
> Whose kiss is like a soldier's kiss which will not be denied!
> The whole night long we dream of you, and waking think we're there –
> Vain dream, and foolish waking, we never shall see Clare.
>
> The wind is wild to-night, there's battle in the air;
> The wind is from the west, and it seems to blow from Clare ...

The Honourable Emily Lawless, born in 1845, was the daughter of Lord Cloncurry. She moved among influential people in both Ireland and England, and managed to have friends ranging from Gladstone to Horace Plunkett, founder with George Russell of the Irish agricultural co-operative movement. She was a painter and botanist and playwright. Lennox Robinson gives us a picture of her happily diving deeply into the wild Atlantic and bringing to the surface strange sea-creatures that no Clare fisherman had ever seen. She inherited at least some of the looks of her mother, of whom Lady Gregory said that 'once when she went into the House of Lords the assembly had stood up in tribute to that beauty, perhaps a gift from the sidhe, who inhabit the hill of Cruachmaa at the foot of which was her home.'

Emily Lawless (1845-1913)

John Betjeman felt the magic of Clare:

John Betjeman (1906-1984)

> Stony seaboard, far and foreign
>   Stony hills poured over space,
> Stony outcrop of the Burren,
>   Stones in every fertile place,
> Little fields with boulders dotted,
> Grey-stone shoulders saffron-spotted,
> Stone-walled cabins thatched with reeds,
> Where a Stone Age people breeds
>   The last of Europe's stone age race... (*Ireland with Emily*)

Poulnabrone Dolmen

Brian Merriman (1749?-1803)

The Stone Age people left their burial places for us to discover today, at **Poulnabrone**, and **Gleninsheen** and elsewhere. Centuries later, a fleeing Bronze Age chieftain, or perhaps a thief, folded a collar of gold in two and hid it among the stones close to Gleninsheen. He never returned to collect it. It lay there for maybe three thousand years, until a boy hunting rabbits in 1930 came upon it. At first it was discarded, as it looked like a bit from a coffin, but was eventually rescued and identified. It is now one of the most prized exhibits of prehistoric gold ornaments in the National Museum.

In **Lisdoonvarna** of the Spa, or **Lahinch** by the sea, or some other Clare town, you may be startled on an August day to come across a mixed bag of people, not in general too 'hippy' but not too conventional either, involved in an intricate dance of the Clare Set in mid-afternoon, in the middle of the street, or gathered around a bearded scholarly-looking man orating from a stone wall. Chances are that you would have stumbled on a group from Cumann Merriman, the Merriman Summer School, which has come to be known waggishly as the Lark in the Clare Air.

Merriman was an obscure country hedge-school master, born somewhere near Ennistymon in the middle of the eighteenth century. Very little is known about him, apart from the fact that he taught and farmed near **Feakle**, in east Clare, before moving to Limerick City where he died in 1803. His entire literary output appears to consist of one lengthy work, in colloquial rather than formal Irish. It is *Cúirt an Mheán Oíche*, or, in English, *The Midnight Court*, and poet Thomas Kinsella has described it as 'a poem of gargantuan comic eloquence and energy, (which) carries within it a rich tradition of conventions and ideas associated with the more burlesque medieval love-songs and Courts of Love.' Frank O'Connor's translation is given here.

In its opening stanzas, we appear to be meeting up with a conventional Aisling poem, where an enchanted maiden appears to the poet. After a lyrical description of the countryside around **Lough Graney**, he goes on:

Ar maidin inné bhí an spéir gan cheo,
Bhí Cancer ón ngréin 'na caorthaibh teo,
Is í gofa chun saothair t'réis na hoíche,
Is obair an lae raeimpi sínte.
Bhí duilliúr craobh ar ghéaga im thimpeall,
Fiorthann is féar go slaodach taobh liom,
Glasra fáis is blátha is luibheanna,
Scaipfeadh chun fáin dá chráiteacht
   smaointe.
Bhí mé cortha is an codladh am thraochadh,
Shín mé thoram ar cothrom sa bhféar glas.

> Yesterday morning the sky was clear,
> The sun fell hot on river and mere,
> Her horses fresh and with gamesome eye
> Harnessed again to assail the sky;
> The leaves were thick upon every bough
> And ferns and grass as thick below,
> Sheltering bowers of herbs and flowers
> That would comfort a man in his dreariest hours.
> A longing for sleep bore down my head,
> And in the grass I scooped a bed

However, it was no exquisite vision woman that appeared:

> I had only dozed when I felt a shock
> And all the landscape seemed to rock,
> A north wind made my senses tingle
> And thunder crackled along the shingle,
> And as I looked up, as I thought, awake
> I seemed to see at the edge of the lake
> As ugly a brute as a man could see
> In the shape of a woman approaching me,
> For if I calculated right
> She must have been twenty feet in height

> Ba ghairid mo shuan nuair chuala, shíl mé,
> An talamh máguaird ar luascadh im thimpeall
> Anfa aduaidh is fuadach fíochmhar
> Is calaithe an chuain ag tuargain tínte.
> Siolladh dem shúil dár shamhlaíos uaim
> Do chonac mé chugham le ciumhais an chuain
> An mhásach bholgach tholgach thaibhseach
> Chnámhach cholgach ghoirgeach ghaibhdeach;
> A haeirde cheart, má mheas mé díreach,
> Sé nó seacht de shlata is fuíollach,

The lady had come with a legal warrant for his arrest, summoning him to appear at the Court of the palace of Moy Graney, where Aoibheall, Queen of the fairies, is presiding over a judicial enquiry into the state of the country and, in particular, as to why Irishmen choose to hang on to their bachelor status as long as possible, while fine women lack husbands and lovers. Witnesses are called: a young woman explains how she attends dances and races and every occasion, and how she fasted devoutly, and rinsed her shift against the stream, and left her nails in the ash and resorted to other such charms, all in vain. But a wheezy old man leaps to his feet and launches into a lengthy and furious attack on her morals, virtue and ancestry:

Merriman Summer School proceedings in the 1970s — the lark in the Clare air!

> 'Damnation take you, you bastard's bitch,
> Got by a tinkerman under a ditch, ...
> Your seed and breed for all your brag
> Were tramps to a man with rag and bag:

And so the invective goes backwards and forwards. It is proposed that vigorous young men, and well-fed priests, should be compelled to marry. After all,

> Is there living a girl that could grow fat
> Tied to a travelling corpse like that;
> That twice a year wouldn't find a wish
> To see what was she, flesh or fish,
> But dragged the clothes about his head
> Like a wintry wind to woman in bed?

The epic goes on for over 1,000 lines. Eventually, Queen Aoibheall issues her judgment. Our poet is the first to be chosen for punishment:

> Take the rope and give him a crack,
> Earth it up the small of his back.
> That, young man, is the place to hurt you,
> We'll teach you to respect your virtue,
> Steady now, till we give you a sample —
> Women alive, he's a grand example!

'And the Queen of the Fairies sat alone At the end of the hall on a gilded throne' Illustration by Brian Bourke from The Midnight Court, *translated by Frank O'Connor.*

*'Has the Catholic Church a glimmer of sense
That the priests won't marry like anyone else?'
Illustration by Brian Bourke from* The
Midnight Court, *translated by Frank O'Connor.*

Detail, Corcomroe Abbey

As she invites the women to invent further tortures, the poet wakes in terror.

It is highly Rabelaisian and uproariously funny. Part of the opening verses in its original Irish often appeared in schoolbooks, but most of the mock-heroic epic lived obscurely among scholarly Irish texts for generations, until it burst like a bombshell on the English-speaking world with Frank O'Connor's translation in 1945, when it was promptly banned. There have been several translations since, but it was not until many years later that Merriman was regarded as respectable enough to deserve a commemorative plaque, which was erected with much ceremony at his burial place in Feakle. We will come to all the territory of the *Cúirt* later on in this trip.

The first Merriman Summer School was held in 1968 and the subject was the poet and the poem. Every year since it has been devoted to various aspects of Irish literary, political and social life, with a high degree of scholarship, and an equal degree of merriment. Twenty years ago, Susan and Thomas Cahill wrote in a *Literary Guide to Ireland*:

The session is a week-long Celtic drinking bout replete with the thrusts and parries of slashing wit, traditional music and song, late-night liaisons, and sunrise swimming in cold pools scooped out of the lava cliffs. As with Senan's monks, endurance is paramount. The revellers are not lords and ladies ornamented in gold torq collars and colored capes, but writers, professors, media people, and a handful of intellectual politicians. But in a country where few traditions ever really die, this assembly has gladly assumed the old mantle of unregenerate aristocracy, and Club Merriman is probably as close as any ordinary, twentieth-century mortal can come to the pagan pride, liveliness, and treachery of the old Gaelic order.'

No doubt the proceedings — and the personnel — have mellowed somewhat over the years. Still, if you find a bunch of elderly academics and industrious-looking Japanese students jigging to a fiddler at a street corner or a dusty crossroads, you will guess that it's a bit of Merriman. And it's all great fun.

Along the coast road from **Ballyvaughan** to **Kinvara**, a signpost leads you to **Corcomroe Abbey**, half a mile inland. Here, in the midst of a desert of rock, the Benedictines of the twelfth century dedicated their monastery to Sancta Maria de Petra Fertilis, to Holy Mary of the Fertile Rock. Was it an expression of will, or of appeal, or of faith? We can admire the industry of those monks of old who built fertile fields high up into the unrelenting stone hills. But there is a way in which the stone itself is fertile. The vegetation which springs from between the cicatrices is rich in nutrients. Cattle are grazed on the hillsides all year round. It has been suggested that the dedication has a metaphysical rather than naturalistic context and certainly Corcomroe is a place of unutterable peace. Even in its roofless state an air of harmony surrounds it. The arches are graceful, the carving is delicate, and the lancet windows draw the eyes and the heart upwards. John Betjeman has better words for it:

> A ruined abbey, chancel only,
> Lichen-crusted, time-befriended,
> Soared the arches, splayed and splendid,
> Romanesque against the sky.

It is little wonder that William Butler Yeats, drawn always to places of beauty and transcendence, chose Corcomroe as the setting for his play *The Dreaming of the Bones*. In it the ghosts of Dervorgilla O'Rourke of Breffny and Dermot MacMurrough, king of Leinster, the lovers whom Irish folk-memory names as the traitors who initiated the Norman invasion of Ireland in the twelfth century, are condemned to wander through time, together but not able to touch, until they find an Irishman or woman who will forgive them. Their punishment stretches to infinity.

On some old maps, a broken dotted line is marked 'Bóthar na Miasa', the Road of the Dishes. The dishes were the overflowing food-filled dishes of King Guaire (**Dún Guaire Castle** is the gem-like one with its feet in the water just beyond **Kinvara**: medieval banquets with a literary flavour are held there.) While the king feasted, his brother, Saint Colman MacDuach, fasted lengthily at his hermitage a little south of **Cappaghmore** (a visit is recommended to this untroubled place). When the time came to end the fast, Colman prayed for nourishment. At the same moment the good King Guaire was praying that someone in need should share his feast. Immediately the dishes rose in the air and winged their way to the place of the saint. The legend inspired Yeats' *The King's Threshold*.

Back on the Kinvara road, take a moment to follow a signpost and look briefly at **Duras** (sometimes spelled Dooras) House Youth Hostel. At the turn of the century it was owned by Count Florimond de Basterot of Bordeaux, who had inherited the property through several generations of marriage connections with the Frenches, Martins and Lynches of this area. Florimond, last of his line, spent his summers at Duras and had become a good friend of Lady Gregory. We are approaching a region of immense importance in Ireland's literary history.

Mr. Edward Martyn came to see me, bringing with him Mr. Yeats whom I did not know very well, though I cared for his work very much and had already, through his directions, been gathering folklore. They had lunch with us, but it was a wet day and we could not go out.... We sat through the wet afternoon, and though I had never been at all interested in theatres, our talk turned on

William Butler Yeats (1865-1939)

Edward Martyn and W.B. Yeats — cartoon by Max Beerbohm

Edward Martyn (1859-1923)

plays. Mr. Martyn had written two, *The Heather Field* and *Maeve*. They had been offered to London managers, and now he thought of having them produced in Germany, where there seemed to be more room for new drama than in England. I said it was a pity we had no Irish theatre where such plays could be given. Mr. Yeats said that had always been a dream of his, but he had of late thought it an impossible one, for it could not at first pay its way and there was no money to be found for such a thing in Ireland. We went on talking about it, and things seemed to grow possible as we talked; before the end of the afternoon we had made our plan. We said we would collect money, or rather ask to have a certain sum of money guaranteed. We would then take a Dublin theatre and give a performance of Mr. Martyn's *Heather Field* and one of Mr. Yeats' own plays, *The Countess Cathleen*.' (*Our Irish Theatre* by Lady Gregory)

That meeting, so casually occurring just because Martyn had a guest on his hands to entertain on a wet afternoon, turned out to be a momentous one for Irish literature — and, indeed, for Ireland. Out of it grew, eventually, the Abbey Theatre, which marked the beginning of the Irish Literary Revival. If you draw a three-mile circle just to the north of **Gort**, it will encompass **Coole Park**, which was Lady Gregory's home; **Thoor Ballylee**, Yeats' ivory tower; and Edward Martyn's **Tulira Castle**. De Basterot's Duras House near Kinvara, already mentioned, would be just outside the circle. These were the homes, and these were the people, among whom thought was transformed into action.

Both Coole Park and Thoor Ballylee are clearly signposted a few miles north of Gort on the main Galway road. Tulira House is privately owned and not open to the public. Duras House is a Youth Hostel, with some memorabilia displayed on the walls. (Non-hostelling visitors are not, however, particularly welcomed during busy summer months). Because of de Basterot's friendship with Lady Gregory, much of the talking and planning took place while the friends and collaborators strolled in the gardens there. Edward Martyn was of a family that had managed to retain both its wealth and its Catholicism. He was a cultivated, if eccentric, poet and playwright, and something of a religious ascetic: Violet Martin wrote that he looked like 'a starved R.C. Curate — in seedy black clothes — with a large black bow at the root of his long naked throat.' His father had been a legendary rake, which may explain his own unusual piety. Yeats, expecting the worst, was both surprised and impressed on first coming to Tulira Castle to find its walls hung with paintings by Utamaro, Degas, Monet, Corot. The fact that Martyn had just completed a play *The Heather Field* and Yeats had just finished *The Countess Cathleen* sharpened their aspiration to create an Irish theatre rather than having the plays produced in London or Paris, which was the current trend.

But Coole Park, and Lady Gregory, became the centre of things, an intellectual rendezvous for all the major figures of the new movement.

Lady Gregory (1852-1932)

At the time of the first meeting between Yeats and Lady Gregory, Yeats had already founded the National Literary Society, which turned to native sources as inspiration. But it was felt that it would be easier to persuade a public to attend a theatrical performance than to actually go out and buy, and read, the new books.

Lady Gregory's own background was quite different from those of Yeats or even Edward Martyn. She was born in 1852 at **Roxborough House**, not far from **Coole**. She married Sir William Gregory of Coole in 1880. She was twenty-eight, he was sixty-three. When Sir William died in 1891 she inherited the estate, and threw her considerable energies into revitalising the ailing property which was later to take such an outstanding place in Ireland's public life. About that time Yeats describes her as 'a plainly dressed woman of forty-five, without obvious good looks, except the charm that comes from strength, intelligence and kindness.' Sean O'Casey called her 'a sturdy, stout little figure soberly clad in solemn black made gay with a touch of something white

Dunguaire castle, County Galway

The 'Autograph Tree' at Coole

under a long, black silk veil that covered her grey hair and flowed gracefully behind half-way down her back. Her face was a rugged one, hardy as that of a peasant, curiously lit with an odd dignity, and softened with a careless touch of humour in the bright eyes...'

That plain, bright-eyed woman created an ambience in which the finest literary minds of the period gathered, and wandered the woods and lake shore, and found peace, and relaxed and debated and flourished. After that first fateful visit, Yeats spent many summers there:

> I have heard the pigeons of the Seven Woods
> Make their faint thunder, and the garden bees
> Hum in the lime-tree flowers; and put away
> The unavailing outcries and the old bitterness
> That empty the heart ...   ('In the Seven Woods')

The swans in particular stirred Yeats' mystical soul:

> The trees are in their autumn beauty,
> The woodland paths are dry,
> Under the October twilight the water
> Mirrors a still sky;
> Under the brimming water among the stones
> Are nine-and-fifty swans.   ('The Wild Swans at Coole')

Swans still fly in to the lake at Coole, but of the house nothing remains but the foundations. Prophetically, Yeats had written in 1929:

> Here, traveller, scholar, poet, take your stand
> When all those rooms and passages are gone,
> When nettles wave upon a shapeless mound
> And saplings root among the broken stone,
> And dedicate — eyes bent upon the ground,
> Back turned upon the brightness of the sun
> And all the sensuality of the shade —
> A moment's memory to that laurelled head.   ('Coole Park, 1929')

The house cannot be recovered, but at least the estate, now a public park, is being well maintained, the woods — those that are left — properly managed, and the walks and pathways made smooth again. There are car parks, and a modest building houses a café and shows a film of how it all began. The famous 'Autograph Tree' still bears the names cut into it by all those legendary characters — W.B.Y., his artist brother Jack B. Yeats (with a graving of a little donkey), J.M. Synge, George Russell (AE), Douglas Hyde, John Masefield, Sean O'Casey, George Bernard Shaw, 'and,' wrote Lady Gregory, 'this A.J. was cut by Augustus John after his descent from the topmost boughs where he had left those letters also to astonish the birds of the air.' In spite of the loss, it is a pleasant place to roam, and sense the spirits among the trees. After all, didn't the poet claim 'Our shadows rove the garden gravel still, / The living seem more shadowy than they.'

Lady Gregory learned Irish, joined the Gaelic League, translated mythological material from the manuscripts, and wrote several plays of her own. She visited the country people in the surrounding barony of **Kiltartan**, and harvested from them some of their rich store of hero tales and poetry, rendering them in the spoken idiom. In his introduction to her volume *Cuchulain of Muirthemne* Yeats, not a man over-given to modesty, states: 'I think this book is the best that has come out of Ireland in my time.' And he adds: 'When I was a child I had only to climb the hill behind the house to see long, blue, ragged hills flowing along the southern horizon. What beauty was lost to me, what depth of emotion is still perhaps lacking in me, because nobody told me, not even the merchant captains who knew everything, that Cruachan of the Enchantments lay behind those long, blue, ragged hills.'

It was during some of his early visits to Coole that Yeats first came upon the village — or, rather, group of houses, not enough to be called a village — called **Ballylee**. Its name, he tells in the essay 'Dust Hath Closed Helen's Eye', was known through all the west of Ireland because of the saying of a wise woman, Biddy Early, that 'there is a

Lady Gregory at Coole Park

Thoor Ballylee

Anthony Raftery (1784-1835)

cure for all evil between the two mill-wheels of Ballylee.' The saying had caught his fancy, and his interest was deepened by stories of Mary Hynes whose beauty was spoken of in wonder around the turf fires of the district and whom the blind poet Anthony Raftery had written of as 'the shining flower of Ballylee'. Some twenty years later Yeats acquired the old Norman keep of Ballylee, with its adjoining mill and small cottage. He called it **Thoor Ballylee**, restored and furnished it, and wove it through the texture of his poetry. Its every aspect fulfilled for him some emblematic purpose. The winding stone steps represented the twisted course of history.

> Before that ruin came, for centuries,
> Rough men-at-arms, cross-gartered to the knees
> Or shod in iron, climbed the narrow stairs,
> And certain men-at-arms there were
> Whose images, in the Great Memory stored,
> Come with loud cry and panting breast
> To break upon a sleeper's rest
> While their great wooden dice beat on the board.   ('The Tower')

After his death, the stone with his own inscription was set in the front wall:

> I, the poet William Yeats,
> With old mill boards and sea-green slates,
> And smithy work from the Gort forge,
> Restored this tower for my wife George;
> And may these characters remain
> When all is ruin once again.

The tower once more fell into decay, and was once more restored, this time through the inspiration and dedication of the late Mrs Mary Hanley of the Kiltartan Society. It is now a place of pilgrimage for scholars, students and curious travellers. Its café, bookshop and audio-visual aids take little from the magic of

> An ancient bridge, and a more ancient tower,
> A farmhouse that is sheltered by its wall,
> An acre of stony ground,
> Where the symbolic rose can break in flower...

Raftery's 'strong cellar' beneath the castle can still be discerned. One rainy day, that blind poet tells us, near Kiltartan on the way to Mass, he met the maiden

> whose love enslaved me and left me low.
> I spoke to her gently, the courteous maiden,
> And gently and gaily she answered so:
> Come, Raftery, with me, and let me take you
> To Ballylee, where I have to go.   (trans. Douglas Hyde)

Raftery's pursuit of Mary Hynes reflected Yeats' own hopeless pursuit of Maud Gonne. Biddy Early represented both earthy and unearthly wisdom. Such images were powerful fuel for Yeats' imagination. He does not appear to have been aware of the association of another powerful wraith within the locality, that of the Fairy Queen, Aoibheall, (Yeats' 'Aoife') presiding over her Midnight Court from Cragleigh Hill, as chronicled by the poet Merriman. His ordeal opens so innocently:

> Twas my pleasure to walk in the river meadows
> In the thick of the dew and the morning shadows,
> At the edge of the woods in a deep defile,
> At peace with myself in the first sunshine.
> When I looked at Lough Graney my heart grew bright,
> Ploughed lands and green in the morning light,
> Mountains in ranks with crimson borders
> Peering above their neighbours' shoulders.   *(trans. Frank O'Connor)*

> Ba ghnáth mé ag siúl le ciumhais na habhann
> ar bháinseach úr 's an drúcht go trom,
> in aice na gcoillte, i gcoim an tslé',
> gan mhairg, gan mhoill, ar shoilse an lae.
> Do ghealadh mo chroí nuair chínn Loch Gréine,
> an talamh, 's an tír, is íor na spéire;
> taitneamhach aoibhinn suíomh na sléibhte
> ag bagairt a gcinn thar dhroim a chéile.

Loch Gréine, or Graney lies about ten miles south-east of Yeats' tower: first south, then east to the village of Caher, where a road runs along the lake shore so that you can watch how fish, full of fun, jump 'one perch high', allowing their speckled bellies to catch the poet's eye before he fell into his terrifying dream. Merriman lies in an unmarked gave in the nearby village of Feakle, where he taught in a hedge-school for some twenty years.

Biddy Early, the 'wise woman' that Yeats associated with his tower at Ballylee, lived close to here, about two miles from Feakle towards **Tulla**. The wee cottage, close to the road, is difficult to locate without local guidance. When last visited by this traveller it was almost derelict, with a 'For Sale' notice on the gate. A neighbouring young man, when asked would he be thinking of buying it, said very emphatically 'I would not. I'd have nothing at all to do with it!' It is said, however, that there are many who have trawled Kilbarron lough (it's across the field almost opposite to the house) for Biddy's magic bottle, for it was thrown into the lough after her death.

Tuamgraney, described by Edna O'Brien as, 'a small somnolent village with a limestone rock that sprawls irregularly over the village green where sprouts a huge beech tree along with incidental saplings that meander out of it.' The tree is actually a lime tree.

Edna O'Brien (1930-   )

Admirers of Edna O'Brien will want to circle over towards Lough Derg, and the village of **Tuamgraney** (the locals always pronounce it Tomgraney) where she comes from. In spite of her unflattering picture of it in *A Pagan Place*, it is a charming spot, with a little village green and two memorial parks. The interesting old church of St Cronan houses a small Heritage Centre, which is a monument to purely voluntary effort and enterprise. One wonders how many pub quizzes it took to raise the £6,000 to save the stained-glass window that was rescued and brought from Sixmilebridge. The Centre will be happy to arrange a walking tour, a trip to the Holy

Grave of Raftery, the poet, at Killeeneen

Anthony Raftery (1784-1835)

Island of **Inish Cealtra**, search out your ancestors or almost anything else you can think of, all on a happy informal basis. Tel 061-921351.

In her idiosyncratic book *Mother Ireland* Edna writes about her childhood, the delightful and fearful adventure of coming home from school, then:

Out of breath, satchel held onto as if a person, the last bit of road with not a cottage, not a tree, and the high wall bordering our land where someone had chalked "Up the Farmers", and the big wasp-filled hollow tree stump, and the remains of the tree that had fallen long before in a storm. Then the stubborn gate with its screechy hasp, and its faulty hinge, fixed to the stone pier that had on its surface one tiny spot of smooth slate which required to be touched over and over again for good luck, but couldn't be, because of the urgent need to get home, but had to be because ... and then of course the biggest bogey of all, a brush with the supernatural, because under such and such a tree a man appeared, an old gatekeeper who had died of a wrong; then the cattle, their stares, their huge heads, their bulling and their bawling, the chips on their horns glinting in the sunshine, cattle bulling and bawling — and home to what? Once it was the tillage inspector who had come, and had to be appeased with tea and scones before being brought out to inspect the barely adequate patches of wheat and barley ...'

Through all her stories there is that love/hate struggle with her background:

You are Irish you say lightly, and allocated to you are the tendencies to be wild, wanton, drunk, superstitious, unreliable, backward, toadying and prone to fits, whereas you know that in fact a whole entourage of ghosts resides in you, ghosts with whom the inner rapport is as frequent, as perplexing, as defiant as with any of the living. (*Mother Ireland*)

As you're here, and there's time, why not a scenic drive along the lake shore to **Killaloe**, where brood the ghosts of Brian Ború and a band of early saints? We'll meet up with it properly in Chapter 15.

Back to **Gort**, on our journey generally northwards. But before hurrying on to Galway city, a small detour is necessary. At **Kilcolgan**, a right turn by O'Donoghue's pub will bring you to **Killeeneen**, where the gateway to an old ivy-clad church ruin and churchyard carries the solemn legend:

REILIG NA BHFILÍ
CEMETERY OF THE POETS
KILLEENEEN.

Coming on it unexpectedly, one would be forgiven for wondering if this, like the legendary Cemetery of the Elephants, is where all the poets of Ireland must come to die. But in fact it contains only a few: two local poets, the Callanan brothers, and one important one, Anthony Raftery.

There are few Irish adults over the age of fifty who couldn't recite, off the cuff and in Irish, the three verses of 'Raifterí an File':

> Mise Raifterí an file,
>> lán dóchais is grá
> le súile gan solas,
>> le ciúineas gan crá,
>
> ag dul siar ar m'aistear
>> le solas mo chroí
> fann agus tuirseach
>> go deireadh mo shlí;
>
> Féach anois mé
>> lem aghaidh ar bhalla
> ag seinm cheoil
>> do phócaí folamh.

> I am Raftery the poet
>> Full of hope and love
> With eyes without light
>> And calm without torment.
>
> Going west on my journey
>> By the light of my heart,
> Weak and tired
>> To my road's end.
>
> Look at me now,
>> My face to the wall,
> Playing music
>> To empty pockets. *(trans. Frank O'Connor)*

The image that this evokes of a poor pathetic wanderer eking out a humble existence with his fiddle-playing is not quite a true picture. Blind and penniless he may have been, but by all accounts he was a very strong, tough, arrogant and quite charismatic character, regarded with something like awe by the people. His fiddle-playing wasn't up to much, but his songs were so highly thought of that among the more superstitious, his talents were thought to arise from some more than human power.

Raftery was born in or around the year 1784 at Killeadan near Kiltimagh in Mayo, but he spent most of his time wandering in County Galway, especially around Ballylee and Gort — drawn to that area, among other reasons, by the beauty of Mary Hynes:

> My star of beauty, my sun of autumn
>> My golden hair, O my share of life!
> Will you come with me this coming Sunday
>> And tell the priest you will be my wife?
> I'd not grudge you music, nor a feast at evening,
>> Nor punch nor wine, if you'd have it be,
> And King of Glory, dry up the roadway
>> Till I find my posy at Ballylee!   *(trans. Frank O'Connor)*

Mary Hynes wasn't the only beauty that inspired Raftery. His song to Breedyeen Vesey is as fulsome:

> O cheek as blush-abounding,
> O berry of the mountain,
> Thy promises are sounding
>> For ever in my ear.
> And, spite of clerics frowning,
> I'd take you if I found you;
> It's I who would go bounding
>> To see again my dear.   *(trans. Douglas Hyde)*

Douglas Hyde (1860-1949)

Anois teacht an Earraigh beidh an lá ag dul
    chun síneadh,
Is tar éis na Féile Bríde ardófaidh mé mo sheol,
Ó chuir mé i mo cheann é, ní stopfaidh mé
    choíche,
Go seasfaidh mé síos i lár Chontae Mhaigh Eó.

I gClár Cloinne Muiris bhéas mé an chéad oíche
'S i mBalla taobh thíos de tosnófaidh mé ag ól
Go Coillte-Mac raghad go ndéanfad cuairt
    míosa ann
I bhfós dá míle do Bhéal an Átha Mhóir.

Ó fágaim le huadacht é go n-éiríonn mo chroí-se
Mar éirítear an ghaoth nó mar a scaipeann an
    cheo,
Nuair a smaoinim ar Chearra nó ar Bhalla
    taobh thíos de,
Ar Sceathach an Mhíle nó ar phláineadh
    Mhaigh Eó.

Cill Aodáin an baile a bhfásann gach ní ann,
Tá sméara 's sugha-chraobh ann is meas ar gach
    sórt,
'S dá mbeinnse 'mo sheasamh i gceart-lár mo
    dhaoine
D'imeodh an aois díom 's bheinn arís óg.

Douglas Hyde, who became first President of Ireland, collected much of Raftery's songs and poems from the Irish-speaking people of County Galway. He was collecting and translating other material from the oral tradition at the same time, and his *Love Songs of Connacht* changed the life of Lady Gregory of Coole, opening her eyes and ears to what she called 'the learning of the ages walking our roads.' Raftery was dead about sixty years at the time, but she found that the country-side was still alive with stories and memories of the blind poet, and she set herself the task of recording the recollections of 'old people in the cottages, cabins and workhouse.'

Despite Hyde's enormous admiration of Raftery, and the devotion with which he recorded and translated so much material from mainly oral sources, he has this to say:

There is no comparison at all to be drawn between Raftery as a poet and a man like Owen Roe O Sullivan or the Munster poets who lived a hundred years ago. They were learned men. Masters of the Irish language, old and new, were they. They had a vocabulary of their own, but it was not always a too natural one. It was melody they sought for, and melody they found. But they took away too often from the sense to add to their melody. My Raftery never sought out melody at all. He is not without it, but he never went hunting for it. He never used a 'cramp' or hard word in order to increase the mellifluousness of his verses. He spoke out the thing that was in his heart, simply and directly, in his own words; but for all that I am mistaken if even a Munsterman would not understand him to-day better than he would understand Owen Roe.' (*Songs Ascribed to Raftery*)

Raftery's verse may not have been as exquisitely wrought as that of Owen of the Sweet Mouth, but he matched the Munsterman in terms of the hold he maintained for generations on the imagination of the Irish-speaking country people.

In our own time, the best-remembered poem of Raftery's is probably 'Killedan', when the poet resolves to set out for his own home territory in County Mayo:

Now, with the coming in of the spring, the days will stretch a bit;
And after the Feast of Brigid I shall hoist my flag and go:
For, since the thought got into my head, I can neither stand nor sit
Until I find myself in the middle of the County of Mayo.

In Claremorris I should stop a night to sleep with decent men;
And then I'd go to Balla, just beyond, and drink galore;
And next I'd stay in Kiltimagh for about a month; and then
I should only be a couple of miles away from Ballymore!

I say and swear that my heart lifts up like the lifting of a tide;
Rising up like the rising wind till fog or mist must go,
When I remember Carra, and Gallen close beside,
And the Gap of the Two Bushes, and the wide plains of Mayo.

To Killeden then, to the place where everything grows that is best;
There are raspberries there, and strawberries there, and all that is good
   for men;
And were I only there, among my folk, my heart would rest,
For age itself would leave me there, and I'd be young again.
                    (trans. James Stephens)

The headstone over the grave (by the west gable of the ruined church) gives merely the terse respectful Irish: RACTURAIG, which he himself would appreciate. A slab on the ground says, more communicatively for English-speakers, 'Anthony Raftery, Poet.'

The brothers Mark and Patsy Callanan were contemporaries and (usually) friends of Raftery's. He seems to have fallen out with one or other of them from time to time, but they gave each other great value in debate and poetic performance. They are close enough now for the debates to continue for all time.

Clare

Songs Ascribed to Raftery

Douglas Hyde

Introduction by Dominic Daly

In the 1970s, Irish University Press reissued Hyde's Songs Ascribed to Raftery, Love Songs of Connacht *and* The Religious Songs of Connacht.

Opposite: Douglas Hyde portrait by Sarah Purser

7. GALWAY
Citie of the Tribes

Pádraic Ó Conaire (1883-1928)

Galway is the most colourful of Irish cities and its 'Cúirt', held annually in April, is probably Ireland's liveliest Poetry and Literary Festival. An old seaport town, it is the gateway to Connemara, the Corrib Country, the Aran Islands, to a different life, a different culture; gateway to the Gaeltacht — the Irish-speaking district of south Connemara — which means that Irish is often heard on the city streets and in the shops. There are two theatres, the *Taibhdhearc*, all Irish, and the gallant, trenchant Druid. The University of Galway spills out waves of vibrant young people, ensuring that the streets are awash with loquacious bilingual youth with all its vivacity and laughter.

Fine stone houses and towers, carved with family coats of arms, proclaim the Norman/English origins of Galway and its streets — streets where in the old days the Irish fisherfolk of **The Claddagh** village, on the west side of the harbour, were not allowed to 'strutte ne swagger', and in which it was ordered that 'no man, nor manchild, do werr no mantles in the streets, but cloaks or gowns, doublets and hose, shapen after the English fashion, of the country cloth, or any other cloth it shall please them to buy.' The forbidden mantle referred to in the Ordnance of 1538 was the blue Galway cloak, a marvellous garment worn right into the nineteenth century, and of which precious few, if any, have survived to this day. The narrow streets and curious alleyways, intriguing arches and fine converted stone warehouses give Galway itself a strutte and a swagger, added to by the Galwegians' consciousness that Columbus stopped here on his way west, to pick up a crew member and attend Mass in St Nicholas' Cathedral. Few enough of the citizens pause in their animated affairs to watch the sun go down on Galway Bay.

Eyre Square is a green space in the middle of all this fuss and bustle. On the north side, slightly withdrawn, as if in concentration, a small stone-carved figure sits on a stone wall, hat pushed back, well-worn boots dusty as in life. One hand clutches his lapel, the other writes on a sheet of paper spread on his knee. Pádraic Ó Conaire would surely have liked sculptor Albert Power's portrait of him, and maybe looked around for the donkey. This much-loved storyteller wrote always in

Irish, and most of his stories are set in the Galway and Connemara in which he grew up. The short story 'M'Asal Beag Dubh' — 'My Little Black Donkey' — has delighted generations of school-children. It tells of how he thought to buy the little donkey he spotted on a fair-day in Kinvara: of how he bargained with the tinkerman owner, hanselled the twelve kids — ('They gathered about to gaze at me. One child took hold of my coat, one took hold of my trousers, the youngest took hold of my knee. Another one of them put a hand in my trouser pocket. Of course the creature was merely looking to see if I had even the pound — but instead of the pound she got a box in the ear, and not from the gentleman of the roads either...') and set off eventually only to discover that the donkey would move only when he had the wind in his ears, so he fashioned him a wreath of branches, and away they went at a trot.

He was born in Galway in 1883 and after his father died was brought up in Connemara by his grandparents. After some years in the Civil Service in London he returned to Ireland in the early 1900s. It was then he took to writing. He took also to wandering, with his little black donkey and green cart, sometimes sleeping in barns or under a hedge. There are those who remember him arriving in Dublin after a long trek, and tying his donkey to a lamppost on Grafton Street while he turned in for a pint. When he died in 1928, he left just a pipe, some tobacco, and an apple. The poet F.R. Higgins wrote for him a fine tribute.

O'Conaire is largely thought of as an old-style teller of folk-tales, probably because of what is known of his life during his later years, and is generally regarded with more affection than respect. Some critics, however, such as Roger McHugh and Maurice Harmon, remind us that he was ahead of Frank O'Connor and Sean O'Faolain in turning to the great European writers, particularly Zola and de Maupassant, for new models of writing. Cahalan brackets this humbly-born wanderer with the urbane cosmopolitan George Moore, Ó Conaire being as innovative in Irish as Moore was in English. The novel *Deoraíocht / Exile* paints a picture of life in London as experienced by a crippled Irish-speaker. In its mixture of the tragic and comic, it is a forerunner to Flann O'Brien and even Joyce.

As for Joyce, what Galway meant to him was the inspiration of his life — his wife, Nora Barnacle, of whom all his passionate woman characters were images: Molly Bloom, Gretta Conroy, Anna Livia Plurabelle:

Then you came to me. You were not in a sense the girl for whom I had dreamed and written the verses you find now so enchanting. She was perhaps (as I saw her in my imagination) a girl fashioned into a curious grave beauty by the culture of generations before her, the woman for whom I wrote poems like 'Gentle lady' or 'Thou leanest to the shell of night'.

Niall Williams
Martin McDonagh
See *Crossing the Millennium,*
page 259–260

They've paid the last respects in sad tobacco,
And silent is this wakehouse in its haze.
They've paid the last respects and now their
    whiskey
Flings laughing words on mouths of prayer
    and praise...

Ah, they'll say: Padraic's gone again
    exploring
But now down glens of brightness, O he'll
    find
An alehouse overflowing with wise Gaelic
That's braced in vigour by the bardic mind.

(F.R. Higgins' 'Tribute to Pádraic Ó Conaire')

James Joyce (1882-1941)

Right: Nora Barnacle — wife of James Joyce and his inspiration for Molly Bloom,Gretta Conroy and Anna Livia Plurabelle

Below: Nora and James in London on 14 July 1931 where they married in a registry office

But then I saw that the beauty of your soul outshone that of my verses. There was something in you higher than anything I had put into them. And so for this reason the book of verses is for you. It holds the desire of my youth and you, darling, were the fulfilment of that desire. (Letter, August 1909)

The Barnacle family lived at No. 8 **Bowling Green Street**. Nora was actually born in the local hospital, which was unusual in those days, and might indicate difficulties attending the birth. Joyce told his brother Stanislaus, in a letter written from Austria in 1904, that she was one of seven children, and that their father was a baker who had a shop, but 'drank all the buns and loaves like a man'. An uncle, Michael Healy, helped to support the family, and Nora lived betimes with her grandmother at Augustine Street. She was wild and high-spirited and enjoyed dallying with the local lads. It was after another of her uncles gave her a thrashing for keeping company with a Protestant that she took herself off to Dublin, and Finn's Hotel, and immortality.

After Nora's mother died in 1940, the house had a succession of tenants until 1987, when it was put on the market again. To save it from an uncertain future, the sisters Sheila and Mary Gallagher put together their savings and a small legacy, and bought the house. They have gradually restored it to look as it would have at the turn of the century, and opened it to the public. Let us all be grateful.

Joyce made a sentimental journey to Galway in 1909 just to see where Nora grew up, and wrote: 'My dear little runaway Nora, I am writing this to you sitting at the kitchen table in your mother's house!... To think of my being here!' During another visit a few years later, he cycled to **Oughterard** to visit the graveyard there. Nora had told him about an early sweetheart of hers, Michael ('Sonny') Bodkin. Poor Michael had got out of his sick bed to say goodbye to her, singing to her from under an apple tree on **Nun's Island**, before she left for Dublin. He died shortly after. The story made a deep impression on Joyce, so much so that he wove the story around Gretta Conroy and Michael Furey in 'The Dead', the last and finest short story in *Dubliners*. Joyce took coincidence very seriously: what would he have made of the fact that the story became the last and greatest film of John Huston.

After visiting Oughterard, Joyce chose to set the grave of the Michael Furey of his story there. He did not find a Bodkin or a Furey, but he did find a J. Joyce, which pleased him greatly. The real Sonny Bodkin is buried in the cemetery at **Rahoon**, just outside Galway in the direction of Oughterard. Though the markings are unclear, it is easy to identify as it is the only roofed tomb close to the yew-lined wall to the left of the side entrance.

> Rain on Rahoon falls softly, softly falling,
> Where my dark lover lies.
> Sad is his voice that calls me, sadly calling,
> At grey moonrise ... ('She Weeps over Rahoon' by James Joyce)

The tomb of Sonny Bodkin at Rahoon cemetery (not the cross in the foreground, but the box tomb in the middle distance).

Cottage in Rossaveal, Connemara

Scene from the Druid Theatre's performance on Aran of Synge's Riders to the Sea *(the Aran islands' first professional Synge presentation) in 1982*

Scene from the film Man of Aran

(Right and overleaf) The Burren of County Clare. 'Stony fields poured over space' is how John Betjeman described the place.

(Below) At Lough Gur, 12miles, 18km south of Limerick, an extraordinary collection of stone circles, forts, dolmens and other ancient monuments surround the lake. At the gateway to the so-called 'New Church', Teampall Nua — very much ruined — local poets are honoured. The plaque reads:

Sweet Teampall Nua
In an unmarked grave 'sleeps'
Thomas O'Connellan
Renouned poet-harper of Cloonamahon, Co Sligo
Who died in Bourchier's Castle, Lough Gur, in 1698 AD.
This plaque also honours
Owen Bresnan (1847-1912)
local poet & historian whose song 'Teampall Nua'
kept O'Connellan's memory alive.
'Those who love his Irish melodies, enchanting and sublime,
Should raise a wreath of laurels o'er his grave.'
It was finally done by Lough Gur & Dist. Hist. Soc. in June 1991

(Right) Tulira Castle was the home of Edward Martyn, one of the founders of the Irish literary revival at the turn of the century and of the Abbey Theatre. A later owner swapped the castle for a yacht, evidently to the satisfaction of both parties.

(Below) The great fort, Dun Aengus, perches dizzily on the cliffs of Aran, the largest of the three Aran Islands. The islands attracted a long sequence of scholars and poets, and inspired J.M. Synge's 'Riders to the Sea'. Liam O'Flaherty, who became one of the most widely read writers of the early twentieth century, was born practically under the shadow of its walls.

REILIG NA BHFILÍ
CEMETERY OF THE POETS
KILLEENEEN

(Above) Coole Park as painted by W.B. Yeats during one of his many long visits to Lady Gregory's home near Gort.

(Left) The Cemetery of the Poets at Killeeneen, near Kilcolgan, Co. Galway, where the grave of blind Raftery the poet is to be found.

(Right) Padraic Pearse's cottage near Rosmuc on Kilkieran Bay in Connemara, where he spent long summers burnishing his ideal of an Ireland 'free and Gaelic as well'.

(Below) Ballynahinch Lake with Derryclare mountain behind. In the middle distance is Ballynahinch Castle, now a hotel, one-time home of the powerful and, needless to say, eccentric Martin family.

(Right) The deserted village on Achill Island, Co. Mayo. The place fascinated Heinrich Böll on his first visit to the west of Ireland. 'Everything not made of stone eaten away by wind, sun, rain, and time, neatly laid out along the somber slope as if for an anatomy lesson, the skeleton of a village. (Irish Journal)

(Below) The Connemara coastline from Clare Island, headquarters of Granuaile, sixteenth-century 'Warrior Queen of the West'. Her castle (top left, opposite page) overlooks Clare Island harbour.

'The French in Killala Bay (1798)' by William Sadler. The French troops came to aid an Irish uprising, an event which began hopefully but ended in tragedy, for the Irish especially.

(Previous page top) The gaunt burnt-out ruin of Moore Hall; it overlooks Lough Carra, Co. Mayo. The ashes of George Moore are under a cairn on Castle Island, just off-shore.
(Below) The stone Virgin and Child by Friedrich Herkner (1902–1986) stands outside Ballintubber Abbey, between Westport and Moore Hall.

8. ARAN ISLANDS
Riders to the Sea

Someone, whose name I forget, told me there was a poor Irishman at the top of the house, and presently introduced us. Synge had come lately from Italy, and had played his fiddle to peasants in the Black Forest — six months to travel upon fifty pounds — and was now reading French literature and writing morbid and melancholy verse. He told me that he had learned Irish at Trinity College, so I urged him to go to the Aran Islands and find a life that had never been expressed in literature ...

So wrote W.B. Yeats in his autobiographical work *The Tragic Generation*. He adds: 'I did not divine his genius, but I felt he needed something to take him out of his morbidity and melancholy.' We know now that that advice was the turning-point for Synge, both of his life and of his career. From his times in Aran came the book of his experiences there, *The Aran Islands* and perhaps the greatest of his one-act plays, *Riders to the Sea*.

The islands can be seen from anywhere on the coast between Loop and Slyne Heads. They lie stretched tautly on the western horizon, betimes glittering in the sun, more often seeming to dissolve through drifting mists or swept by curtains of rain, but always a lure to the imagination. Synge's first visit was in 1898. Let us have his own simple description:

There are three islands: Aranmor, the north island, about nine miles long; Inishmaan, the middle island, about three miles and a half across, and nearly round in form; and the south island, Inisheer — in Irish, east island, — like the middle island but slightly smaller. They lie about thirty miles from Galway, up the centre of the bay, but they are not far from the cliffs of County Clare, on the south, or the corner of Connemara on the north.

With their proximity to County Clare, the islands share the fissured limestone nature of the Burren, its naked rock terracing, its rich archaeology, and some of its flora. Like the Burren, they can look grey and bleak and sullen. But, again like its counterpart on the mainland, suddenly the magic is revealed by a trick of light or a change of mood. Tim Robinson, in *Stones of Aran: Pilgrimage*, describes his gradual discovery of the island's nature during his first dark winter there.

What captivated me in that long winter were the immensities in which this

Scene from Riders to the Sea

John Millington Synge (1871-1909)

Tim Robinson (1935-   )

little place is wrapped: the processions of grey squalls that stride in from the Atlantic horizon, briefly lash us with hail and go sailing off towards the mainland trailing rainbows; the breakers that continue to arch up, foam and fall across the shoals for days after a storm has abated; the long, wind-rattled nights, untamed then by electricity below, wildly starry above. Then I was dazzled by the minutiae of spring, the appearance each in its season of the flowers, starting with the tiny, white whitlow-grass blossoms hardly distinguishable from the last of the hailstones in the scant February pastures, and culminating by late May in paradisal tapestry-work across every meadow and around every rock. The summer had me exploring the honeysuckled boreens and the breezy clifftops; autumn proposed the Irish language, the blacksmith's quarter-comprehended tales, the intriguing gossip of the shops, and the discovery that there existed yet another literature it would take four or five years to begin to make one's own.

Robinson's *Stones of Aran* is the most remarkable chronicle of the islands in modern times. Step by step he has circled Inishmore (or Árainn, as he insists it is properly called) examining minutely each rock and hollow, recounting the history on a geological time-scale, mining the memories of the elders to retell the stories of the lives lived there over generations, the struggles with poverty, hunger, the sea, and sometimes with each other.

Pat Mullen (1883-1972)

One of the stories he recounts illustrates the thin edge by which families survived less than a century ago, and the mutability of circumstance. The story is told in the first place by Pat Mullen in his book *Man of Aran* published in 1935, which was largely about the making of the famous Flaherty film (they show it all the time in Kilronan, for the 'strangers'). Pat was one of eleven children; finding food for the lot of them wasn't easy. Pat's father Johnny owned 'a bit of a crag' near a beach, a rocky stretch where nothing grew only a couple of thorn

The premier of Man of Aran

bushes. He decided to make a field out of it, a new potato patch. The normal island way to 'make land', as has been explained umpteen times, is by a mixture of sand and seaweed spread over the bare rock. The problem here was that the taking of even wind-blown sand on that stretch of shoreline was forbidden by the local Minister who used it as a backing and protection to his own farm. So in deepest winter Johnny Mullen and his children went out at night, rounded up all the donkeys they could find wandering, and under cover of darkness dragged up loads of sand on to his crag, smoothing the beach behind them. It made fine 'new gardens'.

Robinson comments:

Not long after I had read this raw little creation-myth I happened upon an image from the other end of the spectrum of human dreams. It was a photograph by Cecil Beaton, a carefully confected essence of sophistication; it showed a bar in, I suppose, Manhattan ... with, in the centre, Audrey Hepburn exquisitely reclined across several barstools; on the right S. J. Perelman proffers a silent New Yorkerism, while on the left is an elegant couple in evening dress, tête-a-tête: an actor whose name I forget — and Johnny Mullen's granddaughter.

The granddaughter of the man who had to steal sand to make a field was the film actress Barbara Mullen. Her career began after she married the young cameraman John Taylor whom she met while the film *Man of Aran* was being made.

As even sand helped to bridge the gap between a hungry and an adequate winter, so did sea-wrack. Each townland could harvest only from its own adjoining shoreline: seaweed was thrown on some portions of the shore more than others, but that was the will of God, to be accepted. But in one's own territory, one had to be quick, and strong, and fierce. Liam O'Flaherty, born on the island in 1896 and destined to become an internationally respected writer, paints a savage picture of such a day in 'Poor People', of a sick man harvesting weed 'in the poisonous cold of a February morning'.

Shevawn Lynam, novelist and biographer, once suggested to a group of Aran men that they should buy equal shares in a fine modern trawler and, in those heady pre-EU days, they could fish wherever and whenever they liked. As she tells it: 'They stood, six foot one, two and four, each as sparse as a spruce, with chiselled features, curiously fine little hands and feet and the manners of mandarins. They murmured together in Irish and then one of them smilingly replied "We'd rather each to be going out on his own hook".'

On his own hook. The Aran Islands and its people have been endlessly written about, both from inside and from outside. From inside by such as Pat Mullen, already mentioned, and Máirtín Ó Direáin, a fine poet. And then there's Willie Maidhc, as he's known on Árainn, Liam O'Flaherty to you and me. He was born in 1896 at Gort

Liam O'Flaherty (1896-1984)

Máirtín Ó Direáin (1910–1988)
EDITOR'S NOTE:

Liam O'Flaherty revisits Aran for the last time in 1981

The Reverend Alexander Synge ministered unhappily on Aran for four years or so.

Liam O'Flaherty's birthplace at Gort na gCapall

na gCapall at the back of the island with the high cliffs and Dún Aengus close behind. He had been to school at Rockwell in Tipperary (courtesy of a visiting priest) and at the Queen's College in Dublin (courtesy of a Department of Education scholarship). He joined the Irish Guards using his mother's maiden name. In 1923 he wrote a novel set on Aran, *Thy Neighbour's Wife*, which caused a bit of trouble in spite — probably because — of the fact that it gives the most detailed description of everyday life then. To quote his nephew, Breandán Ó hEithir: 'The roving author continued his sniping from a safe distance and returned home occasionally to collect more ammunition.' One of his best books, *Skerrett*, is based on an island feud between his own schoolmaster and the parish priest. His short stories, most of which draw on his Aran environment, are brilliant gems of perfection reflecting close intimacy with nature in all its realities, and of course his novel *Famine* is an acknowledged masterpiece. O'Flaherty died in 1984: most of his work is again in print. Breandán Ó hEithir, the nephew, was an acute commentator on life in Ireland and in Aran, a journalist and novelist in English and Irish. His early death was a great loss.

For outsiders writing about Aran, try Aidan Higgins, or Leo Daly, or Seamus Heaney, or the Wicklow novelist Richard Power. Emily Lawless or Lady Gregory. Ethna Carbery or that strange man Arthur Symons. Or try even John Messenger, anthropologist and cold commentator. The Aran islanders were not entirely pleased with him — but they include him in the cast of writers worth noting, drawn from the ranks of the 'strangers'. Giraldus Cambrensis had his say in 1220. He seemed to think that the absence of mice was significant. The Reverend Alexander Synge, uncle of the playwright, wrote letters to his relatives that indicate that literary gifts run in families. Padraic Pearse came to Aran and founded a branch of the Gaelic League there. Even James Joyce dropped in on a visit to Nora's Galway connections. Breandán Ó hEithir made a selection from writings over several hundred years and called it *An Aran Reader*. Bring it with you.

Finally there is J.M. Synge. His elemental drama, *Riders to the Sea*, has about it the inevitability of the Greek tragedy. Old Maurya has lost her husband and five sons to the sea. Her last son insists on going out, on a bad night, to a horse fair on the mainland. Maurya feels the black grip of destiny: 'He's gone now, God spare us, and we'll not see him again. He's gone now, and when the black night is falling I'll have no son left me in the world.' By nightfall, his corpse is brought to the house. That is the whole story, but the intensity of it is almost unbearable. No longer so for old Maurya: she has gone beyond pain and hope. 'They're all gone now and there isn't any more the sea can do to me ... I'll have no call now to be up crying and praying when the wind breaks from the south, and you can hear the surf is in the east, and the surf is in the west, making a great stir with the two noises, and they hitting one on the other ... It's a great rest I'll have now, and great sleeping in the long nights after Samhain ...' And finally: 'No man at all can be living for ever, and we must be satisfied.'

Somerville and Ross remarked of the Aran people:

Lying on the warm rocks they see Ireland stretched silent, enigmatic, apart from them and are content that it is so. Their poverty is known to many, their way of thought to a few; they remain motionless, on the edge of Europe, with the dust of saints beneath their feet.

Since the days of Synge and O'Flaherty, 'the electric' has come to the islands, dispelling the soft night-light of candle and rush, the dimly-lit corners where mystery hung. Boats bring loads of day-trippers from Galway and Doolin and Rossaveal. Other arrivals are television, and Hiace vans, and tarred roads, and B&B signs, and outboard motors on the sterns of currachs. But the austere strangeness of these islands resides at a deeper level of experience, not yet eradicated by the casual comings-and-goings of the curious.

Sketch by Harold Oakley: three Aran visitors — left to right, Yeats, Synge and AE (George Russell)
Below: Jeanette Dunne's illustration for the first edition of Liam O'Flaherty's novel The Wilderness

Above: Ballinahinch lake with the Martin house on the right. This sketch was drawn for Maria Edgeworth by her friend Mr Smith during their visit of 1835.

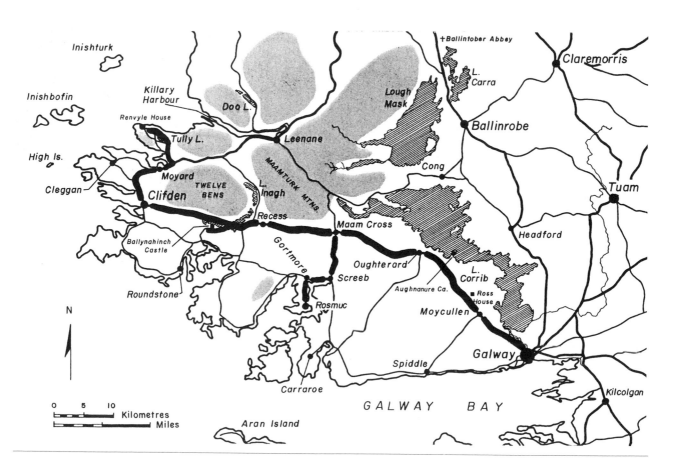

9. CONNEMARA
Sailors, Ghosts and Patriots

Connemara is rock and sedge and bog; it is pools of black peaty water gemmed with white water-lilies; it is small rocky mountains rising so abruptly from the peaty plain that they assume grandeur; it is light and shadow and rain and sunshine all chasing each other at great speed. It is green and brown and deep purple. In between the few roads that make a way around and through the mountains, it is the heart of silence.

The coast is different. Rocky also, much of it, and rust-rimmed with bright seaweed, but much of it given over to sweep after sweep of white, white fine sand. So complex is the interplay between land and sea and lake and island that you might need to taste the water to know whether it is fresh or salt.

At the cost of missing some of the most persistently and genuinely Irish-speaking area of **Cois Fharraige**, instead of taking the coastal road along Galway Bay we will take the inland road westwards. It gradually manages to escape the grip of the Galway suburbs, to slip through the village of **Moycullen**, with the wide expanse of **Lough Corrib** glimpsed towards the right, to arrive at **Oughterard** and to visit, perhaps, the old graveyard where Joyce pictured the grave of Michael Furey of 'The Dead'. Two stops are recommended along the way, both of them close to Moycullen, so well known to salmon and trout fishermen. The first is **Ross House**, 3 miles (5 km) beyond Moycullen: the second is **Aughnanure Castle**, a mile or so farther on (watch for the signpost, towards the right).

Ross House, sometimes called Ross Castle, is an eighteenth-century mansion built on the site of an old fortification by the Martin family. They were for a couple of centuries the greatest landed family of Norman origin in Connacht, and Ross was their first estate. One of the original Fourteen Tribes of Galway, they arrived in Ireland following the Anglo-Norman conquest of 1169. The Tribes lived for centuries within their walled city in a state almost of siege — 'From the ferocious O'Flahertys Good Lord deliver us' was carved above the city gate. When Robert Martin bought the estate of Ross from a ferocious O'Flaherty in 1590, he was the first of the Tribes to venture outside the

Ross House, and its present owner George McLoughlin

Violet Martin (Martin Ross) (1862-1915)

walls. A century later the Martins had acquired about a quarter of a million acres of mountain and bog, and about 80 miles of complex coastline. Violet Martin, the 'Martin Ross' of the Somerville and Ross literary partnership, was born at Ross Castle — it was the house that gave her the pen-name. She was born in 1862, eleventh in a family of fourteen. It was June and, according to her sister, ' a time of roses, when Ross was at its best, with its delightful old-fashioned gardens fragrant with midsummer flowers, and its shady walks at their darkest and greenest.'

When Violet's father died in 1872 leaving the estate in debt, the family moved to Dublin. Years later Mama, with Violet and another daughter, returned to the old house and tried to pull it back from decay. There is a lovely account of a visit from an old retainer who, in his joy at seeing them there, broke into a dance in the hall. 'Mama, who was attired in a flowing pink dressing gown, and a black hat trimmed with lilac, became suddenly emulous, and, with her spade under her arm, joined in the jig. This lasted for about a minute, and was a never-to-be-forgotten sight. They skipped round the hall, they changed sides, they swept up to each other and back again, and finished with the deepest curtseys.'

Violet first met her cousin, Edith Somerville, on a visit to Castletownshend in 1886. Edith wrote: 'It has proved the hinge of my life, the place where my fate, and hers, turned over, and new and unforeseen things began to happen to us.' From then on Violet's life was focused almost entirely on Castletownshend: To quote Edith again: 'For most boys and girls the varying, yet invariable, flirtations and emotional episodes of youth, are resolved and composed by marriage. To (Violet) Martin and me was opened another way, and the flowering of both our lives was when we met each other.'

Various Martins lived on at Ross until 1914, but the estate never really recovered from the effects of the Famine, and the changing political and social climate. Violet had written about her father's death: 'With his death a curtain fell for ever on the old life at Ross, the stage darkened, and the keening of the tenants as they followed his coffin, a tremendous and sustained wail, like the voice of the grave itself, was the last music of the piece.'

But there is a happy ending to the story of Ross House. In recent years it has been magnificently restored by new owners. Slate and stone have been collected from other semi-derelict houses to replace what was decayed or vanished. Granite window-sills from Coole top the garden wall, the chapel has been furnished from others closing down. In the courtyard roses grow anew against the grey stone, and the stables have been turned into splendid holiday homes. The gardens are trim, and an indoor swimming pool is discreetly tucked

View from the front steps of Ross House

behind old barns over which roses climb. Luxury on a small scale: there *is* life after death.

Aughnanure Castle may not have any specific literary connections, but it is worth visiting (open May to September) just because it is such a fine restoration of a small fifteenth-century fortress of the O'Flahertys, who were the chieftain family of Connemara before the Martins.

To get to Ballinahinch from Oughterard, continue along the **Clifden road**, through **Maam Cross** and **Recess**, to turn southwards at a signpost for Roundstone. Two miles along that road brings you to **Ballinahinch Castle**, now a very fine hotel. It has an extra storey now to the original house, and much else has changed, but the Connemara marble fireplace in the dining room was part of the original Martin residence, their first dwelling. The tiles over the hallway fireplace, bearing the date 1813, are thought to have come from Ross.

William Thackeray came that way, where the towering **Twelve Bens** and the **Maamturks** are separated by the valley and lake of **Inagh**. 'The best guidebook that was ever written cannot set the view before the mind of the reader, and I won't attempt to pile up big words in place of the wild mountains,' he wrote in his *Irish Sketch Book*.

William Thackeray (1811-1863)

It was from Ballinahinch that the Martins ruled like monarchs and dispensed legendary hospitality to anybody who managed to reach it — no small feat in those days before any class of a road penetrated there.

Maria Edgeworth made the journey in 1834, with an English party in a four-horse carriage. She had heard her father talk about the 'King of Connemara and his immense territory, and his ways of ruling over his people with almost absolute power, with laws of his own, and setting other laws at defiance.' She described the visit in a long letter to her brother Pakenham, published later under the title *Tour in Connemara and the Martins of Ballinahinch*, and the story is worth retelling. They had been warned that 'no carriage had ever passed or had any one thought of attempting to pass' there, and that as for such a carriage as theirs, the like had never even been seen in these parts.

Maria Edgeworth (1767-1849)

But they set out from Oughterard nonetheless, as they could hardly 'dart over the bog on foot'.

The first bad step we came to was indeed a slough ... the horses sank up to their knees and were whipped and spurred and they struggled and foundered ... and the carriage, as we inside passengers felt, sank and sank ... The postillions leaped off, and bridles in hand, gained the shore and by dint of tugging and whipping and hallooing, and dragging of men and boys, who followed from Corrib Lodge, we were got out and were on the other side.'

At the next bad step 'the horses seeing it was a slough like the first, put back

Maria Edgeworth

Humanity Dick

their ears and absolutely refused to set foot upon it, and they were, the postillions agreed, quite right; so they were taken off and left to look on, while by force of arms the carriage was to be got over by men and boys, who shouting gathered from all sides, from mountain paths down which they poured, and from fields where they had been at work or loitering ... and they talked and screamed together in Irish and Connemara dialect equally unintelligible to us, and ... seized of the carriage, and standing and jumping from stone to stone or any tuft of bog that would bear them, as their practised eyes saw, they, I cannot tell you how, dragged, pushed, carried, screamed the carriage over ... and a great giant, of the name of Ulick Burke, took me up in his arms as he might a child or a doll, and proceeded to carry me over ... just as we reached the bank he stumbled, knee deep sunk, but threw me, as he would a sack, to shore.'

After which Miss Maria actually cuffed an unfortunate lad who had the temerity to laugh!

No doubt as a consequence of all that, by the time they arrived at **Ballinahinch** one of her companions was so unwell that, instead of a single night, they were there for three weeks. Her description of that outlandish household makes fascinating reading, but most intriguing is her description of Mary, the daughter of the house. She found her

one of the most extraordinary persons I ever saw ... Her acquirements are indeed prodigious; she has more knowledge of books, both scientific and learned, than any female creature I ever saw or heard of at her age: heraldry, metaphysics, painting and painters' lives, and tactics. She had a course of tactics from a French officer, and of engineering from Mr. Nimmo. She understands Latin, Greek and Hebrew, and I don't know how many modern languages ... When any allusion was made to books, she could quote whole passages from them, begin or end where you would.

But, for all her accomplishments, she had little knowledge of the world otherwise. She had never learned to speak English well, and spoke in such a thick Connemara accent that they found it difficult to understand her. She adds later: 'Do think of a girl of seventeen, in the wilds of Connemara, intimately acquainted with all the beauties of Aeschylus and Euripides, and having them as part of her daily thoughts!'

But then all the Martins were remarkable, often wildly eccentric as well. They included Nimble Dick, who earned his name because of the neat political and diplomatic footwork which allowed him to build up the vast estates. A great-grandson of his, another Richard, was known variously as Hair-Trigger Dick, because of his duelling propensities, and as Humanity Dick because of his compassion and love for animals. The story of his life, and how he forced through Parliament the world's first legislation protecting cattle and horses, is told by Shevawn Lynam in the biography *Humanity Dick*. Charles Lever's novel *The Martins of Cro' Martin* is loosely based on the family.

Several generations of Martins living lives which combined too much prodigality with too much humanity impoverished the estate in the end. The great famines of the 1800s were the death-blow. Thomas Martin died of famine fever, contracted while visiting his sick tenants. The mortgagees foreclosed on the fair Mary, who had inherited it all. She died penniless in New York, shortly after her arrival; she had given birth during the voyage, in the same boat as some of her poorer tenants.

Will the ancients suffice as exemplars? Frankly, we are afraid not. We must get in touch also with our contemporaries, in France, in Russia, in Norway, in Finland, in Bohemia, in Hungary, wherever, in short, vital literature is being produced on the face of the globe ... Irish literature, if it is to live and grow, must get into contact on the one hand with its own past and on the other with the mind of contemporary Europe.

It might come as a surprise to discover that the author of that statement, in an article written in 1906, is Patrick Pearse. The leader of the 1916 Easter Rising was a most unlikely military leader. He was a shy man, a poet, whose main interests were education and literature.

Padraic Pearse (1879-1916)

The road southwards from Maam Cross leads to Screeb, where another signpost leads to Gortmore and Rosmuc. This is where Pearse built his Gaeltacht retreat, a thatched cottage perched on a knoll overlooking Loc Eiliurach. A sign reading 'Teach an Phiarsaigh' will lead you to it. It is furnished simply and sparsely, as it would have been in his time and is now preserved as a kind of shrine, open to the public. Here in the heart of the Gaeltacht was a perfect world in which to burnish his dream of a free and Gaelic Ireland, and his willingness, or eagerness, to spill his life-blood to bring it about:

Fornocht do chonac thú,	Do bhlaiseas do bhéal	Do thugas mo chúl
a áille na háille,	a mhilse na milse,	ar an aisling do chumas,
is do dhallas mo shúil	is do chruas mo chroí	's ar an ród so romham
ar eagla go stánfainn	ar eagla mo mhillte	m'aghaidh do thugas.
Do chualas do cheol,	Do dhallas mo shúil,	Do thugas mo ghnúis
a bhinne na binne,	is mo chluas do dhúnas;	ar an ród so romham,
is do dhúnas mo chluas	do chruas mo chroí	ar an ngníomh do-chím,
ar eagla go gclisfinn.	is mo mhian do mhúchas	's ar an mbás do gheobhad.

Naked I saw thee,	I kissed thy lips,	I turned my back
O beauty of beauties!	O sweetness of sweetness!	On the dream I had shaped,
And I blinded my eyes	And I hardened my heart	And to this road before me
For fear I should flinch.	For fear of my ruin.	My face I turned.
I heard thy music,	I blinded my eyes,	I set my face
O melody of melody!	And my ears I shut,	To the road here before me,
And I shut my ears	I hardened my heart,	To the work I see,
For fear I should fail.	And my love I quenched.	To the death I shall get

After all that was over, and Yeats's 'terrible beauty' had been born, for better or worse, it was to the stony acres of Connemara that Pearse's mind turned while he waited in his cell for his execution:

> The beauty of the world hath made me sad,
> This beauty that will pass;
> Sometimes my heart hath shaken with great joy
> To see a leaping squirrel in a tree,
> Or a red ladybird upon a stalk,
> Or little rabbits in a field at evening,
> Lit by a slanting sun,
> Or some green hill where shadows drifted by,
> Some quiet hill where mountainy men hath sown
> And soon shall reap near to the gate of Heaven;
> Or children with bare feet upon the sands
> Of some ebbed sea, or playing on the streets
> Of little towns in Connacht,
> Things young and happy.
> And then my heart has told me:
> These will pass,
> Will pass and change, will die and be no more,
> Things bright and green, things young and happy;
> And I have gone upon my way
> Sorrowful. ('The Wayfarer')

Anyone exploring Connemara is drawn inevitably to **Renvyle**. Maria Edgeworth was entertained there, 'within a stone's throw or wave's dash of the vast Atlantic', less lavishly but more elegantly than at Ballinahinch. It belonged to the Blakes, another old Galway family, whose estate extended eastwards to Lettergesh. The Blakes as landlords were a mixed lot, some good, some bad, but like all landed families, the 1840s impoverished them. A later Blake, a woman of strong character who defied the Land League, turned Renvyle into a hotel during the 1880s. It prospered for a while, but eventually had to be sold. It was acquired in 1917 by Oliver St John Gogarty, poet, athlete, wit, raconteur and, almost incidentally, ear-nose-and-throat surgeon, who loved it excessively, using it as a counterpoint to his Dublin life of exchanging wit and malice with the socialites and intelligentsia of the time, although those friends often gathered at Renvyle too.

Oliver St John Gogarty (1878-1957)

My house ... stands on a lake, but it stands also on the sea. Water-lilies meet the golden seaweed. It is as if, in the faery land of Connemara at the extreme end of Europe, the incongruous flowed together at last; and the sweet and bitter blended. Behind me, islands and mountainous mainland share in a final reconciliation at this, the world's end. I am sitting on a little terrace overlooking the lake, watching the wider shimmer of the ocean beyond a thin line of green in the middle distance ... A butterfly, like a small, detached flame, is making

Above: A Robert Gibbings illustration (from his John Graham: Convict)

excellent landings on the faintly pink blossoms of the thorn. Two bees disturb him alternately... In the evening the lake will send the westering sun dancing on the dining-room panels, the oak of which sun and age have reddened until it looks like the mahogany of a later day.'(*As I was going down Sackville Street*)

Those sun-soaked panels, the terrace, and everything else as well, went up in flames in February 1923 when Renvyle House was burned to the ground by anti-Treaty forces. 'They say that it took a week to burn. Blue china fused like solder.' It was rebuilt during the 1930s, as an hotel, which it has been since, a place of rare geniality and comfort, so intimately related to the sea that there have been occasions when Atlantic storms have burst through the gamesroom, depositing rocks and sand and seaweed on the parquet floor.

And what goings-on the place has seen! In those early days, all the literati and intelligentsia came there — Mahaffy, Lady Lavery, AE, the Yeatses. Augustus John spent most of 1930 there, painting landscapes and portraits. Wit and repartee held sway — and so did dabblings in spiritualism. Seances were held, and the resident ghost was persuaded

Derryclare Lake, Connemara

Oliver St John Gogarty with Mrs Gogarty and W.B. Yeats in 1924.

Richard Murphy (1927-   )

to identify itself. Mrs Yeats revealed that it was one of the Blakes, a fourteen-year-old boy who had gone mad and hanged himself, and who now objected to strangers in the house. But W.B. Yeats took the unfortunate wraith to task and set out some rules of behaviour, including that he must desist from frightening the children in their early sleep, and cease to moan about the chimneys. Apparently they came to an agreement, provided that the young Blake was placated with incense and flowers. It is said that he still makes an occasional subtle manifestation, even nowadays.

Gogarty died in New York in 1957. His body was flown to Shannon, and brought to **Ballinakill Cemetery** near **Moyard** as his last resting-place. His gravestone is inscribed with a verse of his own:

> Our friends go with us as we go
> Down the long path where Beauty wends
> Where all we love foregathers, so
> Why should we fear to join our friends?

The Gogarty connection with the area continues, insofar as the Gogarty family still owns Tully House on **Tully Island** on a nearby lake.

Out to sea from here is Richard Murphy's **High Island**:

> A shoulder of rock
> Sticks high up out of the sea,
> A fisherman's mark
> For lobster and blue-shark.
>
> Fissile and stark
> The crust is flaking off,
> Seal-rock, gull-rock,
> Cove and cliff. (*High Island*)

Murphy was born in the West of Ireland in 1927 but spent much of his youth in Ceylon. He came later to live at **Cleggan**, drawn back to the west by remembered boyhood experiences in what he called 'that greatest pleasure ground in the world.' In a long tender poem in memory of his grandmother titled 'The Woman of the House' he recalls those early years:

> It was her house where we spent holidays,
> With candles to bed, and ghostly stories:
> In the lake of her heart we were islands
> Where the wild asses galloped in the wind ...
>
> And those happy days, when in spite of rain
> We'd motor west where the salmon-boats tossed,
> She would sketch on the pier among the pots
> Waves in a sunset, or the rising moon.

Gradually the distillation of that pleasure ground of the west became for him the sea itself and he settled on **Inishbofin**, the 'Island of the White Cow.' He bought the *Ave Maria*, the last of the old sailing hookers built in Galway, and sailed to his own island:

> The boom above my knees lifts, and the boat
> Drops, and the surge departs, departs, my cheek
> Kissed and rejected, kissed, as the gaff sways
> A tangent, cuts the infinite sky to red
> Maps, and the mast draws eight and eight across
> Measureless blue, the boatmen sing or sleep.
>
> We point all day for our chosen island...

The long poem 'The Battle of Aughrim' is an account of an episode in the 'Battle of Kings' for the throne of England. It took place in July 1691 at **Aughrim**, County Galway, which is on the main road to Dublin. A new Interpretive Centre there tells the story.

Below: Poet Richard Murphy (in white cap) on board the Ave Maria with Pat Cloherty at the helm.

Louis MacNeice (1907-1963)

Louis MacNeice, in spite of his 'Valediction' when he takes his final leave of

> ... the black moor where half
> A turf-stack stands like a ruined cenotaph;
> Good-bye your hens running in and out of the white house
> Your absent-minded goats along the road, your black cows
> Your greyhounds and your hunters beautifully bred
> Your drums and your dolled-up Virgins and your ignorant dead...

lays poetic claim to the whole west. We will remember him here, and close this chapter with his more rousing and life-enhancing lines from 'Thalassa', where is concentrated the power and vigour of the Atlantic, and in which he hurls defiance at age or timidity:

> Put out to sea, ignoble comrades,
> Whose record shall be noble yet;
> Butting through scarps of moving marble
> The narwhal dares us to be free;
> By a high star our course is set,
> Our end is Life. Put out to sea.   ('Thalassa')

Co Mayo — Boycotting a tradesman in 1880 — the new word derived from Captain Boycott of Lough Mask House.

10. MAYO
Holy Mountains and Wild Sports

Along our coastal route, the great fjord of **Killary Harbour** separates Counties Galway and Mayo. From the north shore of Killary, **Mweelrea** heaves its mighty shoulder against the sky. The valley of **Delphi** under its evening shadow is paved with gold. Since rich veins of the precious ore were discovered some years back, mining prospectors and conservationists have been locked in mortal combat about the possible rape of the virgin landscape. Sacred **Croagh Patrick**, on the northern horizon, for a while threatened with similar defilement, has by Government decree been rescued from such a fate and allowed to preserve its virtue — but who knows for how long? How beautifully symbolic it is that down through the centuries, endless thousands of devout pilgrims have trampled under their often bare feet the gold that has driven men mad with greed, and that their choice is to continue to do so.

The roads onwards from Killary rival each other in scenic glory. To solve the dilemma of choice, we propose to travel northwards to **Westport**, then to sweep eastwards and down to **Lough Carra**, and to make a circuit of **Lough Mask** before returning to Westport.

So, we loop around the head of Killary harbour by **Leenane** (where all the inhabitants of the surrounding countryside had the time of their lives during the filming of John B. Keane's play, *The Field*), then north through that starkly beautiful Delphi valley, past **Doo Lough**, then along the shore of **Clew Bay** whence the pilgrim path to the mountain summit snakes upwards. The devout pilgrim and the merely curious or compulsive summit-collector will be equally rewarded for the pains of an ascent, with a mighty view of mountain, coast and the bay at the mountain's foot, where all 365 (who counted them?) islands are laid out for admiration. The official Croagh Patrick pilgrimage takes place on the last Sunday of July, and even in these secular days, up to 50,000 people are likely to take part in this extraordinary event. The road brings us to Westport, where Lord Altamont, who traces his lineage back to Granuaile, the sixteenth-century 'warrior queen of the west,' acts as host to the public in his magnificent house and estate.

Heinrich Böll in Achill

The large island of Achill is connected to the Mayo coast by a bridge. Heinrich Böll, Nobel Prize-winning German novelist (1917-1985), had a second home at Dugort on the north of the island under the shadow of Slievemore.

He first visited Achill in the mid-1950s, and kept coming back. In his *Irish Journal* he describes that first visit, the pleasure of reaching 'the outer edge of Mayo' after a difficult journey: 'The house was painted snow white, the window frames dark blue; there was a fire burning in the grate. The welcoming feast consisted of fresh salmon. The sea was pale green, up front where it rolled onto the beach, dark blue out toward the centre of the bay, and a narrow, sparkling white frill was visible where the sea broke on the island.'

It was his wish that his house be used by writers after his death, and his family, in co-operation with a local committee which includes Achill-born poet John F. Deane, respect that wish.

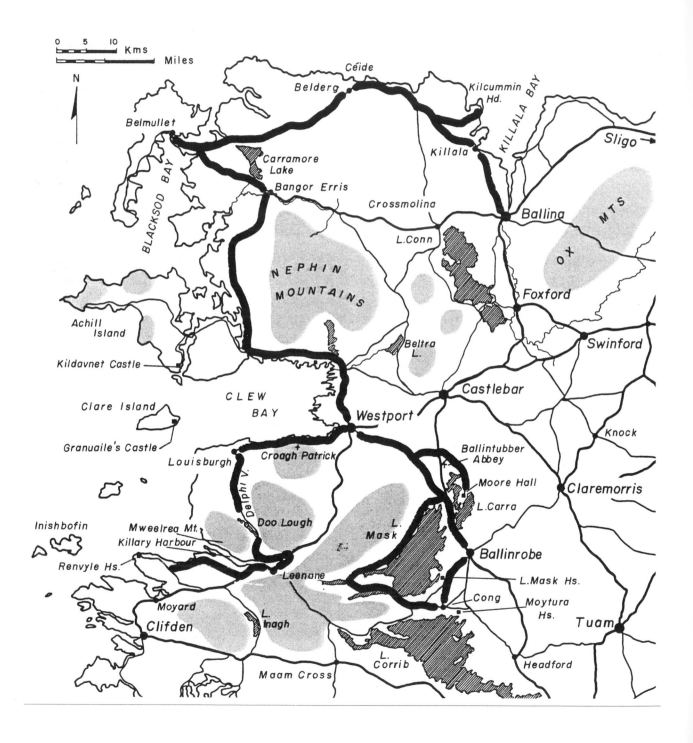

In the history of Mayo, the Moores of **Moore Hall** played a prominent part. The novelist George Moore was one of them, born in 1852. Though he preferred the boulevards of Paris to the bogs of Mayo, in the process of leaving his mark on literary history he gave to the world a picture of Lough Carra, on whose shore stands Moore Hall. Near the topmost corner of Lough Mask, it is one of the loveliest and least-visited of all Irish lakes. To reach it, take the Ballinrobe road out of Westport. The best way to find the way to Moore Hall (and the determinably irreligious George Moore would have found it amusing) is to watch for the signpost to **Ballintubber Abbey**, which you should pick up about 8 miles (13km) along that road. Follow it and it will lead you to our objective (though try to spare a little time to visit that remarkable abbey, in use continuously for over seven hundred years).

We are here, then, at Moore Hall — or, rather, what is left of it, because it too suffered the fate of many great houses, being burned for the greater glory of Ireland in the 1920s. This happened in spite of the fact that the Moores had been the most generous and compassionate of landlords, that several generations of them had fought on the Irish side, and that John Moore had been appointed President of the Republic of Connacht during the brief period of success during the Rebellion of 1798, the 'Year of the French'. We are here to pay homage of a sort to a Moore whom everybody appears to have disliked. 'That egregious ass,' quotes Oliver St John Gogarty. 'The famous novelist that everybody talks about and nobody reads,' said James Stephens. 'Some men kiss and do not tell, some kiss and tell, but George Moore tells and does not kiss,' said Susan Mitchell.

Physically he was rather unprepossessing, with untidy yellowish hair, heavy moustache and white complexion. Yeats said his face looked as if it had been carved out of a turnip, but then Moore described Yeats as looking like an umbrella someone had forgotten at a picnic. He was fiercely anti-clerical, and publicly renounced his Catholicism. He was foppish and acid-tongued. But it seems to have been agreed by all, even by those who only reluctantly admitted it, that he was a truly exquisite writer, an original, a trail-breaker. And *The Lake* is his greatest novel. The Lake is, of course, **Lough Carra**. The shell of Moore Hall stands above it on a hill, with a columned portico and steps that once led to an avenue running between lawns to the lake shore. The atmosphere of the lake, its moods, its surrounding woods, are a constant theme throughout the book:

A thick yellow smell hung on the still air. 'A fox,' he said, and he trailed the animal through the hazel-bushes till he came to a rough shore, covered with juniper-bushes and tussocked grass, the extreme point of the headland, whence he could see the mountains — the pale southern mountains mingling with the white sky, and the western mountains, much nearer, showing in bold

George Moore (1852-1933)

George Moore in his mid-twenties

An island in Lough Carra — by Robert Gibbings

Literary Tour of Ireland

'Mr W.B. Yeats presenting Mr George Moore to the Queen of the Fairies.' Cartoonist Max Beerbohm had scant sympathy for Yeats' mysticism. Below: Poster for Oscar Wilde's 1883 American tour.

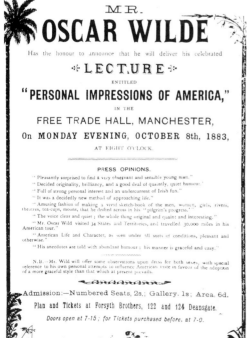

relief. The beautiful motion and variety of the hills delighted him ... It was like listening to music. Slieve Cairn showing straight as a bull's back against the white sky, a cloud filling the gap between Slieve Cairn and Slieve Louan, a quaint little hill like a hunchback going down a road. Slieve Louan was followed by a great boulder-like hill turned sideways, the top indented like a crater, and the priest likened the long, low profile of the next hill to a reptile raising itself on its forepaws.' (*The Lake*)

The story is that of a priest (whom Moore wickedly named Oliver Gogarty just to annoy his 'friend' Oliver St John Gogarty) who denounces a young woman from the altar, causing her to leave the parish. Through subsequent correspondence with her, he is himself led to re-examine his convictions and, ultimately, his soul and the meaning of his life and of his calling. He fakes a drowning, and escapes to America in search of freedom, of Life. How oddly modern are the final words of his last letter to her:

Again I thank you for what you have done for me, for the liberation you have brought me of body and mind. I need not have added the words 'body and mind' for these are not two things, but one thing. And that is the lesson I have learned. Good-bye.

But Moore was a very complex character. He came back to Ireland from Paris, which he loved, to get caught up in the Literary Renaissance with his cousin Edward Martyn, Yeats and the rest. He even wrote some short stories for the Gaelic League, for translation into Irish to act as models for young aspiring writers. Some of these showed a genuine feeling for the grinding poverty of the western peasantry. And despite the fact that his own very fair-minded father had died of a heart attack during a rent strike, he has the principal character in *A Drama in Muslin* commenting on the injustice of 'each big house being surrounded by a hundred small ones, all working to keep it in sloth and luxury.' But eventually this cosmopolitan artist, who in Paris had moved in the society of Degas, Renoir and Monet, grew tired of what he regarded as provincial Dublin amateurs and left for London, leaving behind him a great deal of ill-will for his mocking portraits of the Irish literati in *Hail and Farewell*, his 3-volume reminiscences.

He died in London in 1933 and, as he had requested, had his ashes buried under a cairn on **Castle Island**, a short distance from the lakeshore at **Kiltoom**. The poet George Russell (AE) in his oration (read at the graveside not by AE but by Richard Best), said 'It is possible that the artist's love of earth, rock, water and sky is an act of worship. It is possible that faithfulness of art is an acceptable service.' Years later, perhaps as some kind of recompense for the tragic burning of Moore Hall, a plaque was erected on the wall outside the family burial plot at Kiltoom, among the trees close by on the lake shore. It reads:

Burial place of the Moores of Moore Hall. This Catholic patriot family is honoured for their famine relief and their refusal to barter principles for English gold. Erected by Ballyglass Coy. Old IRA 1964.'

The wheel turns endlessly.

When Moore was a boy playing on Castle Island and around the lake shore, his companions included Oscar Wilde and Oscar's brother Willie, who spent several summers at Moytura House near the village of **Cong** (where the imperishable film *The Quiet Man* was shot, and where stands Ireland's most romantic hotel, Ashford Castle). The Wildes, senior, were a brilliant and highly individualistic pair. Sir William was a real Renaissance man, a distinguished eye and ear specialist whose book *Aural Surgery* became a standard text book. He was also an amateur archaeologist, a leading Celtic antiquarian, and noted womaniser. Mother was Jane Elgee, who became famous for her fervidly nationalist contributions to *The Nation* under the name Speranza, and for her Dublin salons. They were a pretty ill-assorted pair. She was large and flamboyant, he was small and untidy: somebody unkindly said that he was 'a small pithecoid fellow who skulked behind his wife's petticoats'. Sir William spent a large part of his life at his western home — particularly the latter part, after a scandal had dented his reputation — and there wrote his book about the antiquities of the area, *Lough Corrib, its Shores and Islands*, which has been in print almost up to the present.

Lough Mask had another contribution to make to literature — or, at least, to the English language. Half way along the eastern shore of the lake is Lough Mask House. Here, shortly after the death of Sir William Wilde, a drama was played out which created a new word. Captain Boycott, a neighbour of Wilde's along the lake, was agent for Lord Erne, who held a huge estate in Co Fermanagh, and a mere 2,000 acres in Mayo. Boycott was a hard man, a harsh one towards the tenants, and didn't hesitate to evict the unfortunates who couldn't produce their rent in the worst of times. When, in September 1880, process of eviction was served on four tenants, the Land League, an organisation newly established to win tenant farmers some modicum of rights, stepped in. 'What,' had asked Parnell in a famous speech at Ennis, Co Clare, 'are you to do to a tenant who bids for a farm from which another tenant has been evicted? I think I heard someone say shoot him. I wish to point out to you a very much better way — a more Christian and charitable way, which will give the lost man an opportunity of repenting ... You must shun him on the roadside when you meet him — you must shun him in the shop — you must shun him on the fairgreen and in the market place and even in the place of worship ... as if he were a leper of old ...' This was the treatment meted out to Boycott. The Captain's labourers, and his house staff, left: the postman

Oscar Wilde (1854-1900)

Speranza (Jane Francesca) Wilde (1826?-1896)
William Wilde (1815-1876)

Above: Lady Wilde — 'Speranza'. Below: Cover of The Sign of the Three Candles edition in 1938 of Sir William Wilde's famous 1867 book on the history and archaeology of the West of Ireland

Tom Murphy and Tuam

The smallish market town of **Tuam** lies about twenty miles to to the east of Ballinrobe and Cong. Playwright and author Tom Murphy was born in Tuam in 1935 and taught in the local vocational school for several years. You might or might not take Tuam as the setting for several of his plays of provincial life, including the best-known *Conversations on a Homecoming*. You might even try to locate the run-down pub which J.J. its owner, now a drunk, bought in his enthusiastic youth and named The White House in the glow of the Kennedy charisma. In the play, the returning emigrant meets up with old friends there and, as the evening's drinking progresses, their distorted memories and shattered dreams are exposed.

Murphy has a perfect ear for realistic dialogue, but he adds a mythic dimension to the everyday and generates a powerfully emotional impact. In *The Morning After Optimism* two seedy misfits, in an enchanted wood, kill off their idealised counterparts. In *The Gigli Concert* the weary dynamatologist achieves for himself the miracle sought by his client who bales out through lack of courage and conviction. And in *Bailegangaire* an old woman endlessly retells the story of a horrific night of laughter.

John Millington Synge (1871-1909)

stopped delivering. The shops refused to sell him food. A hundred Ulstermen, with troop protection, came to save his crops, but did more harm than good. When they finally departed, so did Boycott, on a boat to England, and a new word was added to the dictionary.

Oddly enough, possibly because of the courage he had shown in the face of the campaign, during which he and his wife themselves worked in the fields like labourers, he was able to return to Lough Mask House a few years later, and live in peace for the rest of his time. Both Moytura House and Lough Mask House escaped the fate of Moore Hall. Roofs intact, they provide most pleasing homes for lucky owners today.

Between Cong and Lough Mask lies the territory of **Southern Moytura**, scene of the first great legendary battle between the Tuatha De Danann and the Fir Bolg. The latter were defeated, but not thoroughly enough. It took a second great battle seven years later, at Northern Moytura which is judged to be near Sligo, for the Tuatha De Danann to rout the Fir Bolg finally. They were driven underground and became the *sidhe*, or shee, the people of the Otherworld, who came to inhabit the mounds and woods and islands and, most strongly, the popular imagination, where this world and the Other were very close. The shee were of uncertain temperament: they could be generous and helpful, but could be hateful if crossed.

Complete the circuit around the western shore of the lake to return to Westport.

Clew Bay is Granuaile country. Granuaile, Gráinne Uí Mháille, Grace O'Malley: all the one. Sixteenth-century chieftain, pirate, warrior, trader. Larger than life in legend, and probably in life also. Anne Chambers has charted her career in *Granuaile: The Life and Times of Grace O'Malley c.1530-1603*. Her strongholds stand at **Rockfleet** west of **Newport**, on **Clare Island**, and at **Kildawnet** on the southern tip of Achill.

Pirate queens and heroes. Christy Mahon was a hero here too for a short time. Synge's *Playboy of the Western World* arrived one cold, dark night in a remote shebeen under the bulk of **Nephin**. The love-light in the eye of Pegeen Mike for this lad who kilt his da transformed a shy, moony young lad into 'a likely gaffer' and a great lepper, who beat them all in the mule races on Doolough Strand. The great sprawling bulk of the Nephins fills the skyline, and Christy's love-talk. 'Yourself and me should be pacing Neifin in the dews of night, the times sweet smells do be rising, and you'd see a little shiny new moon, maybe, sinking on the hills.' And 'you'll be an angel's lamp to me from this out, and I abroad in the darkness, spearing salmons in the Owen or the Carrowmore'. But Pegeen, in torment of soul, betrays

The Céide Fields

> When he stripped off blanket bog
> The soft-piled centuries
>
> Fell open like a glib:
> There were the first plough-marks,
> The stone-age fields, the tomb
> Corbelled, turfed and chambered,
> Floored with dry turf-coomb.
>
> A landscape fossilized,
> Its stone-wall patternings
> Repeated before our eyes
> In the stone walls of Mayo.
>   ('Belderg', Seamus Heaney)

W.H. Maxwell (1792-1850)

Rockfleet — stronghold of Granuaile

him in the end, and helps to snare him for the bullying old man. Her words can find an echo in many of our hearts nowadays: 'There's a great gap between a gallous story and a dirty deed.'

Anyone who wishes to experience the ultimate in remoteness will find it in the bog wilderness of north-west Mayo and the **Mullet** peninsula. One road winds up around the skirts of Nephin. Another hugs the shore of Clew Bay, to turn northwards towards **Bangor Erris** and by the Owen River and Carrowmore Lake of Christy's salmon-spearing, to **Belmullet** and its lonely peninsula. It could hardly be described as beautiful, but it is, in a way, magnificent in its desolation. The northern coast is heroic, with great cliffs breasting the onslaughts of the North Atlantic below bare mountainsides. There was a time it was different. A community who had not yet emerged from the Stone Age farmed these wind-scoured cliff-tops, built their dwellings, surrounded their small fields with stone walls laid out with mathematical precision, and raised tombs to their dead. What became of them we know not. Four and a half thousand years gave the encroaching bog plenty of time to draw a thick mantle over what they left behind, to be discovered only in recent years. Signs of the settlement have been traced over seven miles of hillside. Nothing like it exists anywhere else. It is all 'interpreted' for the passer-by in a concrete-and-glass pyramid standing over the cliffs at **Céide**, near **Belderg**.

Inhospitable as northern Mayo appears at first glance, it has had devotees other than Synge's Christy Mahon. W.H. Maxwell, an 'Anglicised Irishman' on an extended visit to the coast of **Blacksod Bay** in 1829, reached after a journey worthy of Maria Edgeworth's to Ballynahinch or, indeed, invented by Somerville and Ross, discovered for himself a whole new world, marvellously and amusingly described in his book *Wild Sports of the West*. It was still the period of the hard-riding hard-drinking gentry, who ruled in their remote estates like kings, and Maxwell found himself in what tourism promoters would now call a 'sportsman's paradise'. His stories are about the traditional gentry sports — hunting, shooting, fishing — all undertaken with immense gusto. He paints the scene:

To look at the map of Mayo, one would imagine that Nature had designed that county for a sportsman. The westerly part is wild and mountainous; alpine ridges of highlands interpose between the ocean and the interior, and from the bases of these hills a boundless tract of heath and moorland extends in every direction. To the east, the face of the country undergoes a striking change — large and extensive plains cover the surface, and as the lands are generally occupied in pasturage, and consequently not sub-divided into the numerous enclosures which are requisite in tillage farming, this part of Mayo is justly in high estimation as a hunting country ...

And so on. As well as the various sporting stories, there are the oddities of the peasantry, in stage-Irish fashion which we ourselves have almost ritualised.

There is much sound advice, however, on fishing and all other field sports. And seal-hunting was done in the vicinity:

Last summer I was witness to a curious scene. Running through the Sound of Achil in my hooker, at a short distance to leeward I observed several men, who appeared to be practising a quadrille over the thafts and gunnels of a row-boat, as they never rested for a moment, but continued jumping from stem to stern, and springing from bench to bench. Struck by the oddity of their proceedings, I eased away the sheets and ran down upon them — and I was a welcome ally, as the result proved. It turned out, that having espied a seal and her cub sleeping on the sand, they had procured an old musket and rowed over to attack them. They were partially successful and seized the cub before it could regain its native element, although the dam rendered all assistance possible to relieve the young one. Having placed their prize in the boat, they were returning, followed by the old seal, who kept rising beside them, attracted by the cries of the cub — till after many bootless attempts, their gun at last exploded, the ball entered the seal's head, and for a moment she appeared dying. The captors, seizing her by the tail and fins, with an united exertion, dragged her into the boat — but this exploit had nearly ended in a tragedy. Stunned only by the wound, the animal instantly recovered, and, irritated by pain and maddened by the cries of her cub, attacked her captors fiercely. Every exertion they could make was necessary to save them from her tusks, and their oars were too long and clumsy to enable them to strike her with effect. I came most opportunely to the rescue, and by driving a carbine bullet through the seal's brain brought the battle to a close. Never was the old saw of 'catching a Tartar' more thoroughly exemplified, and though we laughed at their terror stricken countenances, the deep incisions made in the oars and gunnels by the tusks of the enraged animal, showing that *gallopading* with an angry seal is anything but pleasure.

Some of Maxwell's comments on the early nineteenth-century Mayo women are interesting too. While admitting that the hard labour, bare feet and exposure to the weather of the women of the western islands did not help their 'personal advantages', there was one who particularly caught his notice:

Her face was uncommonly intelligent — I never saw so dark an eye, and her teeth were white as ivory. But there was a natural ease in all she did — whether she brought a pitcher from the spring, or danced a merry strathspey, every movement was graceful. Even her simple toilet evinced instinctive taste, though no corset was required to regulate a form moulded by the hand of Nature, and her magnificent hair boasted no arrangement beyond the simple cincture of a ribbon ... And yet I have seen that young beauty bending beneath a basket of potatoes which would have overloaded me — and, on one occasion, carry a strapping fellow across the river, who was coming on some state affair to the cabin, which, as he conceived, required him to appear in the presence with dry legs.

Title page of The Godstone and the Blackymor, *a wonderfully idiosyncratic Mayo tour undertaken and reported on by writer T.H. White. 'I stumbled across what Protestants had said was an idol [the Godstone] still being worshipped by Catholics, and a coal black negro selling potent medicines and a real fairy fire which lit our footsteps over the infinite bog — no whimsy.' Long out of print, readers who pursue it will love this pilgrimage in Mayo.*

Literary Tour of Ireland

Paul Durcan (1944-   )

The Main Street, Belmullet

The main street, Belmullet. Illustration by Edward Ardizzone for T.H. White's The Godstone and the Blackymor, a Mayo journey.

Oh! the French are on the sea,
Says the Shan Van Vocht;
The French are on the sea,
Says the Shan Van Vocht:
Oh! the French are in the Bay,
They'll be here without delay,
And the Orange will decay,
Says the Shan Van Vocht.
Oh! the French are in the Bay
They'll be here by break of day
And the Orange will decay,
Says the Shan Van Vocht.

Thomas Flanagan (1923-   )

What is a feminist to make of that? And then there is our own Paul Durcan, who writes about people in oil paintings in National Galleries and mad people with deeply held convictions. He writes about Mayo:

> I walk on, facing the village ahead of me,
> A small concrete oasis in the wild countryside;
> Not the embodiment of the dream of a boy,
> Backside to the wind.   ('Backside to the Wind')

When Mary Robinson, the President of Ireland needed a poem in her acceptance speech, that was one which struck her fancy. And surely it takes a particular kind of poetic genius to entitle a poem 'O Westport in the Light of Asia Minor.' Never mind, say, 'Teresa's Bar':

> Outside in the rain the powers that be
> Chemist, draper, garda and priest
> Paced up and down in unspeakable rage
> That we could sit all day in Teresa's bar
> Doing Nothing.

Journeying eastwards, back towards the twentieth century and into softer country, one reaches **Killala**. In the early summer of 1798, three ships carrying a thousand or so French troops under the command of General Humbert landed in Killala Bay, at **Kilcummin** near **Benwee Head**, to aid an Irish insurrection. There were some brief and glorious victories. But by autumn it was all over, and the optimistic 'Republic of Connacht,' with John Moore of Moore Hall as President, was a dream trampled in the bloody mud of **Ballinamuck** near Longford town. Thomas Flanagan's sweeping novel *The Year of the French* tells the bitter story. Among the many characters in the novel is the poet, schoolmaster, womaniser, Owen MacCarthy, modelled on Eoghan Rua Ó Súilleabháin of Munster, and the well-meaning Protestant clergyman, Arthur Vincent Broome, who keeps a record of all that has passed. He records an abortive effort to decipher some of MacCarthy's Irish verse:

I assured him that I felt keenly the unhappy lot of his fellow countrymen, and suggested that this might somehow be improved if they were able to experience more completely the safeguards of English law. He responded with the verses of some other poet, which he then put into English for me....'Troy and Rome have vanished; Caesar is dead, and Alexander. Perhaps someday the English too will have their day.'

I challenged him as to the meaning that he derived from this dark utterance, and he replied it meant only that Greece and Rome had once been empires, and England was now in its turn summoned to greatness. I told him that I did not for a minute suppose it to mean any such thing.

Flanagan uses the ironic exchange to illustrate the gulf of understanding between what the two represent. MacCarthy, drawn by the excitement and drama into the folly, ends on the scaffold. 'Ballinamuck took the fight out of him, and the poetry as well.' His friend Sean MacKenna visits him the day before, bringing him a new linen shirt from the shop, 'that he might make a good appearance upon the morrow.' As for Moore, he was taken, wounded, to the gaol at Waterford, where he died.

> Then what will the yeomen do?
> Says the Shan Van Vocht;
> What will the yeomen do?
> Says the Shan Van Vocht;
> What should the yeomen do
> But throw off the Red and Blue,
> And swear that they'll be true
> To the Shan Van Vocht.

Right: A scene from The Playboy of the Western World, *Synge's archetypal Abbey play; and below, Mulrany beach.*

Eva and Constance Goore-Booth: 'both beautiful — one a gazelle'

11. SLIGO
Land of Heart's Desire

Sligo is, of course, the territory with which William Butler Yeats has above all become identified. The Yeats Summer School is the oldest of that style of cultural caper that enlivens the Irish summer up and down the country.

Born in Dublin in 1865, he spent much of his early life in London, but Yeats always regarded Sligo as his spiritual home, and he loved it passionately. Away from it, he wrote in 'Reveries over Childhood and Youth', 'I longed for a sod of earth from some field I knew, something of Sligo to hold in my hand. It was some old race instinct like that of a savage, for we had been brought up to laugh at all display of emotion. Yet it was our mother, who would have thought its display a vulgarity, who kept alive that love. She would spend hours listening to stories or telling stories of the pilots and fishing people of Rosses Point, or of her own Sligo girlhood, and it was always assumed between her and us that Sligo was more beautiful than other places.'

His mother was Susan Pollexfen, one of a family of Sligo merchants, millers and sea traders. William's father, the fine portrait painter John B. Yeats, had married her in 1863. The young William spent much of his childhood and youth among his Sligo relatives, absorbing the tales of myth and wonder of the cottiers, fishermen and small farmers. The Pollexfen men weren't given to story-telling. John B, who himself was known as an entertaining raconteur, describes them as 'inarticulate as the sea-cliffs ... lying buried under mountains of silence.' But the sea cliffs and the mountains spoke eloquently to William B, and combined with myth and legend to inspire his image of life and the world and, in his later years, the mystical life of the soul.

The best way to explore **Sligo** and **west Leitrim** — for some of the loveliest and most significant parts of the Yeats Country lie over the county border — is with the *Collected Poems* in one hand, the *Plays* in another, and in the third hand Sheelah Kirby's *The Yeats Country* which hopefully will be in print for ever. You could make room too for Benedict Kiely's illustrated anthology, *Yeats' Ireland*. You may have your own favourites among the hundreds of volumes devoted to the poet, but those three or four will best guide your footsteps and your

William Butler Yeats (1865-1939)

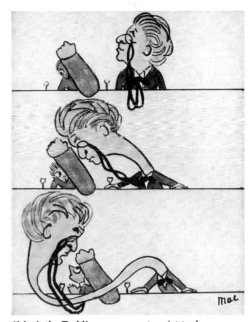

'Mac', the Dublin woman cartoonist took American journalist and writer Harold Speakman to meet Yeats during Speakman's own 'literary' tour of Ireland — journeyed by donkey and cart for the most part. This cartoon later arrived by post from 'Mac' who wrote: 'He — W.B.Y. — was in great form, so I told him about you and your elbow. He hadn't even noticed it and said — [censored].' 'Mac' maintained that Speakman 'just put his elbow on the table as a defense between Yeats and himself — and the cartoon shows what might have happened'. (Here's Ireland, *by Harold Speakman*)

understanding through the landscape.

Sligo town sits at the head of an inlet of Sligo Bay. Close by on the east lies **Lough Gill**, and to the north-west rise the rugged and strangely-sculptured hills of which the prow-shaped plunge of **Ben Bulben** forms the western silhouette. Westwards, the eye is drawn irresistibly to **Knocknarea**. Legend tells that the great mound on its summit, never opened, shelters the mortal remains of Maeve, the warrior queen of Connacht, who led the armies of the west against an Ulster army led by Cúchulainn. But that's another story, and another chapter. From the cairn Maeve, and you, can look down over **Carrowmore**, a plain that is literally packed with the tombs of an earlier race:

> Caoilte, and Conan, and Finn were there,
> When we followed a deer with our baying hounds,
> With Bran, Sceolan, and Lomair,
> And passing the Firbolgs' burial-mounds,
> Came to the cairn-heaped grassy hill
> Where passionate Maeve is stony-still ... ('The Wanderings of Oisín')

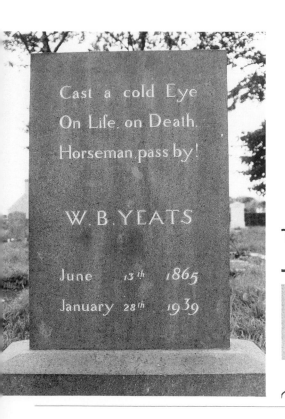

So casually, indeed, do some local entrepreneurs regard 'the Fir-bolgs' burial-mounds' that they have destroyed many of them over the years, and even today some of the precious boulder-circled mounds are collapsing into ever-widening gravel pits.

From Knocknarea one can survey all of that land of sea and hill that is intertwined with the poetry. Close by is **Cummen Strand**:

> The old brown thorn-trees break in two high over Cummen Strand
> Under a bitter black wind that blows from the left hand;

West of Cummen lies **Strandhill**: on such a shore did Cúchulainn, all unknowing, slay his son, then

> Stared on the horses of the sea, and heard
> The cars of battle and his own name cried;
> And fought with the invulnerable tide.

To the south, across the bay, are **Ballysodare** and **Collooney** and the trailing edge of the **Slieve Gamph** (or Ox) mountains. Willows or 'salleys' grown for basket-making at Ballysodare inspired the song 'Down by the salley gardens.' Here also, lived Paddy Flynn, 'a little bright-eyed old man who lived in a leaky one-roomed cabin' who filled the poet with stories, and who replied, when Yeats asked him had he ever seen the faeries, 'Am I not annoyed with them?' meaning he was constantly pestered by them!

Swing south to Collooney, then west towards **Coolaney**. A right turn shortly before that village takes you onto a little road that wanders northwards over the hill. It brings you to the **Hawk's Rock**, an outcrop like a huge tumbling block, less dramatic now than before its feet were clothed in forestry. The **Hawk's Well** is to be found near the summit of the small hill adjoining it — a miraculous well, indeed, to ever hold water in that location, even if it is difficult to prove or disprove the legend that the water ebbs and flows with the tide in the sea beyond. and is fresh or salt accordingly. Here, in the play *At the Hawk's Well*, Cúchulainn meets the old man who has wasted all his life waiting for the magic run of water that will make him immortal.

Beltra Strand of the vivid sunsets brings to him the vision of perishing armies and fallen horsemen; but

> We who still labour by the cromlech on the shore,
> The grey cairn on the hill, when day sinks drowned in dew,
> Being weary of the world's empires, bow to you
> Master of the still stars and of the flaming door.

Rosses Point nowadays rings to the voices of many holidaying families. In Yeats' youth the area was owned by his cousins the Middletons, and for the Yeats children it was an enchanted play-ground. They listened to tales of smugglers and sailors until 'the world

Sebastian Barry
See *Crossing the Millennium,* page 260

seemed full of monsters and marvels'. Later he brought fellow-poet AE (George Russell) to walk the **Greenlands** on the northern side of the peninsula, which he found a real haunt of fairies.

In his later years Yeats turned once more to this land of childhood memories for some of his most profound and enigmatic poems:

> Saddle and ride, I heard a man say,
> Out of Ben Bulben and Knocknarea,
> *What says the Clock in the Great Clock Tower?*
> All those tragic characters ride
> But turn from Rosses' crawling tide,
> The meet's upon the mountain-side.
> *A slow low note and an iron bell.*   (Alternative Song for the Severed Head
> in 'The King of the Great Clock Tower')

A painting by the poet's brother, Jack Yeats, of 'Memory Harbour' shows a village of Rosses Point with, in the middle of the river channel, the navigation marker known as 'The Metal Man'. 'I never did a painting without putting a thought of Sligo into it,' he said.

Drive around **Lough Gill** for its beauty, but listening in your mind to the music of the poetry, and remembering the ghosts of the mythic past that inhabit it. Taking the southern road closest to the river, pass first (or pause at) Tobernalt, the **Penal Mass Rock** where pilgrims gather even today on the last Sunday of July, to come by **Dooney Rock** of the Fiddler, and 'where dips the rocky highland/ of Sleuth (or Slish) Wood in the lake' where as a youth the poet had attempted to sleep and meditate — unsuccessfully, as it happened; he was not built for such discomfort. His other dream-place of a life of inspired simplicity is the tiny island:

> I will arise and go now, and go to Innisfree,
> And a small cabin build there, of clay and wattles made:
> Nine bean-rows will I have there, a hive for the honey-bee,
> And live alone in the bee-loud glade.   ('Innisfree')

Dromahair's ghosts are the unforgiven ghosts of Ireland's long memory. It was the seat of the O'Rourkes, princes of Breffny, and some remnant of their stronghold still survives in that attractive village. The elopement of Dervorgilla, wife of Tiernan O'Rourke, with the King of Leinster led to the first Norman incursion into Ireland in 1169.

Glencar Lake, farther north, is even more beautiful. Sheer cliffs rise on the north side, and, if you are lucky enough to be there on a day when the wind is from the south, you will see how 'the cataract smokes against the mountain side,' the waterfall blown back and upwards from the clifftop so that, up there, you could stand under it as under a shower. *Sruth-in-aghaidh-an-aird* is its name: the stream against the height. There are other cascades too 'Where the wandering water gushes / From the hills above Glencar.' If you have time to spare, drive around the mountain range, by **Glenade Lough** and the small roads that lead around under the singular peak of **Ben Weskin**, hovering like a mighty wave about to break over one's head and swamp the plain.

Though we pass close by it, we are not yet ready to visit **Drumcliff**. Regaining the main road follow, instead, a signpost west for **Lissadell**.

Lissadell House was one of the great formative influences on Yeats' life. When he first visited that solid Georgian house by the sea, the Gore-Booths still lived a life of elegant ease which appealed enormously to the young poet's sense of order and good taste. He was especially entranced by the two sisters, Constance and Eva, spirited and gracious, living the life of their class and time, riding to hounds and entertaining. He could not foresee then that they would rebel against their background, Eva to organise factory girls in England, Constance, as Countess Markievicz, to become a suffragette, an Irish revolutionary earning a death sentence which was reprieved, and becoming the first woman MP elected to Westminster.

The light of evening, Lissadell,
Great windows open to the south,
Two girls in silk kimonos, both
Beautiful, one a gazelle.

Aideen Gore-Booth, the last chatelaine of Lissadell, died in 1994. She belonged to a family of fine people, people of courage and determination, who gallantly resisted time and circumstances which would have defeated lesser spirits. The house is open to the public from May to September and should not be missed, though the days of its grand style are long gone.

The little roads back bring us at last to **Drumcliff**, 'under bare Ben Bulben's head,' and the poet's last resting-place. It is a fitting place for the poet to lie, under the enchanted mountain where legendary Diarmuid, lover of the beautiful Gráinne, was killed by a wild boar. A small graceful Church of Ireland church, where an ancestor of his was Rector, an old high cross, the fragment of a round tower. The grave is to the left, inside the gate:

No marble, no conventional phrase;
On limestone quarried near the spot
By his command these words are cut:
    Cast a cold eye
    On life, on death.
    Horseman, pass by!

The words are enigmatic, and come at the end of a long poem affirming the natural life-force and the responsibilities of poets. It was written at a stage in his life when he had left behind the romantic period of his youth, and the stirring days of war and insurrection during which he had given affirmation to 'a terrible beauty'. Now he sees death as part of a transformative experience, a state beyond the tyranny of physical and temporal law, where he can walk with mystical beings. Rather than casting a cold eye on life and death, let us think of him now truly blended with the spirits of all the mythological figures that had inhabited his imagination, and reliving the archetypal heroic life:

Because we love bare hills and stunted trees
And were the last to choose the settled ground,
Its boredom of the desk or of the spade, because
So many years companioned by a hound,
Our voices carry; and though slumber-bound,
Some few half wake and half renew their choice,
Give tongue, proclaim their hidden name — 'Hound Voice.'

The women that I picked spoke sweet and low
And yet gave tongue. 'Hound Voices' were they all.
We picked each other from afar and knew
What hour of terror comes to test the soul,

And in that terror's name obeyed the call,
And understood, what none have understood,
Those images that waken in the blood.

Some day we shall get up before the dawn
And find our ancient hounds before the door,
And wide awake know that the hunt is on;
Stumbling upon the blood-dark track once more,
Then stumbling to the kill beside the shore;
Then cleaning out and bandaging of wounds
And chants of victory amid the encircling hounds.

('Hound Voice')

The Hawk's Rock, near Coolaney

12. DONEGAL
Scholars and Battlers

Adieu to Belashanny, where I was bred and born;
Go where I may I'll think of you, as sure as night and morn
The kindly spot, the friendly town, where every one is known,
And not a face in all the place but partly seems my own ...

The music of the waterfall, the mirror of the tide,
When all the green-hill'd harbour is full from side to side,
From Portnasun to Bulliebawns, and round the Abbey bay,
From rocky Inis Saimer to Coolnargit sandhills grey;
While far upon the southern line, to guard it like a wall,
The Leitrim mountains clothed in blue gaze calmly over all,
And watch the ship sail up or down, the red flag at her stern —
Adieu to these, adieu to all the winding banks of Erne!

Ballyshannon, where the Erne meets Donegal Bay, is the gateway to Donegal. William Allingham names all the local landmarks in his long poem 'The Winding Banks of Erne'. However, he never really said goodbye to Belashanny, or Ballyshannon as it is better known today. He lived in London from his middle years, editing *Fraser's Magazine*, but continued to visit Ballyshannon regularly. Nor has Ballyshannon said adieu to Allingham. There is a bust of him in the bank where he worked as a young man, now the Allied Irish Bank, the large stone building at the bottom of the main street. A plaque marks the house on the Mall where he was born, 'the most westerly of a row of 3 in a street running down to the harbour'. And there is a memorial tablet on the bridge over the Erne whose sound continued to haunt him: 'The little town where I was born has a voice all its own, low, solemn, persistent, humming through the air day and night, summer and winter'. The sound is not so pervasive nowadays, because an electricity power dam destroyed the falls which tumbled so dramatically towards the sea.

Allingham was given to lengthy epic poetry, but one of his most-loved poems is his child's song:

Up the airy mountain,
    Down the rushy glen,
We daren't go a-hunting

William Allingham (1824-1889)

> For fear of little men;
> Wee folk, good folk,
>   Trooping all together;
> Green jacket, red cap,
>   And white owl's feather!

In London, Allingham was at the centre of the liveliest literary circle, his friends including such writers as Tennyson, Browning and Rossetti. His diaries, kept faithfully for half a century, give fascinating pen-pictures of many of the great literary figures of the time and are an invaluable historical resource. He was a close friend of Tennyson's and kept him company on one of his visits to Killarney. He is buried at St Ann's Church, on the hill at the top of the town.

North from here you are coming into the region that contains some of the wildest and most remote areas of Ireland, at times and in places magnificent, bleak, fierce, gentle, remote, populous, but at all times beautiful, despite the rashes of discordant recently-built dwellings sited without any consideration for the lie of the land. Donegal's anomalous position of belonging with the Republic — the 'South' — while in fact being the most northerly point of all Ireland and almost cut off by the westernmost corner of the Border with Northern Ireland, has given it some sense of being an independent territory, a sense carried well by the people who live here. Even historically, Donegal has looked less to Dublin or Belfast than to Glasgow, because it was to Scotland that its 'tatie-hokers' went, to work through the summer digging potatoes in awful conditions to earn the year's sustenance.

The Four Masters

The town of **Donegal** is a modest, relaxed, unhurried place, a good introduction to its hinterland. It stands at the head of Donegal Bay. Roads from north, east and south converge at its central 'Diamond', and an O'Donnell castle guards the quays. Remnants of a Franciscan Friary stand gauntly on a little promontory in the estuary of the River Eske. It commemorates one of the largest literary enterprises ever carried out in Ireland, that is the compilation of the Annals of Ireland by the 'Four Masters'. It was a time of great political strife and the work was carried out because it was feared that the ancient records of Ireland might be lost forever. The four 'Masters' were Franciscan Brothers Micheal O'Clery, Peregrine Duignan, Peregrine O'Clery and Fearfeasa O'Mulconry, and they compiled their monumental work between the years 1630 and 1636. The Annals were no less than a chronology of all that was known — and surmised — of Irish history since the flood. The dedication page states 'On the 22nd of January 1632 this work was undertaken in the Monastery of Donegal and was finished in the same place on the 16th August 1636.' Despite the statement, little enough of the work was actually carried out in the Donegal friary, as it had been largely destroyed in the Elizabethan wars which had devastated so much of the country. The work was done 'on the run' as the monks fled from one place of refuge to another, and much of it was done at **Bundrowes**, over the Leitrim border. The friary had been established by an early Red Hugh O'Donnell in 1474, and he and his wife Nuala are buried there. Donegal is above all O'Donnell country. Both the Abbey and the Castle had been founded by O'Donnells. When Red Hugh O'Donnell and the other great chieftains of the North set sail for Spain with their followers after their final defeat at Kinsale in 1601, in that exodus which came to be known as the Flight of the Earls, it was said the heart of Ireland could be heard to break. It was the end of Gaelic Ireland.

But as kings and chieftains come and go, people endure. The land of Donegal is rich in rugged beauty, but poor in fertile soil. Like their landscape, the people have always had a a strong and rugged individuality, but they were, perforce, poor. Scratching a living from such stony highlands and valleys was a hard survival. Peadar O'Donnell was one who came from such stock. He was born in 1893, on a small coastal farm at Meenmore near **Dungloe**, the fifth of nine children. He taught school, first on the small island of **Innisfree**, later on **Aranmore Island**. His novels are set against the background of his own stony acres and rough shores, and a way of life which even at the time was probably unique in Europe. The O'Donnells' five-acre farm ran down to the Atlantic shore, and by all accounts it was a lively household. In the pattern of the people of that place and time, his father was a migrant worker, spending the summer on the potato fields of Scotland once the spring sowing was done and the turf cut at home. He was a great musician, with the house always full of people in the evenings, and to the end of his days Peadar O'Donnell was at his best and most joyful in a room full of talk, argument and good-humoured disputation.

Nobody else has written so compassionately about these people of the glens and townlands. His stories were simple, many would say naive, the language strong and colourful, and Peadar himself would have been amused if anyone thought of them as high literature. Indeed he was primarily a revolutionary and political agitator, spending several episodes in jail as a result of his 'activities'. It was during a sojourn in Mountjoy Prison that he began writing, 'to take his mind back to Aranmore and Innisfree' and 'the hearty bustle of the flood tide.'

As Brian Friel put it, 'At a time when the social reformer was being denounced as a Red and an anticleric, the writer quietly took over and wrote beautifully of birth and death and love in one of the remotest parts of Europe'.

'There will be Another Day' is his account, written many years after the events it recalls, of the campaign against the payment of Land

Peadar O'Donnell (1893-1986)

Anseo ag Stáisiún Chaiseal na gCorr
d'aimsigh mise m'oileán rúin ...
Anseo braithim seasmhacht
is mé ag feiceáil chríocha mo chineáil
thart faoi bhun Eargail
mar a bhfuil siad ina gcónaí go ciúin
le breis agus trí chéad bliain
ar mhínte féaraigh an tsléibhe
ó Mhín 'a Leá go Mín na Craoibhe ...
Thíos agus thuas tím na gabháltais
a briseadh as béal an fhiántais.
Seo duanaire mo mhuintire;
an lámhscríbhinn a shaothraigh siad go
  teann
le dúch a gcuid allais ...
                    (Cathal Ó Searcaigh)

Here at Caiseal na gCorr Station
I discovered my hidden island ...
Here I feel permanence
as I look at the territory of my people
around the foot of Errigal
where they've settled
for more than three hundred years
on the grassy mountain pastures
from Min 'a Lea to Min na Craoibhe ...
Above and below, I see the holdings
farmed from the mouth of the
  wilderness.
This is the poem-book of my people,
the manuscript they toiled at
with the ink of their sweat ...
                (trans. Gabriel Fitzmaurice)

Life on the west coast, — ballot box under Garda escort on the way to Innisfree island, Co Donegal in the general election

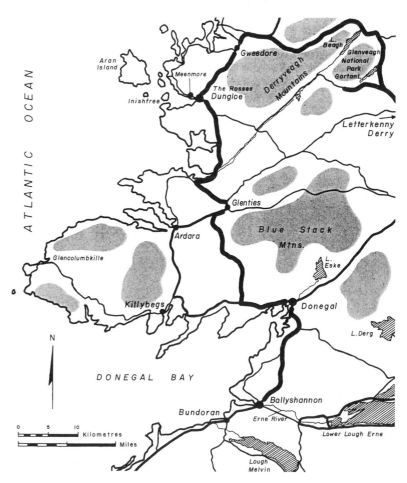

Annuities during the troubled days after the Civil War. This was history, not fiction, the true story of the struggle of his 'people of the townlands' and those people stand out vividly from the pages, tough, proud and gallant. Like his description of Black James Duirnin, asked in court if he was willing, like some others, to give in and pay up:

Black James was asked if it was need exposed him to so great a hardship as jail at his age — he was over seventy at the time — or was he influenced in any way by politics. Duirnin was always slow to find words, but you felt that his delay was forced on him by the care he took to sort out his thoughts before he spoke. This time he was even slower than usual, and his neighbours waited in a tense silence. He said he thought politics entered into it. All this began, he explained, a good few years back. On a Sunday it was, and in the parochial hall. He minded the day fine. There were a number of young men in a line and they raised their hands and took an oath. He took no oath for he was too old, although he was then of the same mind as those men. A resolution was put before the people that day, disowning rent, and he said his word on it and he put his hand up for it. 'Some of the men who took an oath that day didn't abide by their oath, but my hand is up yet.'

Peadar O'Donnell

The Big Windows is the story of a woman from the islands, brought into the glens as a bride, and how her strange open ways were felt as a threat to the glenspeople, coming to a head with her decision to break out the tiny windows which were the pattern there, and install big ones which would allow her to see the sky above the mountains. It's a touching story, but obviously Peadar had a moral in it too: much as he loved his people and honoured the life they led, he knew that change had to come. 'Light also opens the mind.'

Peadar edited *The Bell* for many years, with the kind of gaiety, gusto and flamboyance that he brought to everything he undertook. Founded as a literary magazine by Sean O'Faolain, but always of wider scope than most journals of its kind, under Peadar it extended itself also to social and even political commentary.

Some of the opening lines of *The Big Windows* are worth quoting. Brigid Dugan was about to leave the island for her new home on the mainland:

The neighbours would have time enough to move in when smoke arose over the grey flags on the mainland to make it known that Brigid's man, Tom Manus Sharkey, had arrived there with his cart. It would be their task then to raise a cheery noise and gather the whole Dugan family into it, so that any sadness in them would get no chance to show itself, and, above all, so that Brigid herself might enter the boat in a right way; for the island, attentive to all things that touched on its people, had a saying that the girl who went forth in tears got good reason for tears before life was finished with her. 'So, bear in mind now, cheer let you, and shout.'

'Cheer, let you, and shout.' That was the way Peadar O'Donnell approached life, with gaiety and defiance, and roused others. He died

Patrick MacGill (1891-1963)

Gartan

in Dublin in 1986 aged 93, his mind razor-sharp to the end. Some will recall the old revolutionary, agitator, jailbird, novelist, polemicist, playwright, raconteur, editor of *The Bell*, co-founder of the Irish Academy of Letters. Those closest to him will remember the stories around the fireside, the great compassion, the shouts of laughter.

Let us also look briefly through the eyes of another Donegal man, Patrick MacGill from Glenties, at a hiring fair in Strabane. He was twelve years old at the time, and joined up with a group many of whom had walked all night.

We stood huddled together like sheep for sale in the market-place of Strabane. Over our heads the town clock rang out every passing quarter of an hour. I had never in my life before ever seen a clock so big. I felt tired and placed my bundle on the kerbstone and sat down upon it. A girl, one of my own country-people looked at me.

'Sure, ye'll never get a man to hire ye if ye're seen sitting there,' she said.

I got up quickly, feeling very much ashamed to know that a girl was able to teach me things. It wouldn't have mattered so much if a boy had told me.

There was great talk going on about the Omagh train. The boys who had been sold at the fair before said that the best masters came from near the town of Omagh, and so everyone waited eagerly until eleven o'clock, the hour at which the train was due.

It was easy to know when the Omagh men came, for they overcrowded an already big market. Most of them were fat, angry-looking fellows, who kept moving up and down examining us after the manner of men who seek out the good and bad points of horses which they intend to buy.

Sometimes they would speak to each other, saying that they never saw such a lousy and ragged crowd of servants in the market-place in all their life before, and they did not seem to care even if we overheard them say these things. On the whole I had no great liking for the Omagh men.

A big man with a heavy stomach came up to me.

'How much do ye want for the six months?' he asked.

'Six pounds,' I told him.

'Shoulders too narrow for the money,' he said, more to himself than to me and walked on.

Standing beside me was an old father, who had a son and daughter for sale. The girl looked pale and sickly. She had a cough that would split a rock.

'Arrah, an' will ye whisth that coughin'!' said her brother, time and again. 'Sure, ye know that no wan will give ye wages if ye go in in that way.'

The father never spoke. I suppose he felt that there was nothing to be said. During one of these fits of coughing an evil-faced farmer who was looking for a female servant came around and asked the old man what wages did he want for his daughter.

'Five pounds,' said the old man, and there was a tremble in his voice when he spoke.

'And maybe the cost of buryin' her,' said the farmer with a white laugh as he passed on his way.

High noon had just passed when a youngish man, curiously old in appearance, stood in front of me. His shoulders were very broad, and one of them was far higher than the other. His waist was slender like a girl's, but his buttocks were heavy out of all proportion to his thin waist and slim slivers of shanks.

'Six pounds!' he repeated when I told him what wages I desired. It's a big penny to give a wee man. I'll give ye a five-pound note for the six months and not one white sixpence more.'

He struck me on the back while he spoke as if to test the strength of my spine, then ran his fingers over my shoulder and squeezed the thick of my arm so tightly that I almost roared in his face with the pain of it. After a long wrangle I wrung an offer of five pounds ten shillings for my wages and I was his for six months to come.   (*Children of the Dead End*}

They were, as he said, merely a ware purchased in the market-place, something less valuable than a plough, and of no more account than a barrow.

That happened at the beginning of the twentieth century. The hiring fairs lasted long after that, into the memories and experiences of many still living. Some years later MacGill went to labour in Scotland, as was the pattern of the men and many of the women too, and it was he who first brought to public notice the inhuman conditions under which they lived and worked.

To the east of the Rosses the Derryveagh Mountains hide the **Glenveagh National Park** among their craggy foldings. Streams and waterfalls cascade down their slopes to the lake which mirrors the castellated Glenveagh Castle. Red deer come to sip the water; they roam the wooded slopes above and around the terraced gardens which are graced with statuary and exotic shrubs and vines. Close by is a smaller lake, Gartan Lough. In contrast with Glenveagh's rugged fierceness, at **Gartan** there are gentle lawns and rustling trees, a sweet and fitting place in which to commemorate a saint — though the saint, Columba or Columcille as he is more generally known, was of no naturally sweet and gentle disposition but a man of energy and resolution. He was born here at Gartan in the year 521. One of his more important monastic foundations was at Derry, which is the starting point for our next chapter.

Glenveagh

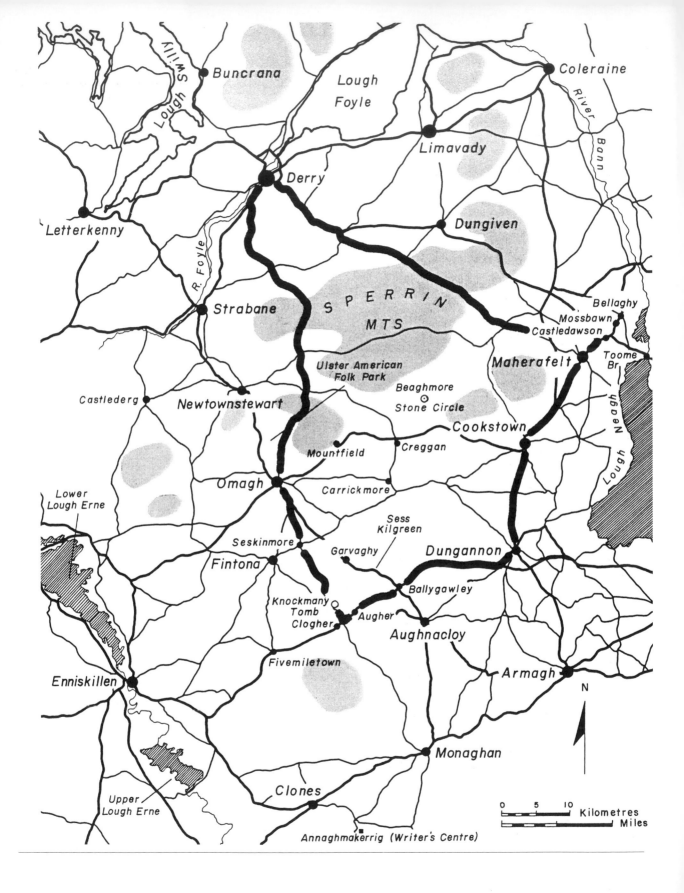

13. DERRY AND TYRONE
Saints, Mad Kings and Rough Fields

Derry, or **Londonderry**: Derry is from the Irish *Doire*, an oak grove. Originally Doire Columcille, Columcille's oak grove, 'London' was added after the city was granted to a group of London merchants in 1608. Both name-styles have their advocates nowadays. Local wags enjoy calling it Stroke City, as it is so often written Derry/Londonderry in an attempt at general diplomacy.

Columcille is important for several reasons. He was an aristocrat of the royal household of the Uí Néill, and a man therefore of considerable power and influence — and, no doubt, some of the arrogance that can go with such status. He founded a string of monasteries, including that at Derry where St Columb's Cathedral now stands, before taking off to Scotland to found Iona. He was a cultivated and scholarly man, and a poet of some standing, some of whose work has come down to us. It is on this account that, as is recorded, in the year 575 a message was sent to him to Scotland from 'the men of Ireland' to come and attend the Convention of kings at Druim Cett. The reason: to defend the poets of Ireland from banishment.

Saint Columba (Columcille) (521-597)

Now, whatever might be our own views about poets, this might seem a bit severe. To understand the threat, one has to think back to the status (which today's poets would surely envy) that the poets — the *ollam* and the *filid* — of that period had established for themselves. They had large retinues, and unlimited hospitality was their rightful due. Furthermore, according to custom they could be refused nothing they asked for. Many of them exploited their privileges to an outrageous degree and the High King pointed out that 'there is great vexation regarding them.'

It is a tribute to the diplomatic skills of Columcille that he managed to save them from banishment with the argument that the praise made by the poets lasts eternally: that whereas the rewards for eulogies are transitory, the praises live on after them. What concessions he succeeded in winning from the poets themselves is not on record.

There is another Columcille story of special interest to us, the one which has come to be known as 'the first ever copyright case'. It relates to an earlier stage of his career, during his presumably haughty and

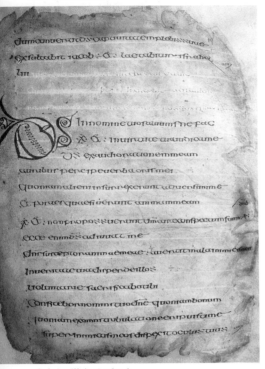

Columcille's Cathach

Jennifer Johnston
See *Crossing the Millennium*, page 260

hot-headed youth. With his literary leanings, he admired greatly the renderings of the psalms in a psalter belonging to Finian, founder of Clonard, so he copied it, not bothering to ask the owner's permission. Finian was furious, and demanded the copy. Columcille refused to hand it over, and the dispute finally was put before the High King. The king's famous judgment: 'to every cow its calf, to every book its copy' is one which still operates today. But even this judgment Columcille would not bow to. Such bad blood was created that the battle of Cuil Dreivne ensued, in which many died. Columcille, overcome with remorse, sailed to Iona, to exile.

The book in question — Columcille's copy, in his own hand, — is thought to be *The Cathach*, that is, the Battler, carried into battle by the warlike O'Donnells as a talisman. The Battler, after its centuries of war-scarred history, rests in the calm harbour of Dublin's Royal Irish Academy, undisturbed except for an occasional reverential opening by scholars. Its elaborately-wrought silver shrine, which was made before the year 1100, is in the collection of the National Museum.

That Battle of the Books was fought in the year 561 AD. In Iona, the penitent Columcille established the famous monastery which is still a place of pilgrimage and retreat today. But Columcille grieved for Derry:

> Were the tribute of all Alba mine,
> From the centre to the border,
> I would rather the site of one house
> And it in the midst of Derry.

and:

> The dearest of any in Ireland's ground
> For its peace and its beauty I gave my love;
> Each leaf of the oaks around Derry is found
> To be crowded with angels from heaven above.

And back at Gartan there is the Flagstone of Loneliness, Leac an Uaignis, on which the saint spent a night of penance the night before he sailed. Right into our own time, people going into exile would come in pilgrimage to the glen, and spend a night on that flagstone, praying to the saint to save them from the pangs of homesickness. It is interesting to note, finally, that over in Iona in Columcille's monastery, travelling poets were welcomed. It was customary to invite them to sing 'a song of their own composition, sung to a tune' before departure.

Derry is a lovely old city, built on a hill which was originally an island in the River Foyle, and spilling down its sides to the river. The core, on the hilltop, is completely walled, with streets radiating from its central medieval 'diamond' to a series of gateways.

The Siege of Derry in 1689, when a group of apprentice boys slammed the city gates against the army of the lawful James I at a period when the throne of England was being claimed by William of Orange, was a turning point in the long-drawn-out War of the Kings, and the final defeat of James affected the course not only of English history but that of Ireland as well.

At Derry, one has crossed the Border into territory governed not from Dublin but from London. That circumstance, created in 1921, has led to some decades of bitter conflict, around and about and through which life has gone on in quite remarkably normal a fashion throughout most of the North. The territory is beautiful, often spectacularly so. Its placenames are widely sung: The Derry Air; Star of the County Down; Carrickfergus; Ballycastle-o, and legend clusters densely around places like Derry/Londonderry, Armagh, Antrim, Downpatrick. Concurrent with the rise of 'The Troubles', a whole school of poets, and dramatists too, has emerged where poetic voices were few before — deeply troubled voices, torn between the sense of need and/or duty to deal with contemporary events, and the urge to follow the intimate pathways of their own sensibilities and find expression for their personal truths. For several of these writers the landscape, and the naming of it, becomes a metaphor in an exploration of almost metaphysical realities.

The naming of places is a central theme of Brian Friel's play *Translations*. It is 1833, and the British Army has come to Ballybeg, Co. Donegal, in the process of creating the new Ordnance Survey of all of Ireland. This involves the naming, or rather the rendering in English form, of every town, village and feature of the landscape. But the name of a place embodies mythic and psychic power. How can the significance of a name, acquired through time and history in one language, be rendered with any meaning in another deriving from a totally different cultural experience? And does Ballybeg and its district, and the culture they represent, disappear, it has been asked, when re-named? As the Irish-speaking hedge-school is also to be replaced by a new 'national' school where English is the exchange, the people will have to learn to go not from Lis na Muc to Poll na gCaorach, but from Swinefort to Sheepsrock. Will they find their way? The threat is implied that a whole culture will disappear. But, with Friel's typical flourish of ambiguity, he gives the last words to the old hedge-schoolmaster: 'it can happen that a civilisation can be imprisoned in a linguistic contour which no longer matches the landscape of ... fact.'

And yet. In *Faith Healer*, Frank, the uncertain healer, uses a litany of placenames, the mean little Welsh or Scottish villages through which he passes, as a kind of incantation, repeated ritualistically over and over: 'for the mesmerism, the sedation':

Brian Friel (1929-   )

17-28 March 1981·TWO WEEKS ONLY·Brian Friel's
FAITH HEALER
KATE FLYNN · DONAL McCANN · EAMON MORRISSEY
Director JOE DOWLING · Design WENDY SHEA · Lighting LESLIE SCOTT
"Spectacularly brilliant acting...a triumph of immense proportions"
"A major contribution to Irish dramatic literature"

ABBEY THEATRE

Frank McGuinness (1953-   )

George Farquhar (1677-1707)

Above: Cover of the first edition of The Factory Girls *(Monarch Line/Wolfhound Press 1982) design based on the Peacock Theatre poster for the first performance*

Aberarder, Aberayron,
Llangranog, Llangurig,
Abergorlech, Abergynolwyn,
Llandefeilog, Llanerchymedd,
Aberhosan, Aberporth ...

They become an almost abstract sound, a mantra, until he is faced ultimately with the exploding savage reality of violence in Kinlochbervie.

Translations was the first production of the Field Day Theatre Company, founded by Friel and Stephen Rea in 1980. Though its main emphasis was on touring drama, Field Day was not just a theatre company, more a movement which became a notable cultural force in the north-west. As well as producing a series of publications analysing the symptoms and causes of, let us say, 'the current situation,' Field Day was the publisher of the immense — and controversial — *Anthology of Irish Writing* covering 500 years of literary, social and political output.

Brian Friel was born in **Omagh**, spent much of his life in Derry, and now lives in Donegal. His world-acclaimed *Dancing at Lughnasa* is set, like so many of his plays, in the Donegal village he names Ballybeg. Think **Glenties**, near the west coast. But *The Freedom of the City* is explicitly **Derry**, the Derry of today, with its divisions and complexities. As is the location of Frank McGuinness's *Carthaginians*. Both reflect on the aftermath of the 1972 incident known as 'Bloody Sunday', when a peaceful civil rights march was fired on by troops.

McGuinness was born and reared in the hinterland of Derry, in **Buncrana** on the Inishowen Peninsula, and that is the location of his first play, *The Factory Girls*, a story arising from the tradition in Derry and east Donegal of the women being the family breadwinners through their work in the shirt factories. The play illustrates their growing assertiveness and self-awareness as they demand better conditions, not only in their work, but in their lives. Derry city is also the model for the Rome of McGuinness's *Innocence*, based on the life of Caravaggio. In Caravaggio's time, Rome was much the same size as Derry is now, and the playwright imagined him walking through those same hilly streets and through the gateway arches.

George Farquhar, playright of an earlier age, was another Derryman and is thought to have been present at the famous Siege of 1689. His first foray into the theatrical world was as an actor, in Dublin's Smock Alley. He was cast in Dryden's *Indian Emperor* but having, in an excess of enthusiasm, run a sword into a fellow actor, he left for London and rarely visited Ireland again. His abandonment of acting led him to writing as an alternative livelihood, to the great benefit of the English-speaking world. *The Beaux Stratagem* and *The Recruiting Officer* are masterpieces of the period.

The County of Derry takes a long stride across the North to dabble a toe in a corner of **Lough Neagh**.

> The lough will claim a victim every year.
> It has virtue that hardens wood to stone.
> There is a town sunk beneath its water.
> It is a scar left by the Isle of Man.

So Seamus Heaney opens his Lough Neagh Sequence. Like many of his poems, it points out that lives are lived by myth and folk memory rather than barren facts or stripped evidence. The fishermen up the shore never learn to swim. '"We'll be quicker going down" they say.' But it's not far to shore? No matter. 'The lough will claim a victim every year.'

Seamus Heaney (1939-   )

Eel-fishing has been the life-blood since time immemorial of those living by the shores of that great shallow water. Up to two hundred boats fish brown eels with long lines, some of them up to 5 miles (8km) long with hundreds of hooks. And in autumn at the waning moon with a westerly wind and preferably with rain, the weirs above the lake harvest the eels, now silver, that are setting out on one of nature's most mysterious migrations, back to the sea where they were born, far away in the Sargasso.

> ...and when did this begin?
> This morning, last year, when the lough first spawned?
> The crew will answer, 'Once the season's in'.

The slither of those invisible wrigglings in the grass across childhood toes is still a sudden remembered shock in grown men:

> ...years
> Later in the same fields
> He stood at night when eels
> Moved through the grass like hatched fears
> Towards the water.

Seamus Heaney was born in 1939 in the townland of **Mossbawn**, hard by the northern shore of the lake. The family moved some years later to **Bellaghy**, a bit further 'up the road' but Mossbawn inspired a whole sequence of poems centred on family. Heaney has come to embody the contemporary Irish consciousness for a world-wide audience. He, like the others, has had to wrestle with interior and exterior conflicts, the paramount riddle of identity. Their farm, he points out, lay between **Toome Bridge** and **Castledawson**, each a symbol and a monument to opposing resonances, the former for the glorified death of Roddy MacCorley, the latter for the ruling ascendancy. In the collection *Wintering Out* he explores those oppositions. Images of what lies concealed, covered over by bog and moss, treasures and bone pieces, but darker images too, the Tollund Man, the

Earth-pantry, bone-vault,
Sun-bank, embalmer
of votive goods
and sabred fugitives.

Insatiable bride.
Sword-swallower,
Casket, midden,
floe of history.

Ground that will strip
its dark side,
nesting ground,
outback of my mind.
(*Kinship*)

drowned strangled woman of Scandinavia, unexpectedly rising to the surface in their glory or horror.

And meanwhile the shade of Mad Sweeney, the cursed king, beyond all help and eventually to die in a dung-heap, goes screeching and lurching from bush to thorn-tree, up the **Bann Valley**, through **Antrim** and **Down**. 'For thirty years I lived on the verges of that territory, in sight of some of Sweeney's places and in earshot of others — Slemish, Rasharkin, Benevenagh, Dunseverick, the Bann, the Roe, the Mournes,' says Heaney.

Sweeney was resurrected from a collection of medieval, or earlier, tales into popular consciousness by Flann O'Brien / Brian O'Nolan in his brilliant quirky novel *At Swim-Two-Birds*. Flann O'Brien's deranged monarch, cursed by a saint (the worst kind of curse from all accounts) to live like a bird of the air, is excruciatingly comic in his unspeakable miseries. Heaney, in his version 'Sweeney Astray' finds in him a reflection of our mass schizophrenia.

> One night
> I walked across the Fews —
> the hills were dark, the starlight dead —
> when suddenly five severed heads,
> five lantern ghouls, appeared and rose
>
> like bats from hell, surrounding me.
> Then a head spoke — another shock!
> — This is the Ulster lunatic.
> Let us drive him into the sea ...
>
> His brain convulsed,
> his mind split open
> Vertigo, hysteria, lurchings
> and launchings came over him ...

After the deeps and labyrinths of such visions, in the collection *Seeing Things* we seem to be in a lighter, more ordered world, where differences if not resolved are at least less turbulent. But the search is not over: what is it that hides just out of sight — or in the offing?

> The emptier it stood, the more compelled
> The eye that scanned it.
> But once you turned your back on it, your back
> Was suddenly all eyes like Argus's ...

But there is trust that there will come

> 'That day I'll be in step with what escaped me'.

One morning about the year 1810, a boastful youth swallowed a half pint of whiskey to give him courage and elevation, and hurled himself across a river in a mighty leap, to the cheers of a great crowd of onlookers. 'I had done that which has never been done from that day to this, although many persons, confident in their own success at leaping, came to the place with an intention of following my example, but after looking at it they shook their heads, and very calmly returned home. This I have been told many times. It is called "Carleton's Leap" until this day'.

We are in the **Clogher Valley**. The spot is about a mile out the Fintona road from **Clogher**, close to a bridge over a small tributary of the River Blackwater. Work-shy and wayward, and given to showing off at leppin' and weight-lifting, William Carleton showed little signs of becoming 'the greatest novelist of Ireland by right of the most Celtic eyes that ever gazed from under the brow of a story-teller', which is how Yeats appraises him. Carleton was an original. He was, as he himself said, the chronicler of 'a class unknown in literature, unknown by their own landlords, and unknown by those in whose hands much of their destiny was placed.' Until he made them seen.

He was born at **Prillisk** near Clogher in the year 1794. The family moved around a bit; the cottage at **Springtown** where they lived for some time still stands picturesquely at the end of a winding lane shaded by trees, about one mile south of **Augher**, where they were tenants of Squire Storey of Corick House (the Storey family still lives there). 'On a green upland lawn ... stood an old ecclesiastical ruin, grey from time ... The country in the distance lay charmed ... the motionless lakes shone like mirrors wherever they caught the beams of the evening light, as did several bends of the broad river which barely moved within its winding banks through the meadow below.'

His stories open a curtain on life in pre-Famine Ireland. He was the first to write in English about the ordinary people — the poor, the ignorant, the dispossessed, from the inside. He was able to because he was one of them, and shared their poverty, their turbulence, their humour and their inconsistencies. He abandoned his religion to join up with the Rev Caesar Otway in villifying the superstitions of Popery, but castigated the clergy of both churches equally for their pride and arrogance. He wrote in favour of temperance, and on the virtues of poteen; he celebrated drunkenness and praised sobriety, derided what he saw as the naive revolutionary ideas of the Young Irelanders, but burned with rage at the deprivations suffered by his people under the power of agents, proctors, bailiffs and usurers.

In *Traits and Stories of the Irish Peasantry* we meet them in all their extravagance, their teeming energy and inconquerable humour. There are wonderful pen-pictures — like that of Dr Turbot, Parson:

William Carleton (1794-1869)

William Carleton's cottage, near Augher

Literary Tour of Ireland

Carleton Summer School brochure cover shows the painting by J. Twigg in 1860 of the view 'from the books room window' at Corick House

Below: On Knockmany hill is Knockmany Cairn, Augher, photographed c.1910

when walking, he drove forward as if his head was butting or boring its way through a palpable atmosphere, keeping his person from the waist up, so far in advance that the a posteriori position seemed as if it had been detached from the other, and was engaged in a ceaseless but ineffective struggle to regain its position ...

Then there is Buckramback with his lessons at dancing and etiquette, 'not jigs and reels, no rude lepping and bounding, but quadrilles and waltzes, the Sir Roger de Coverley '— all in a broken-down barn at Kilnahushogue.

In *Valentine McClutchy* a fist fight erupts between Darby O'Drive who has converted to Protestantism and Bob Beatty who has converted to Catholicism, after an argument during which each supports the religion to which he originally belonged. The neighbours come to join in the fight, the Catholics fighting for Bob, and the Protestants 'owing to a similar mistake fought like devils for Darby and the Pope'.

In more sombre mood, we are shown the rascally Skinadre over his scales 'weighing out with a dishonest and parsimonious hand, the scanty pittance which poverty enabled the wretched creatures to purchase from him'. And in *The Black Prophet* there is the terrible picture of Famine:

The features of the people were gaunt, their eyes wild and hollow, and their gait feeble and tottering. Pass through the fields, and you were met by little groups bearing home on their shoulders, and that with difficulty, a coffin, or perhaps two of them. The roads were literally black with funerals; and, as you passed along from parish to parish, the death bells were pealing forth.

That book he dedicated to the Prime Minister of Great Britain and Ireland.

This peasant life ended with the famine of the 1840s, when the population halved and the face of the countryside changed for ever.

This same Clogher Valley is John Montague's *The Rough Field*. Writing a century and a half later than Carleton, he remembers a homecoming:

> To a gaunt farmhouse on this busy road,
> Bisecting slopes of plaintive moorland,
> Where I assume old ways of walk and work
> So easily, yet feel the sadness of return
> To what seems still, though changing ...
> Rough Field in the Gaelic and rightly named
> As setting for a mode of life that passes on:
> Harsh landscape that haunts me,
> Well and stone, in the bleak moors of dream.

His grandfather's farm at **Garvaghy**, literally the Rough Field, is four miles from **Ballygawley**, and in the collection of that name Montague talks about a kind of vision of historical destiny, to be

John Montague (1929-   )

You do not forget
and I always come back.
Stepping from the car
outside Clogher, I saw
a brilliant rainbow
lifting its prismatic arch
across Knockmany Hill
as in a healing dream
in savage Chicago. It
shone both a secret
and a sacrament, a promise
and its fulfillment.
I still live by it.
                    ('Mount Eagle', John Montague)

evoked by the communal memory: 'Like Dolmens round my child-hood, the old people.'

Over all this valley, and its vivid ghosts, stands **Knockmany Hill.** Its crown is a chambered tomb. Several thousands of years before Carleton's small farmers and hedge schoolmasters and landlords lived out their tumultuous lives, a community of people about whom we know little carved mysterious messages on massive rocks, then stood them around their burial and closed it over.

To reach the top of the hill where the cairn is you will have to leave your car and take a fairly steep ascent through the forest. If you should cease to be vigilant and take a wrong turn you might find yourself endlessly circling the hill without ever reaching your objective and perhaps have to return to the beginning and start again. And this too is appropriate: it is not given to mere mortals to reach too easily or casually to the heart of power and mystery.

It is unfortunate that the cairn is now, for protection, encased in concrete, but we can peer through the barred gate, as through the barriers of time, to try to read the meaning of circle, spiral and lozenge. How different were the carvers from Carleton's people, if at all?

Four miles to the east of Knockmany a pile of boulders is topped by what is called '**St Patrick's Chair**' but belongs to an age long before Christianity. Whoever presided at that throne, for ritual or inaugura-tion, it was not St Patrick! Up until recent times, people celebrated the old feast of Lughnasa or Lammas here. Other tombs of the ancients dot the surrounding countryside, protected less by decree than by their numinousness. A little further off at Beaghmore, north of Creggan, a web of intertwining stone circles deepens the sense of time's relativity:

> Ancient Ireland, indeed! I was reared by her bedside,
> The rune and the chant, evil eye and averted head,
> Fomorian fierceness of family and local feud.
> Gaunt figures of fear and of friendliness,
> For years they trespassed on my dreams,
> Until once, in a standing circle of stones,
> I felt their shadows pass
> Into that dark permanence of ancient forms.   ('Home Again')

Like all the northern writers, Montague has to deal with 'the fissure between traditional loyalties and the sense of a world elsewhere'. But deep complexities are, over and over, subsumed in the mystical energy of place. As in 'A Slow Dance':

> greenness, rain   The whole world
> spatter on skin,   turning in wet
> the humid pull   and silence, a
> of the earth.   damp mill wheel.

ANNAGHMAKERRIG
The Tyrone Guthrie Centre

Many fine poems have been written, novels commenced or concluded, biog-raphies researched, canvasses painted, sculptures shaped, musical suites com-posed, at Annaghmakerrig's studios and workshops near Newbliss, County Monaghan, about 30 miles (40 km) south of the Clogher Valley.

Sir Tyrone Guthrie, the actor and thea-tre director, left his home to be a retreat and workplace for artists of all kinds from Ireland and abroad. It is a gracious house surrounded by old gardens, overlooking a lake within a 400-acre for-ested estate.

Anyone engaged in creative work may apply to stay for anything from a week to a year in this peaceful place away from all distractions, either in the 'Big House', which is run like a good country hotel, or in well-designed self-catering units in what used to be the farmyard.

There are individual studios for art-ists, a music room and a large rehearsal /performance space for groups. It is a unique working ambience in which to pursue the muse. Residents usually come together for a sociable evening meal.

Some payment is required, but rates are negotiable.

Applications should be to Bernard Loughlin, Director, Tyrone Guthrie Centre, Annaghmakerrig, County Monaghan. Tel. 047-54003 Fax 047-54380.

Opposite: Leganany dolmen south-west of Belfast in nearby County Down

We leave the Clogher Valley and its rough field carrying with us, if we have dared to climb to it, the aura of John Montague's **Seskilgreen**:

A circle of stones
surviving behind a
guttery farmhouse,

the capstone phallic
in a thistly meadow:
Seskilgreen Passage Grave.

Cup, circle,
triangle beating
their secret dance

(eyes, breasts,
thighs of a still
fragrant goddess).

I came last in May
to find the mound
drowned in bluebells

with a fearless wren
hoarding speckled eggs
in a stony crevice
while cattle

swayed sleepily
under low branches

lashing the ropes
of their tails
across the centuries.

We circle back towards Derry. At **Omagh** the totally individual mellifluous voice of Benedict Kiely, familiar to so many radio listeners, seems to hang in the air, endlessly story-telling, weaving marvellous intricate webs of recollection, about places, people, wanderings, songs, ballads, fables, of captains and kings and dogs and horses and gods and heroes and, in a different, angry mood in recent times, of the terrorism and cruelty of the divided North.

Benedict Kiely (1919-   )

This is Kiely's town. 'Close to Omagh I was born, and in its streets and on the roads around it I grew up. Or was reared. We also had a house.' Dromore was where he was born. He moved to Omagh, he says, when he was 'about as big as a Jameson bottle.' It is the 'Ballyclogher' of so many of his tales.

Kiely has written ten novels, ranging from quasi-fantasy such as *The Cards of the Gambler* to darkly realistic works like *Proxopera* and *Nothing Happens in Carmincross*. His biography of William Carleton is the best written about that original man. But, perhaps because he is, as his neighbour John Montague says, 'almost overcome by the variety of life', he is at his best in his short stories. He is a born story-teller, and his account of his youth and young manhood in Omagh, *Drink to the Bird*, is richly peopled with personalities who may, in fact, be ordinary enough but around whom his rich imagination has built the stuff of legends. Like Margaret O'Reilly, the ballad-singing woman who had most of the words of a song so long 'that a man driving a horse and cart over the Barrack Hill in Omagh Town began to sing it and was still singing, without having repeated a verse, eight miles away at **Seagully Crossroads**.' And the farmer who would leave a team of

Ben Kiely with Annie McKenna at Carleton's cottage.

horses standing in a half-ploughed field and follow a brass band all day and, since Omagh had two bands, 'his sowing was always dilatory and his harvests very close to Christmas'. And the townsman who joined the British Navy and survived the sinking of three destroyers, and later again was found by a fellow-townsman, in the middle of a bombardment of Crete, curled up in a hole in the ground reading the *Ulster Herald.* 'He said hello and went on reading.' And before all that, how Kiely first discovered that it was a man's world, at three years old, when he 'bested' a nun, though he might have wondered about that later.

The Cannonhill road went up from the Town in three steps, but those steps could only be taken by Titans ... If you looked back from Cannonhill, the prospect, or perhaps it should be the retrospect, was really something: the whole Town, spires and all, you could even see clear down into some of the streets: the winding river or rivers, the red brick of the county hospital, already mentioned, as also Arethusa Glenhordial of the pure mountain springs, and Gortin Gap and Mullagharn and the tips of Sawel and Dart in the high Sperrins.

Alice Milligan (1866-1953)

Ulster-American Folk Park

While you're in Omagh, it's worth looking in at a world that many of our own ancestors have encountered. The old homestead of the Mellon family, who became powerful magnates in Pittsburgh, is the centrepiece of the 70-acre Ulster-American Folk Park. It is cleverly conceived insofar as you step aboard an emigrant ship there, and disembark on the other side into the New World of the Americas.

Talking about the **Sperrins**, in the same book Kiely gives an intriguing account of his first visit, as a young man, to Alice Milligan, 'a great lady and a poet, the two in one,' who lived in the foothills of the Sperrins. 'The house stood in the sharp angle between the **Killyclogher** road which led to **Mountfield** and the road which we called, elegantly, the Asylum Road and which led ultimately to **Carrickmore**.' The country people said that if you met her on the road you'd give her a penny, but in fact she lived in a one-time rectory in the remnants of graciousness, and as to the drawing-room of her home, 'About such drawing-rooms I had at that time, or up to that time,' he says, 'heard something from Dickens and Thackeray, chiefly perhaps from Thackeray,' but never had stood in one until then. She had been one of the first Abbey playwrights, and wrote poetry for the *United Irishman* and other nationalist periodicals.

Something of Friel's incantations is echoed in Kiely's recital of the postal place-names: 'Aghee, Altamuskin, Arvalee, Aughaleague, Augher, Ballynahatty, Beragh, Bomacatall, Brackey, Cavanacaw, Clanabogan, Claramore, Clogher, Clohogue ...'

'The ground,' he says, is 'littered with things, cluttered with memories and multiple associations.' Reading the products of his prodigious memory, we can see how apt is the memoir's title. It is from 'Mr Flood's Party' by Edwin Arlington Robinson:

> Well, Mr. Flood, we have the harvest moon
> Again, and we may not have many more;
> The bird is on the wing, the poet says,
> And you and I have said it here before.
> Drink to the bird ...

Lyric Theatre c.1976.
Back row left to right: Paul Muldoon, John Hewitt, Patrick Galvin, Frank Ormsby, Ciaran Carson.
Front row left to right: Seamus Deane, John Boyd, Michael Longley

14. BELFAST AND ANTRIM
The City and the Glens

So we come to **Belfast**, Capital of Northern Ireland, that place of so much complexity and paradox, like the title of Ciaran Carson's poem (and book of poems) *The Irish for No*. (There isn't any, of course.)

We have mentioned the burgeoning of northern writers which began in the 1960s. One of the 'enablers' of the movement was one Philip Hobsbaum, himself a poet, literary critic and English university lecturer. Under his wing a group began meeting to read and discuss each other's work. 'The Group', as they later came to be known included Michael and Edna Longley, James Simmons, Stewart Parker, Derek Mahon, Seamus Deane, and Marie Devlin and Seamus Heaney, who later married. Their sessions were based on those of the 'Movement' poets of the 1950s whom Hobsbaum had also organised and guided. When Hobsbaum departed in 1966 Heaney took over as host and when he left in 1970 the group had come to include Paul Muldoon, Frank Ormsby and Michael Foley.

For most Northern writers, there has been the element of struggling with the quandary of place and displacement, the politic and the literary, in their different ways. Carson's is a voice sure of its place. His

Ciaran Carson (1948-   )

Some northern voices in the 1970s, at Queen's University, Belfast, c. 1977
Back row: Anthony Weir, John Hewitt, Padraic Fiacc, Ciaran Carson
Front row: John Morrow, James Simmons

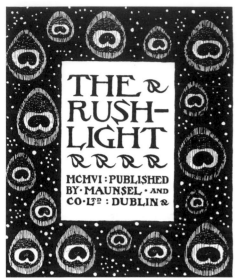

Title page design by Joseph Campbell

Michael Longley (1939-   )

Derek Mahon (1941-   )

Joseph Campbell (1879-1944)
W.R. Rodgers (1909-1969)

is the authentic voice of today's Belfast, his work and the city inextricably intermeshed. The poems are complex, digressive, layered, witty, blackly humorous, comically conversational — and heartbreaking. With him, the shadow of the local conflict permeates all everyday actions and exchanges. A car backfiring creates a tense silence; a late-night knock at the door may betoken a very unwelcome guest. The innocent and sinister become indistinguishable, each is a parable or parody of the other. Like in 'Belfast Confetti':

Suddenly as the riot squad moved in, it was raining exclamation marks,
Nuts, bolts, nails, car keys. A fount of broken type. And the explosion
Itself — an asterisk on the map. This hyphenated line, a burst of rapid fire ...
I was trying to complete a sentence in my head, but it kept stuttering,
All the alleyways and side streets blocked with stops and colons.

Although born and bred in Belfast, Carson's first language is Irish, and he is inclined to use some of the stop-start, story-within-story method of the oral tradition, though in a very non-traditional manner. He was a musician before he was a poet, and has published a *Guide to Irish Traditional Music*. At the time of writing he is Traditional Arts Officer for the Arts Council of Northern Ireland. As for 'The Irish for No', the fact that such a word doesn't exist in Irish is counterpointed by the very definite *No* that exists in Northern English: 'Ulster Says No' declares every street-corner.

Michael Longley shifted his focus to the west of Ireland and his own emotional innerscape: Derek Mahon detached himself fairly thoroughly from any local sense of place at all. But even for him, the string pulls:

But the hills are still the same
Grey-blue over Belfast.
Perhaps if I'd stayed behind
And lived it bomb by bomb
I might have grown up at last
And learnt what is meant by home.   ('Afterlives')

and, in 'The Spring Vacation':

One part of my mind must learn to know its place.
The things that happen in the kitchen houses
And echoing backstreets of this desperate city
Should engage more than my casual interest,
Exact more interest than my casual pity.

Two Belfast writers of an earlier period have a loyal if relatively small following. Joseph Campbell, born in 1879, and W.R. Rodgers, born in 1909, the Presbyterian minister who wrote such joyful celebrations of sexual love. They were lucky enough to grow up in an Ireland undivided by any borders except those of the mind. We remember

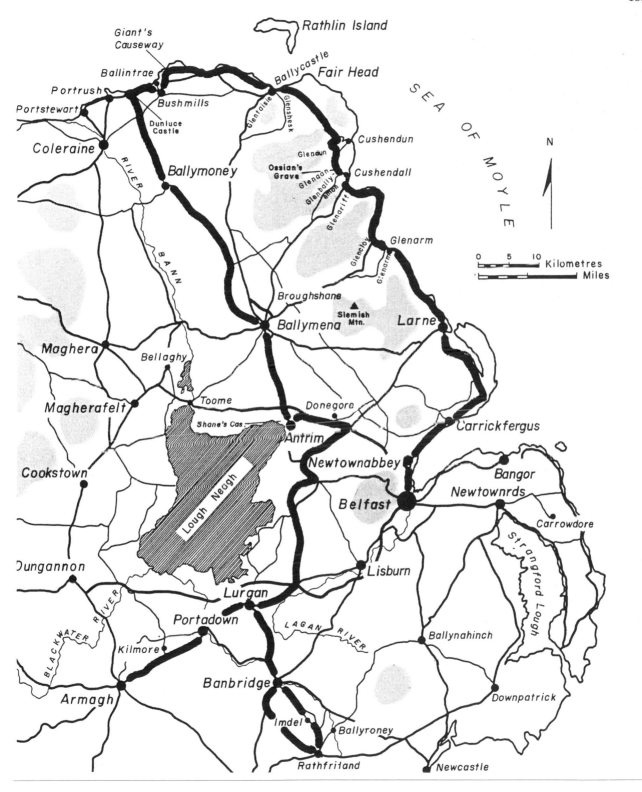

Rathlin Island

Giant's Causeway

Ballintrae

Portrush

Portstewart

Bushmills

Dunluce Castle

Coleraine

Ballycastle

Fair Head

SEA OF MOYLE

N

Glentaisie

Glenshesk

Ballymoney

RIVER

BANN

Cushendun

Glendun

Ossian's Grave

Glenaan

Glenballyemon

Cushendall

Glenariff

Glenarm

Glencloy

Glenarm

0   5   10   Kilometres
              Miles

Maghera

Bellaghy

Broughshane

Slemish Mtn.

Larne

Ballymena

Magherafelt

Toome

Donegora

Shane's Cas.

Antrim

Carrickfergus

Cookstown

Lough Neagh

Newtownabbey

Bangor

Newtownrds

Carrowdore

Belfast

Dungannon

Lisburn

Strangford Lough

Lurgan

Portadown

LAGAN RIVER

Ballynahinch

BLACKWATER RIVER

Kilmore

Downpatrick

Armagh

Banbridge

Imdel

Ballyroney

Rathfriland

Newcastle

Where Lagan stream sings lullaby,
There blooms a lily fair,
The twilight gleam is in her eye,
The night is on her hair;
And, like a love-sick *leanán sidhe*
She hath my heart in thrall:
Nor life, I owe, nor liberty
For love is lord of all ...   ('My Lagan Love')

Helen Waddell (1889-1965)

Brian Moore (1921–1999)

Louis MacNeice (1907-1963)

Campbell most gratefully as the man who wrote the magic words to match that haunting melody 'My Lagan Love.'

Campbell was related by marriage to a remarkable woman, Helen Waddell, who was twenty years his junior. Daughter of a Presbyterian missionary from Belfast, she was born in Tokyo, read Chinese, Latin and old French, was educated at Oxford and feted in Dublin, Britain and America. But she was first, foremost and forever a daughter of the manse, a missionary's girl. Her two great achievements in scholarship, *The Wandering Scholars* in 1927 and *Medieval Latin Lyrics* in 1933 shed a shaft of brilliant light into a forgotten world of arcane knowledge for which a whole generation stood in her debt. Her flawed but fascinating novel *Peter Abelard* has never gone out of print. She died, her fine mind long clouded over, only in 1965.

Sir Samuel Ferguson, George A. Bermingham, Forrest Reid, Robert Lynd, St John Ervine, C.S. Lewis were all Belfastmen, each making his different contribution to inspiring or entertaining us. Belfast too is the place where the Lonely Passion of Judith Hearne, in her mid-life crisis, drove her to lose herself in fantasy, in Brian Moore's novel of that name. And Belfast is the setting for three others of his novels: *The Feast of Lupercal, The Emperor of Ice-Cream* and *An Answer from Limbo*.

In spite of all that has happened, in spite of the gaping gaps in the walls and the occasional heaps of uncleared rubble, in spite of Maurice Craig's much-quoted 'May the Lord in his mercy be kind to Belfast', Belfast is experienced as a kindly, hospitable, even gracious place, and its **Europa Hotel** one of the most gallant, genial and welcoming hostelries to be found anywhere, in peace or in strife, loved and appreciated by journalists from all corners of the earth, where *Pravda* swaps yarns with *The Chicago Tribune* and men who couldn't be seen even talking to each other in public can swop pints and jokes.

From Belfast it is a pleasant drive along Belfast Lough to **Carrickfergus**, once you get off the motorway and leave the smoke and chimneys behind. It is an old port town whose main feature is the massive Carrickfergus Castle which stands dramatically on a rock overlooking the harbour, balefully watching all shipping routes into and out of Belfast.

Louis MacNeice, born in Belfast in 1907, spent his youth here and grew up within sight of the castle:

> I was born in Belfast between the mountain and the gantries
> To the hooting of lost sirens and the clang of trams:
> Thence to Smoky Carrick in County Antrim
> Where the bottle-neck harbour collects the mud which jams
>
> The little boats beneath the Norman castle,

The pier shining with lumps of crystal salt;
The Scotch Quarter was a line of residential houses
But the Irish Quarter was a slum for the blind and halt. ('Carrickfergus')

It is a sour poem, but then MacNeice was often sour about Ireland and things Irish. He spent a miserable childhood in the rectory at Carrickfergus, where his father was minister and from where his mother was removed to an asylum. Later he was able to write an intensely moving epitaph for his austere and unapproachable father: 'dead in daffodil time / Before it had come to Easter.' He came to see him as 'courteous / And lyrical and strong and kind and truthful / A generous puritan ...

MacNeice was conscious of the isolated life of the Protestant upper middle classes, particularly in relation to the people of the countryside who were their neighbours; he and his like were 'banned for ever from the candles of the Irish poor.' He was unhappy at home, but even more unhappy at being sent to England. He was shocked at industrial England, having 'always lived near the sea and the sight of high ridges.' But London and its life claimed him, and in the end he felt more at home there than in Ireland, despite occasional nostalgia for the west of Ireland where he had spent happy holidays.

The vickarage at Carrickfergus has been demolished and in its place now stands the institution called the MacNeice Fold which is a 'sheltered accommodation'. A plaque outside acknowledges him further, stating — Louis MacNeice / Poet / lived here. He is buried in the village of **Carrowdore** on the other side of Belfast Lough, in the graveyard of Christ Church.

Moving up the coast from Carrickfergus we come to **Larne**, and to a writer who is as far removed from the sensibility of MacNeice as it would be possible to get. Anna Margaret M'Kittrick, known as Amanda M'Kittrick Ros, is celebrated as the worst novelist ever published. She left her native Larne and entered an extravagant landscape on the inside of her head. She was actually born at **Ballinahinch**, about fifteen miles (24 km) south of Belfast, where her father was a teacher at nearby **Dromaness**. She came to Larne as a schoolteacher and stayed to marry first Andy Ros, the stationmaster at Larne, then, after he died, a local businessman, Thomas Rodgers. She recorded her 'real' name as Amanda Malvina Fitzalan Anna Margaret McLelland M'Kittrick Ros. She seems to have restrained herself from adding the 'Rodgers'. For their tenth wedding anniversary Andy gave his lady wife the money to publish her first novel, *Irene Iddesleigh*, written as a result of her great admiration of the popular novelist Maria Corelli. More novels followed, each uniquely dreadful.

A cult following emerged at Oxford, led by Aldous Huxley, who

Amanda M'Kittrick Ros (1860-1939)

enjoyed himself hugely corresponding with her. Ornamented with alliteration to excess, populated by personalities unknown in the real world — there is no beating Amanda at her own peculiar game.

Madam, How dare you? I say — how dare you? You have dragged my poor innocent dove — my wife — my angel into your seething saloon of sin and shame, to rob her of all the charm and grace and place her in the singed list of the loose to be in Co. with your train of degraded elegance. Give me my little rural ruby set in the folds of innocence she wears, whose mind is as pure as the balm of heaven, within whose breasts sin hath never concealed itself. I say — give her me with a robe of rags, a mind of modesty, a heart of horror for all things unclean and hands untainted by the gruesome grasp of vice, rather than a princess — a duchess — a countess — a mimicking madonna decked with diamonds the purest, rubies the rarest, pearls of matchless lustre (produced by mechanical and mischievous means) and the defiled non-trappings some of our ugly-faced have-you-believe cream of aristocracy don to impersonate heaven's purest virgin of Babylonian blood and bearing, thereby aiming to achieve humanity.

(Helen Huddleson)

Amanda M'Kittrick Ros (1860-1939)

Someone left her a lime kiln, of all things, and she became embroiled in years of litigation. This, and her reaction to literary critics, fuelled a series of sarcastic poetic activities published in two collections, *Poems of Puncture* and *Fumes of Formation* which almost ignite on the page. But there is no doubt that she delighted in language, even re-inventing it to suit her purpose. She may well have been right when she wrote: 'I expect I will be talked about at the end of 1,000 years.'

And how's this for a poem on Westminster Abbey:

> Holy Moses! Have a look!
> Flesh decayed in every nook.
> Some rare bits of brain lie here,
> Mortal loads of beef and beer.

EMAIN MACHA — NAVAN FORT

Emain Macha (pronounced *Ow*-en *Mock*-a) lies two miles (3km) west of Armagh. What is to be seen now is a great grass-covered mound, with a surprisingly wide view of the surrounding countryside.

The mound conceals the evidence of an astonishing history, only recently deciphered by archaeologists. To quote John Montague: 'Myth and reality warmly met as we swarmed over Navan Fort.'

In legend Emain Macha was the great Royal Site of the Ulster kings. It features in several of the ancient stories, particularly the Táin Bó Cuailgne, the Cattle Raid of Cooley, which has a chapter to itself in this book. Excavation has revealed that, after a couple of thousand years of use as a homestead and stockade, an enormous round wooden structure was built, containing five concentric rings of posts. It was later filled with rocks with the posts still standing, to form a cairn, then the whole structure was ritually burnt, and afterwards covered with sods.

That event is dated, as are the hero-tales of the Ulster Cycle, to the interface of the Bronze and Iron Ages, about the first century BC. But no stories have come down to us. As to its doing, or meaning, records, tradition and folk-memory are silent.

The resultant mound is what one strolls over today. A Visitor Centre close by, through an audio-visual show and other displays, tells the story of Emain Macha, in legend and in history.

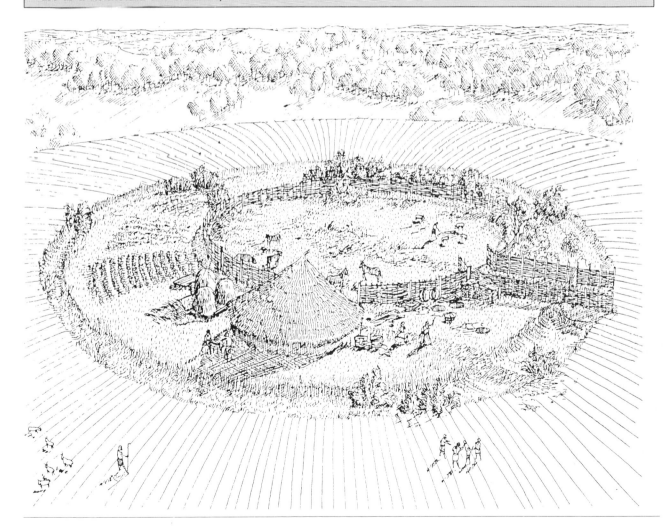

Northwards from here the Antrim Coast Road is a sixty-mile symphony of sea and rock and cliff and sand. It is one of the most spectacular routes in Ireland. It hugs the coast close to the sea for most of its forty-mile length, culminating in the grand flourish of the Giant's Causeway. Inland a series of glens pierce the moorland. Going northwards you pass, or penetrate, the glens one by one: Glenarm, Glencloy, Glenariff, Glenballyeamon, Glenaan, Glencorp, Glendrum, Glenhesk, Glentaisie. Until the coast road was opened up in the 1830s, these glens were among the most remote in the land. The communities who lived in them lived in extreme isolation. As a consequence, an immensely rich heritage of old ways and old stories, traditional usages and customs were preserved into recent times.

These deeply-probing glens are most lovingly celebrated by John Hewitt, for long regarded almost as the North's laureate. He was born in Belfast in 1907, at 96 Cliftonpark Avenue, and some of his earliest recollections relate to the dramatic sweep of Cave Hill, and to the Glens of Antrim where he spent childhood holidays and most of the latter part of his life after he retired from his post with the Ulster Museum. He made his home at Leamore Lodge, which had been the gatelodge to Glenville House in Cushendall. To reach it you take the fiercely steep hill past the Curfew Tower (built by one Francis Turnly as a monument to the Brotherhood of Man) in the middle of the little town, and take a right turn immediately after passing some modern bungalows, and continue for less than half a mile. It is a place of splendid views.

John Hewitt (1907-1987)

The Giants' Causeway c.1895

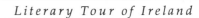

(Left) Lissadell House, Co. Sligo, home of the Gore-Booth family. To Yeats the sisters, Constance and Eva, were 'Two girls in silk kimonos, both Beautiful, one a gazelle.'
(Below) 'Under bare Ben Bulben's head In Drumcliff churchyard Yeats is laid.'

(Above) One of the pre-Bronze Age tombs at
Carrowmore, with Knocknarea in the background.
The Fianna in their hunt
'... passing the Firbolgs' burial-mounds,
Came to the cairn-heaped grassy hill
Where passionate Maeve is stony-still.'

(Right and opposite page) The Rosses of Donegal

(Left) Omagh town near the foothills of the Sperrin hills.

(Below) Evening light over Derry city: Doire Colmcille, named for the saint who fought a battle over a book and was exiled to Iona to repent.

John Hewitt chose to have his ashes placed under a
'beehive' mound on a hill close to his home at
Cushendall, beside the neolithic tomb known as
Ossian's Grave (below).
'... asleep till Fionn and Oscar rise
to summon his old bardic skill ...'

(Below and opposite page, bottom) Last resting-places. Louis MacNeice's at Carrowdore and Sir Samuel Ferguson's at Donegore, both in County Antrim.

Your ashes will not stir, even on this high ground,
However the wind tugs, the headstones shake.
This plot is consecrated, for your sake,
To what lies in the future tense. You lie
Past tension now, and spring is coming round
Igniting flowers on the peninsula.
Derek Mahon, from 'In Carrowdore Churchyard'
(for Louis MacNeice)

(Above) Slemish Mountain is a strong feature in the Antrim landscape. On its slopes St Patrick, Ireland's patron saint, herded cattle as a slave during his early years. For an ascent, the best approach is through the village of Broughshane.

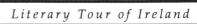

Donegore, County Antrim

East Prospect of the Giants' Causeway c.1739
by Susanna Drury

Hewitt's poems from the glens are a treasure-chest of old folkways and customs, encapsulating a whole way of life: the woman telling him about the tramp who begged shelter in the house, and how her mother 'sat with him all night/ beside the warm fire singing song for song'; of the wake where he snicked the latch 'constrained by ancient courtesy'; the equally necessary courtesies that needed to be extended to the 'wee folk'; the tales of the travelling fiddler; the to him exotic rituals of the young girls' Confirmation, of the evening family rosary.

Watching but never able to belong, he imagines, probably correctly, that the locals see him as 'a strange bird observed about the house'. He is both fascinated and repelled by the rituals of the glens people:

> O country people, you of the hill farms,
> huddled so in darkness I cannot tell
> whether the light across the glen is a star,
> or the bright lamp spilling over the sill.
> I would be neighbourly, would come to terms
> with your existence, but you are so far;
> there is a wide bog between us, a high wall.

Writing mainly in calmer times than those of the present and recent past didn't insulate Hewitt from the problems of identity and the need to define his own. He wrestles with it over and over in poems like 'Once Alien Here.' In the long poem 'The Colony' he sets out the history of the Plantation and its legacy.

At the end he states his emotional claim convincingly:

> ... for we have rights drawn from the soil and sky;
> the use, the pace, the patient years of labour,
> the rain against the lips, the changing light,
> the heavy clay-sucked stride have altered us;
> we would be strangers in the Capitol;
> this is our country also, no-where else;
> and we shall not be outcast on the world.

Kilmore is the village from whence his ancestors, on his father's side, came — old country which to him was like 'a spring well under a gentle thorn, a never-ceasing source and jet full of magic and meaning'. In 'Planter's Gothic' he tells 'When I discovered, not long ago, that the old Planter's Gothic tower at Kilmore Church still encloses the stump of a round tower and that it was built on the site of a Culdee holy place, I felt a step nearer to that synthesis. It is the best symbol I have yet found for the strange textures of my response to this island of which I am a native. I may appear Planter's Gothic, but there is a round tower somewhere inside, and needled through every sentence I utter.'

Kilmore is a tiny old-feeling place between Portadown and Armagh, deep in apple orchard country. If you are following this

> ... fear quickened by the memory of guilt
> for we began the plunder — naked men
> still have their household gods and holy places,
> and what a people loves it will defend.
> We took their temples from them and forbade them
> for many years, to worship their strange idols.
> They gathered secret, deep in the dripping glens,
> chanting their prayers before a lichened rock.
>
> We took the kindlier soils ... We took it from them
> We laboured hard and stubborn, draining, planting
> till half the country took its shape from us.
> ('The Colony')

itinerary and travelling north on the Antrim coast road, a visit to Kilmore is more conveniently made on the return journey southwards. If you do go, try to make it Maytime, to drive through drifts of apple blossom.

Hewitt's romantic imagination did not allow him to be put in some conventional graveyard. He chose to be buried close to Ossian's Grave, in the townland of Lubitavish close to his home at Cushendall, on a high point of these tumbled mountains from where sometimes Scotland can be seen. Though it is known as Ossian's Grave, the site belongs to a period at least 2000 years before Ossian was thought of, who seems so remote:

> Ossian lies
> beneath this landmark on the hill
> asleep till Fionn and Oscar rise
> to summon his old bardic skill
> in hosting their last enterprise.

Follow the signpost for Ballymoney on the left, about a mile out of Cushendall, and then a laneway to the left which leads to the hilltop. Close to the bare stones of Ossian, a small monument resembling a miniature beehive cell marks the poet's resting place. It says only, on a small slab at the foot of the monument:

> John Hewitt
> 1907-87
> My chosen ground.

Another voice is heard in the glens — that of Moira O'Neill, a very different one from that of John Hewitt. She assumes the glenspeople's own 'folk' dialect, as here in 'Putting out from Cushendun':

> The wrack was dark an' shining when it floated in the sea,
> There was no one in the brown boat but only him an' me;
> Him to cut the sea wrack, me to mind the boat,
> An' not a word between us the hours we were afloat.
>> The wet wrack,
>> The sea wrack
>> The wrack was strong to cut.　　　　　　　　　　('Sea Wrack')

Folksy it might be, but in her simple verses she touches the true note of the glen folk-memory, in the exiles' grieving.

> Wathers o' Moyle I hear ye callin'
> Clearer for half o' the world between
> Antrim hills an' the wet rain falling ...
> What is the half of the world between?

Born Agnes Nesta Shakespeare Higginson, she took the name Moira O'Neill as more appropriate for the type of poetry she was writing. Her 'house upon the sea sand, a white house and low' is

Moira O'Neill's house at Cushendun

Moira O'Neill (1870-1951)

perched at the northern end of the curve of Cushendun beach. It is now the property of the National Trust. She was the mother of Mary Nesta Skrine who wrote under the name of M.J. Farrell.

Further north are the great cliffs of Fair Head and the town of Ballycastle whose annual Lammas Fair has a long tradition. Six miles (9.5 km) offshore is Rathlin Island with its one-hundred-strong community. Rathlin is 'The Island' of Michael MacLaverty's best-known novel *Call my Brother Back* and is the place to which the main character returns in *Truth in the Night*.

Up at the northern tip of Antrim, if four white swans breast the foam towards you, you will know that you have seen the ghosts of the Children of Lir. Here the sea hurls itself against the towering cliffs of Fair Head, throwing spray far inland. The jagged cliffs and towering rocks, interspersed with the occasional sweep of smoothed sand, tell of a tremendous battle with the sea. The Sea of Moyle stretches between here and the Scottish Hebrides; it always seems cold and fierce. This was the comfortless home of the Children of Lir in their swan form for three hundred years. Carrignarone, the rock where they found each other after being scattered by the fiercest storm, is surely the one seen just breaking the surface of the water well out from shore, below the cliffs at the western end of Ballycastle, and locally known as the Carraig. Carraig Uisneach, where Deirdre of the Sorrows and the sons of Uisneach came ashore on their return from Scotland, is on this same shore. *The Children of Lir* and *The Fate of the Sons of Uisneach* are two of the great tragic tales of Ireland. They, with a third, *The Children of Tuireann*, have come to be known as the Three Sorrows of Storytelling.

The Children of Lir, Finola and her three brothers, were turned to swans by their jealous stepmother, doomed to spend three hundred years each on Lough Derravaragh in Co. Westmeath, then on the Sea of Moyle, then on Inish Glora in the west. They were allowed to keep their power of speech and their sweet singing voices. Their worst times were those on the Sea of Moyle.

Though the Children of Lir is not of the greatest antiquity, many of the stories associated with it are from a literature far older than Christianity, though in their manuscript renderings, mainly penned by the early monks, these happenings of the old pagan world are often made respectable by a meeting with a saint or the sound of a church bell. So in the version that has come down to us, the Children of Lir regained their original form just in time to be baptised by a saint, and to die decently 'in a state of grace.'

The sons of Uisneach were 'the three bright candles of the Gael.' Naoise was the fated lover of Deirdre — Deirdre of the Sorrows — who was promised to the king, Conor MacNessa. Deirdre and Naoise eloped to Scotland, accompanied by the two brothers. Conor enticed

Michael Mac Laverty (1907-1993)

Padraic Fiacc
Robin Glendinning
Marie Jones
Maurice Leitch
Robert MacLiam Wilson
Maedbh McGuckian
Bernard McLaverty
Conall Morrison
Glenn Patterson
Tom Paulin
Vincent Woods
See *Crossing the Millennium* page 260–261

The Giant's Causeway

The Giant's Causeway has been written about as much as Killarney has, ever since Victorian times and probably earlier. We'll content ourselves with the words of Arthur Young from his *Tour in Ireland* in 1776:

'Rode from Mr. Leslie's to view the Giant's Causeway. It is certainly a very great curiosity, as an object for speculation, upon the manner of its formation. Whether it owes its origin to fire, and is a species of lava, or to crystallisation, or to whatever cause, is a point that has employed the attention of men much more able to decide upon it than I am, and has been so often treated, that nothing I could say could be new.'

Exactly. An elaborate Information Centre will tell you all you want to know about this extraordinary place, and more.

Antrim town:
The home of Alexander Irvine, author of the much-loved My Lady of the Chimney Corner, *can be found next door to the Tourist Information Office, in Pogue's Entry.*

them back with fair promises, but betrayed and killed the three young warriors. In one telling of the story Deirdre decently died of her sorrow; in another she goes finally with the old king 'for what else is a woman to do?'

Stories of the Fianna continued to evolve well into late medieval times, and chronicle their own decline in the face of the new religion. Even the great Oisín in his last lament cries:

I am the last of the Fianna, great Oisín, son of Finn, listening to the voice of the bells; it is long the clouds are over me to-night!

To the Fianna, the sound of bells brought not peace and sanctity but an end to their great elemental days of hunting and feasting, fighting and courting. There is a marvellous account of a long debate between an aged Oisín, back from his centuries in the Land of Youth, and St Patrick, Oisín arguing that Finn and the Fianna, and the lives that they led, were better far than the rewards offered by Patrick's god. Oisín complained that he couldn't understand all that fuss about just an apple: Fionn had in his time given whole orchards away. When Patrick told him that Finn was in bonds in hell for his disrespect to God, Oisín boasted that if the sons of Morna were there, or if Faolan and Goll were living, 'and brown-haired Diarmuid and brave Osgar, Finn of the Fianna could not be held in any house that was made by god or devils.'

Old **Bushmills** is a name which resonates with a different kind of spirit: Uisce Beatha, the Water of Life. Bushmills has been making fine whiskey since 1608, and you will be shown how if you care to visit the distillery. It may make you appreciate its fiery virtues even more to know that water from St Columb's Rill, a tributary of the River Bush, runs into the source of the water used in the manufacture — so it could be claimed that holy water is used. It also explains 'St Columb's Beef' on the local hostelry menu — the dish is laced with Old Bushmills.

As you're so far along, you may as well continue to pretty **Ballintrae** with its sand-fringed shore, and to **Dunluce Castle**, the ultimate of romantic ruins, standing perched on a sea-girt rock. One stormy night in 1639 a portion of the castle broke away and fell into the sea during a night of revelry. Legend has it that the kitchen and all the kitchen staff went with it, disappearing into a watery grave — possibly unnoticed by the revellers.

Returning southwards by way of Ballymoney and Ballymena, the striking isolated shape of St Patrick's **Slemish** mountain dominates the skyline to the east of the latter town. There is the opportunity to visit Antrim town, which has Ireland's most perfect Round Tower, and the demesne of Shane's Castle extending west from the town. But our literary wanderer will be more interested in the tiny alleyway called Pogue's Entry. It was here that Alexander Irvine, who wrote *My Lady* *of the Chimney Corner*, was born. His house has been nicely conserved as a memorial to him, with a little garden adjoining. John Hewitt was a great admirer, and says that it was it was from Irvine that he grew to value often-told stories that had been honed and polished by repetition.

Alexander Irvine (c.1860-1926)

Four miles to the east, in the valley of the Six Mile Water, is the village — hardly even a village — of **Donegore**. It is signposted from the Belfast motorway. There can be few places on earth with an air as peaceful as that of the Church of St John at the foot of Donegore Hill. Old trees overlook it and doves flutter about. In the churchyard is the grave of Sir Samuel Ferguson:

> Nor may I less be counted one
> With Davis, Mangan, Ferguson

prayed W. B. Yeats. And it is true that Yeats was a follower of those three, not just in time but in impulse.

Ferguson came from the background of literary Protestant gentlemen of the nineteenth century. He was born in Belfast in the early days of that century, but the family seat had been Donegore, and he continued to identify with it, and often visited it. He was a lawyer and archaeologist, and in his later years became President of the Royal Irish Academy. He became interested in traditional music and the Irish language when he was quite young, moved to Dublin, to Trinity College, and become one of a group comprising among others John O'Donovan, the Ordnance Survey scholar, and Eugene O'Curry. He turned with great enthusiasm to the old mythologies, and began to write long narrative poems such as 'Congal', which recounts in epic style a battle between an Ulster prince and his foster-father the King of Ireland which took place in AD 637, and 'The Vengeance of the Welshmen of Tirawley', another tale of bitterness and revenge. Yeats described him as being 'consumed with one absorbing purpose, the purpose to create an Irish school of literature, and overshadowed by one masterful enthusiasm, an enthusiasm for all Gaelic and Irish things.' His was a beautiful translation of Cashel of Munster, a much-loved and popular song in the *sean-nós* (old mode) tradition:

> I'd wed you without herds, without money, or rich array,
> And I'd wed you on a dewy morning at day-dawn grey;
> My bitter woe it is, love, that we are not far away
> In Cashel town, though the bare deal board were our marriage-bed this day.

and of the love-poem 'Ceann Dubh Dílis' or 'Darling Dark Head':

> Put your head, darling, darling, darling,
> Your darling black head on my heart above;
> Oh, mouth of honey, with the thyme for fragrance,
> Who with heart in breast could deny you love?

Samuel Ferguson (1810-1886)

The three Brontë sisters, Charlotte, Emily and Anne, painted by their brother Branwell.

The Brontës

His also was the plaintive 'Lament for Thomas Davis', leader of the idealistic Young Irelander movement of the nineteenth century, who died when he was only thirty years of age:

> I walked through Ballinderry in the spring time,
>   When the bud was on the tree,
> And I said, in every fresh-ploughed field beholding
>   The sowers striding free,
> Scattering broad cast for the corn in golden plenty
>   On the quick, seed-clasping soil,
> 'Even such this day among the fresh-stirred hearts of Erin
>   Thomas Davis, is thy toil.'

The Famine interrupted this early Gaelic Revival, and it was some decades later before, as William Trevor put it, 'the half-lost Ireland of the hedge-schools, of the oral tradition and the Irish language, crept into the warmth of Anglo-Irish hospitality' under the guidance of Douglas Hyde, Lady Gregory and Yeats.

Donegore Hill itself (entered through a Garden Nursery) is an ancient earthwork. It has not been excavated, and is thought to cover a passage-grave. Flint arrow-heads are frequently found around the place. Ferguson, that great romantic, is happy no doubt in company with the ancients, on his own ancestral ground.

Continue on southwards to **Banbridge**.

Brunty. Branty. Prunty. O'Prounty. They are all Anglicisations of the Irish name Ó Pronntaigh, and are not uncommon around the north-east. But the version which has achieved literary note is, of course, Brontë. And Patrick Prunty, or Brontë, father of that extra-ordinary Haworth family, came from Emdale, or Imdel, between Rathfriland and Banbridge. The church where he preached and the school in which he taught at Drumballyroney is kept as a small museum relating to the family. The church is prominent on top of a hill 1 mile (1.6 km) out from Rathfriland (tel. 0808 206 31152). The Curator, Carol Brontë, is not herself a relation but is married to James Wallace Brontë, the oldest surviving member of the clan. A signposted Brontë Homeland Drive takes visitors to various locations associated with the family, including the old home, now little more than a shell.

It is said that Emily, Charlotte and the others inherited their literary genius from Patrick's father, Hugh, who grew up in the Boyne Valley near Newgrange, and was a noted storyteller even in an area which in the mid-nineteenth century was rich in Ossianic tales and poetry. Patrick himself brought plenty of tales of ghosts and monsters and other supernatural manifestations with him, which intrigued and frightened his children. The Pruntys were Protestants, so that Hugh's marriage to Catholic Eilish 'of the luminous gold hair' was a runaway one. They had ten children and by all accounts they were a lively and boisterous lot. Patrick, the eldest, appears not to have been anxious to have much to do with his siblings after he went to England. Charlotte did not visit them when she came to Ireland on her honeymoon — though there is a story of one of the uncles setting off for England with a shillelagh to deal with the reviewer who had criticised *Jane Eyre*. Presumably Patrick, in his clerical status, wished to preserve his appearance of an adequately respectable background.

Kilmore mentioned earlier, where John Hewitt's ancestors came from and about which he has written so affectionately, is just off the main road halfway between Portadown and Armagh.

Armagh has always been an important place. It has been the ecclesiastical capital of Ireland since St Patrick established his principal church there around the year 444. The Catholic and Church of Ireland Cathedrals observe each other from adjoining hilltops. There is little left untold about Armagh's claims to glory between the Heritage Centre which has been created at what used to be the Palace Demesne of the latter's Archbishop, and the extensive tourist and 'interpretive' complex which is named St Patrick's Trian.

In the Trian, amongst the various subjects represented by 'three-dimensional models and tableaux displays combined with hi-tech atmospherics' as the brochure describes them, will be found a fantasy based on 'The Land of Lilliput'. Jonathan Swift was a frequent visitor to Armagh during the 1720s, spending long visits with the Copes at Loughgall and with the Achesons at Markethill. In several poems he confesses to being a difficult guest. He bullied the Achesons into elaborate garden 'improvements,' probably not always to their taste and very much at their expense, and dragged poor Lady Acheson into long walks up hills and 'through bogs and through briars.' He had a fine time too swopping banter with the Irish workmen and learning bits of Irish, sure he was being man to man with them.

Many treasures were created during Armagh's long ecclesiastical history, not least among them the Book of Armagh. Despite its small size and relative lack of decoration, it is regarded as by far the most important of Ireland's historical manuscripts, and contains the earliest extant copy of 'The Confessions of St Patrick'. The manuscript was nearly lost to Ireland forever around 1680 when the hereditary Keeper, Florence Mac Maor, pawned it for £5 (and didn't redeem it) in order to pay for his trip to London to testify against Oliver Plunkett, the Archbishop, who was being tried and was executed for high treason. It is now preserved in the library of Trinity College, Dublin.

Derek Mahon's 'The Banished Gods' could almost be an echo from the old manuscript collections :

It is here that the banished gods are in hiding,
    Here they sit out the centuries
      In stone, water
    And the hearts of trees,
Lost in a reverie of their own natures —

Of zero-growth economics and seasonal change
    In a world without cars, computers
      Or chemical skies,
    Where thought is a fondling of stones
And wisdom a five-minute silence at moonrise.

Jonathan Swift (1667-1745)

St Patrick's Breastplate

Christ with me, Christ before me, Christ behind me,
Christ in me, Christ beneath me, Christ above me,
Christ on my right, Christ on my left,
Christ when I lie down, Christ when I sit down, Christ when I arise.
Christ in the heart of every man who thinks of me,
Christ in the mouth of every one who speaks of me,
Christ in every eye that sees me,
Christ in every ear that hears me.

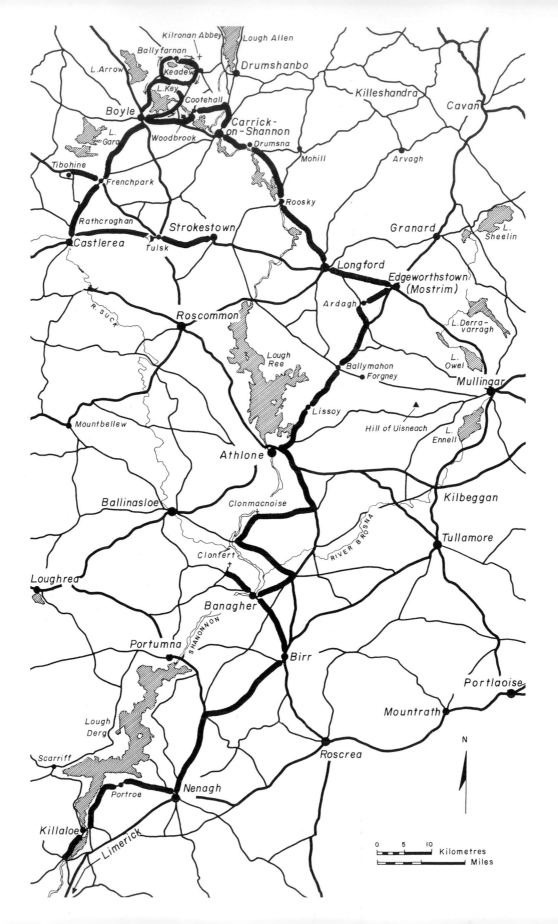

Kilronan Abbey
Lough Allen
Ballyfarnan
Drumshanbo
L. Arrow
Keadew
Killeshandra
Cavan
L. Key
Cootehall
Boyle
Carrick-on-Shannon
Woodbrook
Drumsna
L. Gara
Mohill
Arvagh
Tibohine
Roosky
Frenchpark
Granard
L. Sheelin
Rathcroghan
Strokestown
Castlerea
Tulsk
Longford
Edgeworthstown (Mostrim)
Ardagh
R. SUCK
Roscommon
Ballymahon
Forgney
L. Derra-varragh
Lough Ree
L. Owel
Mullingar
Lissoy
Hill of Uisneach
Mountbellew
L. Ennell
Athlone
Kilbeggan
Ballinasloe
Clonmacnoise
RIVER BROSNA
Tullamore
Clonfert
Loughrea
Banagher
Portumna
Birr
Portlaoise
SHANNON
Mountrath
Lough Derg
Roscrea
Scarriff
N
Portroe
Nenagh
Killaloe
Limerick

0 5 10 Kilometres
Miles

15. MIDLANDS
By the oldest Highway

So far our journeys have kept us fairly close to the coast, forming something of a circuit of Ireland. That has left untouched the whole midland area with its many literary landscapes.

In early days, before roads and railways, the rivers were the highways. The Shannon is Ireland's major river, flowing all the way from close by the Border with Northern Ireland to the sea at Limerick. 'The spacious Shannon spreading like a sea,' as Spenser has it. If we follow some of those early travellers, and stay close to the Shannon, we will meet up with such diverse figures as Oliver Goldsmith and Maria Edgeworth, Douglas Hyde and Percy French, Anthony Trollope and Charlotte Brontë. We will travel northwards, as did the early explorers, both welcome and unwelcome. So, leaving Limerick behind we come to Killaloe.

> Oh, where, Kinkora! is Brian the Great?
>   And where is the beauty that once was thine?
> Oh, where are the princes and nobles that sate
>   At the feast in thy halls, and drank the red wine?
>   Where, oh Kinkora? ...
>
> I am Mac Liag, and my home is on the Lake:
>   Thither often, to that palace whose beauty is fled
> Came Brian to ask me, and I went for his sake
>   Oh, my grief! that I should live, and Brian be dead!
>   Dead, oh, Kinkora!

So does the poet James Clarence Mangan render yet another Irish lament for departed glories, this one attributed to MacLiag who was Brian Ború's own bard. It could be argued that the present-day glories of luxury cruising-craft, for which Killaloe is a major centre, match any that are ages departed. Be that as it may, they so far haven't earned a place in the pages of literature. Brian Ború, Brian the Great, has inspired quite a share. The founder of the great O'Brien dynasty, he was High King of Ireland from 1002 until he was killed while defeating the Vikings at the decisive Battle of Clontarf near Dublin in 1014.

The town of Killaloe stands on a hill overlooking the river and

Above: St Molua's Oratory, Killaloe

Marina Carr
See *Crossing the Millennium*, page 261

Charlotte Brontë (1816-1855)

northwards towards Lough Derg. Brian's royal residence, Kincora, stood on the hilltop, a site now occupied by the Catholic Church. All traces of the 'palace' have disappeared, but there are other links with the past. The oratory which stands in the grounds of the church, the oratory of St Molua (for whom Killaloe is named), originally stood on Friar's Island. It was re-erected here when the island was submerged in the creation of the Shannon Hydro-Electric Scheme. (The notice erected by the Office of Public Works states guardedly that it is 'a reasonably exact' replica of the original church). It could date back to Brian's own time, or near it. St Flannan's stone-roofed oratory, in the grounds of the Protestant Cathedral at the foot of the hill, is almost as old. A lofty tree-planted ringfort about a mile (2 km) along the western shore of the lake is associated with Brian Ború by name, although dating from centuries before his time. From here we can look north-wards towards Cragleigh hill, and the rock near the hill-top called Carrickeeval, the seat of Aoibheall, Queen of the shee, whom we left in County Clare presiding over the taunting and torture of an unfor-tunate poet.

A lake-side drive, more interesting than the main road, brings us to Nenagh with its striking circular donjon, part of a thirteenth-century Butler stronghold, from where we can continue to Birr, County Offaly.

Birr is an elegant town, an orderly eighteenth-century place, and seat of the Parsons, Earls of Rosse, the gardens of whose castle open from the town's streets. The Parsons were a remarkable family of scientists, the best known of whom was the third Earl, Charles Parsons, a noted astronomer. In the 1850s, the scientific world was buzzing with rumours of the extraordinary discoveries relating to the celestial bodies being made by the enormous telescope, largest in the world, that the Earl had built in the garden of his estate at Birr (the frame still stands there). It is probable, however, that the revelations about the spiral nature of nebulae were not foremost in the mind of Charlotte Brontë when on 8 July 1854 she alighted from the train at Birr railway station (which is, unlike the telescope mounting, now gone). With her was her new husband, Rev. Arthur Bell Nicholls, and it was their honeymoon trip. They were on their way to Banagher to visit Arthur's relatives.

Her visit to Cuba Court, Banagher, marked a transformation in Charlotte's brief married life. Arthur and his brother Alan had grown up there, where his Uncle ran a school for boys. (The house got its name from its builder, George Frazer, who had been Governor of Cuba). At home here with his numerous warm-hearted and carefree relatives, the shy, awkward, clumsy curate so despised by Charlotte's father, whom Charlotte had married with grave reservations and in the teeth of her father's opposition, came 'out of himself' and became a different man entirely. She was most pleasantly surprised and pleased by the gentility, as well as the gaiety, of the family. Mrs Bell, Nicholl's uncle's widow, was widely read, and played the piano. 'She is like an English or Scottish matron,' wrote Charlotte to a friend — evidently, in her eyes, the very height of praise. She was compelled to look at her lowly curate with new eyes. As his personality and looks improved in this happy and loving atmosphere, Charlotte Brontë fell deeply in love with her husband. Before they left for home they visited Kilkee, Glengarriff and Killarney, where Charlotte fell off one of the Gap of Dunloe ponies, but apparently to no ill-effect.

Poor Charlotte had only nine months to enjoy her unexpected happiness. Within the year she was dead, from the combination of a severe chest infection and a difficult pregnancy. Nicholls stayed on at Haworth Parsonage until the death of old Patrick Brontë. He then returned to Banagher, married one of the Bell cousins, and lived out the rest of his life at Hill House, still the Church of Ireland Rectory. Little is left now of the Cuba Court, the home of Arthur Nicholls' relatives, but the grand gateway still stands just beyond the northern fringe of the town. We can only imagine what the finely-proportioned early eighteenth-century house would have been like in its heyday, with young people spilling out of its porticoed doors on to well-kept lawns, planning picnics and boating trips on the Shannon.

At the time of the Nicholls' honeymoon visit, Anthony Trollope, still unknown as a novelist, had just recently left Banagher, where he had first begun to discover the joys of living, to take up residence in Clonmel. He had arrived in Ireland in 1841, an unhappy, impoverished, dejected Post Office clerk, twenty-six years old, who took up the Irish posting more in despair than in anticipation.

His mother Fanny Trollope, a popular novelist, had no time for her youngest son; she was having the time of her life being lionised on the Continent. Anthony was graceless and lacking in confidence, and in London had carried out his work extremely badly, because he hated it so much. But that all changed. From his first setting foot in Ireland, he writes, 'all these evils went away from me. Since that time who has had a happier life than mine?'

In his early days he stayed at the bow-fronted Shannon Hotel. The Post Office was just a bit up the street on the left, a two-storeyed double-fronted house with fanlight and a tiny cottage next to it which he and his superior used as an office. Here he carried out his work with enthusiasm and, it seems, a newly-acquired authoritarian air. His job gave him contacts and a better social standing, and he got taken up in the usual Irish jollity. He joined the Galway Blazers, and his adven-

Headstones of various Bells in the churchyard of St Paul's Church, Banagher, including that of the Reverend Arthur Bell Nicholls, who had been Charlotte Brontë's husband. The headstone does not mention Charlotte; it merely states that he was 'formerly curate of Haworth, Yorkshire'

Anthony Trollope (1815-1882)

EDITOR'S NOTE:
Unfortunately, nothing of Arthur Nicholls' home is left standing today.

tures 'in the field' gave him material for his 'Hunting Sketches' which were serialised in *Pall Mall* magazine during 1865-6.

His work entailed much travelling around the country (indeed his income depended on it, as he earned more from 'expenses' than from salary), and his impressions and experiences are reflected in his Irish novels. *The Macdermots of Ballycloran* was his first novel, followed by *The Kellys and the O'Kellys*. The first took shape in his mind around a derelict house he happened upon during a walk near Drumsna, in the higher reaches of the Shannon, though in the novel he made the absentee Lord Birmingham the owner of the estate of Mohill, which he described as a place of miserable hovels, unvisited and ignored by his lordship, although they were the source of much of his wealth. At Drumsna also, in the middle of the night an intruder entered his room. He grappled with him and threw him downstairs, to discover to his embarrassment that the 'intruder' was the local priest, whose room it properly was. That incident gave rise to 'Fr Giles of Ballymoy'.

The only blot on his happy days of dancing and hunting appears to have been the awful Irish cooking. From that point of view alone, it must have been a great joy to him when he was able to bring his bride, Rose, to Banagher. Rose might not have been too flattered by his statement that he depended completely on the laziness of young ladies for his livelihood; that he, as a novelist, was their moral teacher, as most of their education came from novels!

Though Trollope came to Ireland with the usual prejudice of his class and period, he gradually became more politically conscious, and in *The Land Leaguers* and *An Eye for an Eye* he addressed the problems of the relationship between England and Ireland, and the question of Home Rule, to which he was bitterly opposed, while indignant at what he saw as England's neglect of her responsibilities. He stayed in Ireland for about seventeen years, based in turn in Banagher, Clonmel, Mallow and Midleton. He eventually became Post Office Surveyor in Belfast, later taking off on assignments to Egypt and other far-flung places, before eventually dying — laughing, it is recorded — in London in 1882.

Both Brontë and Trollope had their views on the state of matrimony. Charlotte wrote indulgently and apparently happily that a woman's time was never her own thereafter: that her husband's wishes dominated in all matters: that his opinions were automatically right. Trollope, on the other hand, in several of his stories indicated that matrimony — even engagement — was for the woman a triumph, for the man it was 'as though the man had been subdued, brought at length into a cage and tamed, so as to be made fit for domestic purposes, and deprived of his ancient freedom among the woods' — or so he has Colonel Stubbs thinking in 'Ayala's Angel'.

We now come to Clonfert, in County Galway, closely associated with St Brendan the Navigator. He it was that, according to the story which was well known throughout Europe in the Middle Ages, made the fabulous journey westwards via an Island of Birds, an Island of Sheep, an Island of Smiths and other wondrous landfalls until eventually coming to a Land of Fruit and the Island of Delights. Modern scholars have argued convincingly that the land he arrived at was, in fact, North America — and this a thousand years before Columbus.

He voyaged to this part of the midlands too, possibly by the Shannon river. He founded a monastery at Clonfert (about 5 miles, 8 km, north-east of Banagher) about the year 600 AD. It was ravaged by Vikings in 844 and several times by fire — by whose hand is not recorded. The present Protestant church was built in the twelfth century as a Cathedral to succeed Brendan's church. As a Christian church it is practically unique: the Romanesque arcading of the door-way is surmounted by serried ranks of heads — of saints or bishops, no doubt, but in fact their stark presence summons up the age-old celtic cult of the severed head, surviving seven hundred years after Saint Patrick's conversion of the Irish. Clonfert is Brendan's last resting place. Appropriately, a mermaid is carved there, a strange addition from the fifteenth century. With her comb and her mirror, she is a gentler reflection of monastic imagination.

Back to Banagher, then northwards to one of the sweetest places in all of Ireland. Clonmacnois is the 'St Kieran's City Fair' of an old Irish poem, well-known in the Victorian version by R.W. Rolleston:

> In a quiet water'd land, a land of roses,
>   Stands Saint Kieran's city fair;
> And the warriors of Erin in their famous generations
>   Slumber there.
>
> There beneath the dewy hillside sleep the noblest
>   Of the clan of Conn,
> Each below his stone with name in branching Ogham
>   And the sacred knot thereon.

And he names as resting there the seven kings of Tara, the sons of Cairbre, the men of Teffia, many a son of Conn the Hundred-fighter, and so on. Rory O'Connor, the last king of Ireland, whom Rolleston doesn't mention, is actually buried there.

It is indeed a gentle and peaceful place for a last sleep. Its atmosphere is palpable as you reach it even by road, but to come upon it by water, as did the travellers of old — emulated by the pleasure-cruisers of today — is a deeply moving experience.

St Kieran founded what became one of Ireland's foremost monasteries

Oliver Goldsmith (1728-1774)

The parsonage (by R.H. Newell), Pallas, Co Longford, reputedly the birthplace of Oliver Goldsmith on 10 November 1728 ... 'the village preacher's modest mansion'.

here in the year 545. What remains are eight churches, two round towers, three high crosses, and hundreds of early gravestones. Clonmacnois was regarded as representing the final triumph of Christianity over paganism:

> 'Rathcroghan, it has vanished with Ailill offspring of victory: fair
> the sovranty over princes that there is in the monastery of Clonmacnois.
> Choirs lasting, melodious, around Ciaran, if thou shouldst mention him:
> with the victorious tumult of great Clonmacnois'

claimed the *Martyrology of Oengus* about the year 800, with perfect faith.

But these reflections could deflect us from our literary ramblings — though it be time well spent. Let us turn to face the road again, and the town of Athlone, County Westmeath, and then northwards, on the eastern shores of Lough Ree, to the territory of Oliver Goldsmith. It is not dramatic country, but Goldsmith loved it dearly. It shines through his verses in *The Deserted Village*: his Sweet Auburn is Lissoy in disguise:

> Sweet Auburn! Loveliest village of the plain
> Where health and plenty cheered the labouring swain,

Where smiling spring its earliest visit paid,
And parting summer's lingering blooms delayed.

He was born in the year 1728, though the exact day appears to be in dispute. And the same with the place. Was it at the house at Pallas which his father rented while rector of Forgney near Ballymahon? Or at Ardnagowan, which would then have been called Smith Hill, the house of his grandmother? Both claim him. In any case, the family moved to Lissoy shortly after. He attended a hedge-school there, and wrote an appreciative, or ironic, description of his schoolmaster, Thomas Byrne, which includes the much-quoted lines:

> While words of learned length, and thundering sound,
> Amaz'd the gazing rustics rang'd around;
> And still they gaz'd, and still the wonder grew,
> That one small head could carry all he knew.

School, however, wasn't of great interest to him. The author of some of the great masterpieces of the English language idled away his youth, throwing stones at ducks and spending his nights playing cards. He was a great hand at the local sport of handball, won a prize throwing the hammer at Ballymahon fair, drank and gamed with the locals, played the flute and sang in the pubs, gambled and fought.

He attended Trinity College in Dublin, but left without a degree. At one stage he decided to set out for America, and bought his passage, but was at a party when the ship sailed, and arrived home penniless. After his father died, an uncle sent him to the Inns of Court in London, but he gambled away the money before he got there. His exasperated family then sent him to Edinburgh to try to make a doctor of him, and he seems to have gained a dubious degree, and set off wandering around Europe earning his way playing the flute, before returning to London and various odd jobs.

By then he had taken up writing to supplement his income. And his life changed. 'Poor Noll', the reluctant scholar from the Irish midlands, within a couple of years had entered the most select literary society in London and become the friend of Dr Samuel Johnson, Sir Joshua Reynolds, James Boswell. They loved him, and showered praise on him and his writing. But he never acquired real social confidence. 'I have spent more than a fortnight every second day at the Duke of Hamilton's, but it seems they like me more as a jester than as a companion,' he wrote to a cousin. Despite all the gaiety and colour of London society, his mind returned nostalgically to his home ground. He begged for news: 'I know you cant send much news from Ballymahon but such as it is send it all everything you write will be agreeable and entertaining to me. Has George Conway put up a signe yet has John Binley left off drinking Drams; or Tom Allen got a new wig?'

Forgney church

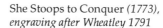

She Stoops to Conquer *(1773),*
engraving after Wheatley 1791

Maria Edgeworth (1767-1849)

His most famous work, *The Deserted Village,* is the story of a hamlet destroyed by the greed of an absentee landlord, and the portrait is recognisably that of Lissoy. But there are few material connections with 'poor Noll' left to see today. The church at Forgney in which his father and brothers used to preach has been replaced, though a stained glass window in the 'new' one commemorates our Oliver. The house at Lissoy is no more, and The Three Jolly Pigeons, though a congenial place, is not the original Ale House of *The Deserted Village.* To add to the difficulties, the signposts cannot be relied on, as the old sport of twisting them around, almost disappeared from the rest of the countryside, still thrives in the Ballymahon area.

More tangible is the house at **Ardagh**, County Longford, an exceptionally pretty village tucked away off the road towards Longford, where Goldsmith took shelter one wet wintry night and started ordering around Sir George Fetherstone, the owner, and his daughter, thinking he was in an inn and was talking to the proprietor and servant girl. That incident he turned into his first real commercial success, the play *She Stoops to Conquer.* The house is now a rural science college, and doesn't look much like it did in those days. The literary pilgrim in search of Goldsmith should pay a visit also to the County Library at Mullingar, County Westmeath. *The Vicar of Wakefield*, for which the author was paid £60, is thought to be the world's most illustrated English novel. The library holds the Kirby Collection of some 250 different volumes, which include the work of almost every major illustrator over more than a century.

Even at the height of his success this genius who 'touched nothing that he did not adorn', according to Samuel Johnson, was still pining. 'I sit and sigh for the Lissoy fireside, and Johnny Armstrong's Last Good-Night from Peggy Golden.' Presumably at the alehouse, his friendly neighbourhood Three Jolly Pigeons. Goldsmith would have been familiar too with the estate of **Edgeworthstown**, at Mostrim, where Maria Edgeworth, 'the great Maria', broke through the barriers of a man's world to publish a series of novels that were not only successful, but pioneering in their time. She inspired the regional novels of Sir Walter Scott, and Turgenev said that he would never have found his own subjects were it not for her stories of landlords and peasants. King George III, after reading it, said 'I know something now of my Irish subjects.'

Castle Rackrent tells the story of the decline of a family of profligate landlords. It is told in the colloquial narrative voice of a workman on the estate, one Thady Quirke ('though in the family I have always been known by no other than 'Honest Thady'') who is modelled on an estate steward, John Landy. A succession of land owners ruin themselves and the estate through dissipation, lawsuits, bad marriages and absence. In the end they have to sell out, to Thady's hated son Jason. The novel was an immediate success, and was closely followed by *Belinda, The Absentee, Ennui* and many others. *Ormond* is a kind of Irish *Tom Jones*, and traces the maturing of a wild young Irishman after a gay life in England, in learning to manage his Irish estate. The kingdom of Cornelius O'Shane of the novel is The Black Isles near the centre of nearby Lough Ree. These books were all written in close collaboration with Maria's father, with whom she also produced a series of educational treatises. Together they also produced an *Essay on Irish Bulls*, which was remarkable for its lack of humour, despite the fact that neither father nor daughter were at all lacking in humour or wit.

Maria wrote at length about the extraordinary household of the Martins of Connemara (see Chapter 9). Her own household at Edgeworthstown was remarkable enough. She herself was a tiny lady, less than five feet tall, with a large nose, red-rimmed eyes and thin straight hair — a real ugly duckling, and a strange figure to find lionised in London and Paris. But her father, after several unsuccessful attempts to get her married, made her his companion and collaborator, and involved her in all his affairs. Richard Lovell Edgeworth was an inventor, scientist, educationalist, politician, writer and humane landlord. He had four wives and twenty-two children, and boasted when he was almost sixty that he could still jump on to a table from a standing position. His inventions included a velocipede — a kind of forerunner to the bicycle which unfortunately ran away with someone before he had added the brakes; a wind driven carriage with a triangular sail like a yacht which, also unfortunately, frightened the horses and, besides, got stuck on the narrow bridges while on a beat; a telegraph system, a perambulator for measuring land, a turnip-cutter and something he called a portable railway. He instigated a new way of building a church spire, by building it inside the church and hauling it up inside like an umbrella — which he carried out on the church at Edgeworthstown. His talents were so many and so various that he overspread himself, flitting from one thing to another sometimes before he had completed the first, jumping on to the next with an excess of zest and enthusiasm.

All the children participated in conversations with callers to the house, no matter how distinguished, and in discussions on mechanical and scientific topics. In the evenings everyone was gathered together in the library to hear what Maria or their father had written that day, and to comment on it.

Tiny Maria may have been, and, in her early years at any rate, shy and awkward, but she was a formidable lady. Apart from her large literary output, she travelled quite a bit and carried on lengthy correspondence with numerous members of her family and friends. After

Richard Lovell Edgeworth

her father's death she took over completely the running of the estate, rescuing it from a state of decline. She died at Edgeworthstown on 22 May 1849, aged 82, and is buried in the cemetery of St John's Church (Church of Ireland) just off the main street (where, incidentally, is buried also a sister of Oscar Wilde's who died as a child). The Edgeworth tomb is immediately outside the church door and there are memorial tablets to several Edgeworths inside the church. There is also a small collection of memorabilia relating to Maria Edgeworth. This includes a marble-topped table given to her by Sir Walter Scott. The house, now greatly altered, is run as a nursing home by the Sisters of Mercy.

The Edgeworth family (by Aidan Buck), 1787, shows Maria on left facing Richard her father. His third wife sits beside him with an infant in her arms, and her four little children cluster around. The four older children from left are Emmeline, Lovell, Anna and Honora.

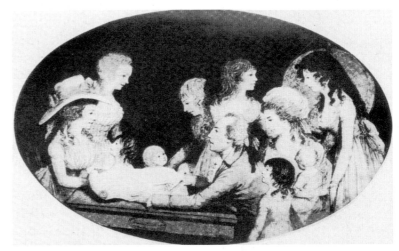

Pádraic Colum (1881-1972)

Next comes **Longford** town. The workhouse sounds a strange and chilly place to be born, but the workhouse at Longford was where the poet Pádraic Colum, that highly respected man of letters on two sides of the Atlantic, first saw the light. His father was master there at the time, that is in 1881. Grim places these workhouses were. Only the totally destitute were taken in, wives were separated from husbands, and all rights to even the tiniest smallholding had to be renounced. However, young Colum and his seven siblings at least benefited by the tales and reminiscences of the inmates, and a visiting doctor who quoted Shakespeare. Father drank himself out of the job eventually, and the youngsters were despatched to relatives in County Cavan, before they all moved to Sandycove in the Dublin suburbs. Later, when Pádraic was working in Dublin and became involved with the Literary Renaissance group, he was lucky enough to be awarded a scholarship by an American banker, which allowed him to devote himself completely to writing. He justified it by an enormous output during subsequent years.

Back to the Shannon, and through the riverside villages of Roosky and Drumsna to Carrick-on-Shannon, a surprisingly drab town in view of its marina of gleaming and glamorous pleasure-cruisers. A road northwards from here follows the Shannon proper through Drumshanbo and along the shores of Lough Allen. Our route, however, takes us in a more or less westerly direction, through winding roads which tread their way through and around the complex lakelets of the Boyle River, which is part of the Shannon navigation, to the village of **Cootehall**.

Lough Key is the most beautiful of all the cruising waters. It is a little difficult to relate this bright and water-glinting landscape to that of John McGahern's *The Barracks* and *The Dark*, beautifully-written novels indeed, but gloomy. It takes more than pretty scenery to nourish a soul withering with hopelessness or poverty, and McGahern has a great gift for describing the attrition of provincial life. He grew up in Cootehall, in the barracks where his father was a police officer and which gave him the setting for his first novel *The Barracks*. The landscape takes shape in the novels and short stories, 'the sluggish Shannon flowing between its wheaten reeds,' Lough Key, Gloria Bog, Slieve an Iarainn — 'names bedded for ever in my life, as eternal.' Bedded also in his life, as eternal, must be the fact that he lost his job as a schoolteacher after the publication of *The Dark*, a story about the pains of adolescence, banned in 1965 despite high critical acclaim.

John McGahern (1934-   )

Not far away from Cootehall, on the other side of the river, stands Woodbrook House. To it, in the year 1932, came eighteen-year-old David Thomson, then an Oxford student, who had taken a summer job as tutor to young Phoebe Kirkwood. The foundations were laid for a gentle evocation of two loves — for Phoebe, and for the house and its surroundings, which appeared in Thomson's book *Woodbrook*, published in 1974. It beautifully evokes the life of an Anglo-Irish family just before the war, and the countryside around Lough Key:

David Thomson (1914–1988)

Approaching Carrick (on-Shannon) from Boyle on the Sligo-Boyle road, you pass Woodbrook on your left, then two miles farther on Clongoonagh where the other branch of the Kirkwood family had lived for several generations. Then the road slopes down. You cross the Shannon by an old stone bridge, pleasantly narrow and long, with low parapets that give a view of the wide river that shines like gun-metal in cloudy weather and on clear days is blue like a calm sea bay ...

This is an area to linger in, to drop anchor and give yourself time to explore the network of little roads and small and big lakes: perhaps to settle in with a copy of Thomson's *Woodbrook* or McGahern's *Amongst Women* (there are several gracious and comfortable guest houses in the region). **Lough Key Forest Park** is a glorious place. The land was once the property of the MacDermots, for centuries the princes of Moylurg, before it passed into the hands of the Harmon-King family to become the Rockingham Estate. Rockingham House burned down in 1957, after which the estate was bought by the State. It was part of the world which young Thomson shared briefly with the Kirkwoods:

We often used to visit Rockingham, the nearest large demesne. Its nearest gatelodge — there were five, I think — was at Ardcarne by the church the Kirkwoods went to every Sunday, bringing me with them when I would go; but if you wanted to go down the most beautiful roadway in the country you had to enter by the main gate half a mile farther on and turn into the Beech Avenue, a tunnel of leaves in summer, a lovely long way lined by strong old beeches between which you saw acre upon acre of rich pasture wooded here and there. At the end of it Rockingham House came into view, a splendid house, built on rising ground beside the lake, of the most hideous architecture conceivable.

The lake, scattered with wooded islands, is one of the gems of the Shannon system. On Castle Island, prominent off-shore, Tadhg Mac-Dermot, patron of the arts, feasted the literati of Ireland in the year 1541. In a later century, W.B. Yeats thought to set up a community there: 'I planned a mystical Order which should buy or hire the castle, and keep it as a place where its members could retire for a while for contemplation, and where we might establish mysteries like those of Eleusis and Samothrace; and for ten years to come my most impassioned thought was a vain attempt to find philosophy and to create ritual for that Order' (from *Hodos Chameliontos*). He had come to the lake in search of local memory of the story of Úna Bán and Strong Tom Costello, which he had come across in Douglas Hyde's *Love Songs of Connacht*. There are different versions of the tale: the essentials appear to be that Úna, a daughter of the chief MacDermot, was confined to Trinity Island by her father to keep her from Costello. He was drowned in his efforts to reach her; she, of course, died of grief. Or, she died of grief first, after which he composed his passionate love-lament, and drowned trying to reach her grave on the island. The song is in the 'high tradition' and even today it is sung only in Irish. English translations are clumsy and can't be made to match the music. This is Douglas Hyde's translation, of a few verses only — the oldest manuscript version consists of no less than forty-five verses!

O fair Una, thou blossom of the amber locks,
Thou who art after thy death from the result of ill counsel,
See, O love, which of them was the best of the two counsels,
O bird in a cage, and I in the ford of the Donoghue.

O fair Una, thou has left me in grief twisted,
And why shouldst thou like to be recounting it any more for ever?
Ringleted cooleen upon which grew up the melted gold,
And sure I would rather be sitting beside thee than the glory of heaven.

O fair Una, it is you who have set astray my senses;
O Una, it is you who went close in between me and God,
O Una, fragrant branch, twisted little curl of the ringlets,
Was it not better for me to be without eyes than ever to have seen you?

Thomas was buried close to her on Trinity Island, though the two trees that grew and, in the way of all love stories, intertwined over their graves can no longer be distinguished. Douglas Hyde wrote 'I do not think there is any song more widely spread throughout the country and more common in the mouth of the people than the poem which strong Thomas Costello ... composed over the unfortunate and handsome girl Una MacDermott to whom he had given love.' In local folklore the strength of Thomas Costello is a popular theme, and some of the stories about his feats almost rival those of the Boyhood Deeds of Cúchulainn.

On Trinity Island, in the Abbey of the White Friars, the *Annals of Loch Cé* (its Irish spelling) were compiled about the end of the sixteenth century. They are now in the library of Trinity College, Dublin. Boyle Abbey is a graceful remnant of the Middle Ages. Traces of a much more distant past lie all around. An extensive cemetery, predating the Bronze Age, is to be found magnificently sited on a hilltop of the Bricklieve Mountain, a collection of beautifully constructed vaulted and lintelled chambers; a very fine portal dolmen (known locally as 'the Labby') stands at the north-western corner of Lough Arrow; and Heapstown Cairn, a huge mound close by it, has never been opened to discover what manner of man or god deserved such a tribute.

Turning clockwise in a circle brings you to Ballyfarnan. Halfway from here to Keadue, overlooking Lough Meelagh, is Kilronan Abbey. If ghostly music seems to float on the air, it is because Turlough O'Carolan, 'the last of the bards', is buried in the cemetery there, where brambles twine and the pink blossom of Himalayan balsam scatters its clouds of colour. In any part of the world, lovers of traditional music will be familiar with O'Carolan's Concerto. The blind composer was greatly revered, under the patronage of the MacDermot Roes and, as he put it in one of his own compositions:

Fuair mé seal i n-Eirinn go h-aerach is go sóghamhuil,
Ag ól le gach tréinfhear bhí éifeachtach ceolmhar —
(I spent time in Ireland happy and contented,
drinking with every strong man who was a real lover of music.)

Goldsmith wrote at length about him, and in glowing terms:

He was at once a poet, a musician, a composer, and sung his own verses to his harp ... A song beginning 'O'Rourke's noble fare will ne'er be forgot,' transplanted by Dean Swift, is of his composition; which, though perhaps by this means the best known of his pieces, is yet by no means the most deserving

Turlough O'Carolan (1670–1738)

... He seemed by nature formed for his profession; for as he was born blind, so also he was possessed of a most astonishing memory, and a facetious turn of thinking, which gave his entertainers infinite satisfaction ... Homer was never more fond of a glass than he; he would drink whole pints of usquebaugh, and, as he used to think, without any ill consequence.

Tales of his wake are part of local folklore. It lasted four days, and was attended by a vast concourse of people, including ten harpers.

Speaking of Goldsmith, one could wonder whether Thackeray was getting his personalities confused, or was writing a parody of Goldsmith's words about Carolan, when he wrote about Goldsmith in his series 'English Humorists':

Who, of the millions whom he has amused, does not love him? ... His sweet regrets, his delicate compassion, his soft smile, his tremulous sympathy, the weakness which he owns? Your love for him is half pity. You come hot and tired from the day's battle, and this sweet minstrel sings to you. Who could harm the kind vagrant harper? Whom did he ever hurt? He carries no weapon — save the harp on which he plays to you; and with which he delights great and humble, young and old, the captains in the tents, or the soldiers round the fire, or the women and children in the villages, at whose porches he stops and sings his simple songs of love and beauty.

To return to Carolan, in order to honour the bard the nearby town of Keadue holds a harp festival every year during the first week of August, to which gather musicians from near and far away places for a light-hearted week of serious and not-so-serious music, song and dancing.

Douglas Hyde (1860-1949)

South of Boyle, on the road to Castlerea, is Frenchpark, the home territory of Douglas Hyde, bilingual scholar, folklorist, poet and essayist, and first President of Ireland. Coming from five generations of Anglo-Irish Church of Ireland clergymen, he was an unlikely champion of native culture. But he became one of the earliest proponents of the idea that Ireland should reclaim her Gaelic culture, and helped to provide the inspiration for the Irish Literary Revival.

He was born in January 1860, and shortly the family came to Frenchpark, where his father had been made rector of Tibohine (pronounced Ti-*bow*-hin). They lived in the Glebe House, but much of his childhood spare time was spent roaming the estate of his relatives, the de Freyns, from whose magnificent house and estate Frenchpark took its name, and where his sometime companion was Seamus Hart, the de Freynes' gamekeeper. Hart was fluent in both Irish and English, and full of stories and folklore. He was also full of strong Fenian sentiments. The young Hyde at fourteen was fascinated by all this. He started learning Irish from him, and accompanied him on visits to the surrounding homes, where he began to write down in his own phonetics some of the stories and expressions he heard. When Hart died in 1875, Hyde records his death using, in his own stumbling attempt at Irish, his friend's familiar expression: 'Schocht seravid leat', the nearest he could get to the Irish for 'May God seven-fold prosper you.'

Seventeen years later we find him in the role of president of the National Literary Society. His inaugural address was a turning point in Irish affairs. In it he argued that the first step towards finding a solution to the problems of Ireland was to restore its sense of national identity, through the rediscovery of its culture and language. This led to the foundation of the Gaelic League, of which Hyde was the first president, a post he held for eighteen years. In 1938 he was inaugurated the first President of Ireland. In July 1949 he was brought to his final resting place, in Tibohine, by the church his father served. The Glebe House is now derelict. Ratra House, where he spent his later years, no longer exists. Frenchpark, one of the most glorious houses in Ireland, is gone. All we have is Tibohine church itself, now in use as a modest Douglas Hyde Centre. A nice tribute is the Tree and Ogham Alphabet planted in the garden, linking the present with the heroic past into which he delved with such enthusiasm.

For his writings Hyde took to himself the name 'An Craoibhin Aoibhinn', 'the lovely little branch'. *The Love Songs of Connacht* which he published in 1893, after years of visiting the homes of the Irish speakers to transcribe some of the richness of their phenomenal memories, created a sensation, and inspired Lady Gregory and others to pursue the same course. There followed *Songs Ascribed to Raftery* and the even larger *The Religious Songs of Connacht* which he regarded as 'a leaf plucked out of the Book of Christendom before we come to that chapter which is called the "Reformation".' In it he included not only overtly pious works but poems, prayers, petitions, blessings, curses, charms, stories, 'and everything else of the kind ... these things are all mixed together in this book. There is no special order and arrangement in them ... just as I got them from the mouths of the shanachies and old people.'

As first President of Ireland, Douglas Hyde inspects the guard at Dublin Castle

Bryan MacMahon remembers him as 'a merry, informal walrus-moustached erudite scholar', and recalls how cheerfully he recited one of his translations:

> A honey mist on a day of frost in a dark oak wood
> And love for thee in the heart of me, thou bright white and good.
> Thy slender form rich and warm, thy red lips apart
> Thou hast found me and hast bound me and put grief into my heart.

What sent this unlikely emissary to convert the Irish to their heritage? Could it have anything to do with the mysterious forces of the

PERCY FRENCH 1854-1920

Percy French and Miss May Laffan: added to his other 'accomplishments, French was a good watercolourist.

The author of such well-loved ballads as 'Abdul Abulbul Ameer', 'Phil the Fluter's Ball', 'The Mountains of Mourne', 'Come Back Paddy Reilly' and, best-known of all, 'Are Ye Right There, Michael', an ode to the West Clare Railway, held the distinguished post of Inspector of Drains for County Cavan. He outlined his responsibilities:

He finds out the holding and what it contains,
Then maps out his system in furlongs and chains,
And points out positions for 'minors' and 'mains'
Such wisdom has William, Inspector of Drains.

He eventually abandoned the drains; banjo-playing, singing and painting suited his talents better and he made a fine career out of keeping people amused.

He was born into a comfortable Anglo-Irish family at Cloonyquin, Co. Roscommon. The house is gone but there is a monument on the spot, just outside Tulsk on the Boyle road.

landscape, as Frenchpark lies within the plains of Moylurg, which were spoken of by poets as early as the tenth century? Clonalis House, at nearby Castlerea, has been, and still is, seat of the clan O'Connor Don, one of the ancient royal dynasties of Ireland (visitors are welcomed at the house). An even stronger influence, but less obvious and therefore requiring more imagination, may be met up with where the hills rise gently towards the south-east, on the road to Tulsk and Strokestown. An obscure crossroads here, at Rathcroghan, marks the centre of a fabled territory, the seat of the ancient Kings of Connacht, and the starting-place for one of the great epic tales of Ireland, the Táin Bó Cuailnge.

That story, and the route of its unfolding across Ireland, deserves a chapter to itself.

16. EAST COAST
Great deeds and gentle places

To anyone looking for spectacular scenery, the landscape north of Dublin, the counties of Meath and Louth, may seem somewhat lacking in drama, though it has the charm of well-husbanded land, rich and gently-rolling river and pasturelands and, in envious urban folklore, rich and fat farmers. But much more importantly, it has written on its face the entire history of the land. Every age, every invasion, has left its mark on it and to travel through its relatively small territory is to journey through all known time on this island.

The Boyne Valley is a fabled place. The most spectacular monuments of European prehistory were raised on the banks of the Boyne, even before the pyramids of Egypt. The three great passage-graves known collectively as Brugh na Bóinne, the Palace of the Boyne, are sited in a curl of the river, just east of Slane. Newgrange, Knowth and Dowth belonged to a race and a culture of which we know nothing apart from their compulsion, and their capacity, to erect such tremendous monuments and decorate the stones of which they were constructed with enigmatic symbols. As you stand in the central chamber of Newgrange, or appraise the complex layers of Knowth, think on the surely superhuman potency of the beings who inspired them. Farther west, near Oldcastle, a group of similar, though smaller, monuments are scattered for half a mile across a hilltop.

The plain which extends from Ardee northwards to Dundalk and beyond is the plain of Muirthemne, the home ground of Cúchulainn. The legendary army of Maeve of Connacht swept through Meath and up towards the Carlingford peninsula in pursuit of the Bull of Cooley, in the great tale, The Táin, or the Cattle Raid of Cooley. The heroic culture to which these tales belong is thought to have arisen in the Iron Age, maybe two thousand years after the Boyne monuments were built, though in fact nobody really knows how old the stories are. The Hill of Tara, seat of the High-Kings of Ireland, has a place in all our mythology, and in our sentimental romanticism too since Thomas Moore (the Victorian one) set the nation singing about 'The Harp that once through Tara's halls/The soul of music shed.'

Celtic Tara was at the height of its power during the Iron Age,

Newgrange

The High Cross at Kells

Francis Ledwidge (1887-1917)

probably about the time of the birth of Christ, and the Druidic powers of Tara declined with the arrival of Christianity. Monasterboice was one of the numerous Celtic-style monasteries which mushroomed during the sixth and seventh centuries, and its decorated high crosses are unequalled. The monastery at Kells was a religious centre of European importance. In the shadow of its round tower and high crosses, an inspired artist (or two, or even several of them, it is thought) created one of the masterpieces of medieval Europe, the Book of Kells, now the most priceless possession of Trinity College, Dublin. It was made probably some time later than the oldest surviving manuscript we know of which contains the story of the Táin and was penned by a disapproving monk in Clonmacnois, near Athlone. Some of those early men of God appear to have been of cantankerous disposition. The abbot of Dromiskin monastery (about 10 km south of Dundalk), St Ronan, was the one who cursed King Sweeney so that he became a madman tearing through the trees like a bird. A few centuries later the Normans brought their new brand of monastic order: the meagre remains of the Cistercian abbey at Mellifont radiate an air of calmer reverence, if less individuality.

The Normans brought other architectural modes too, particularly that of castle-building. They needed strong stone castles to consolidate their position in hostile territory. Trim Castle, built about the year 1200, is the finest curving example of medieval military construction in the land. (Its 'epic force' inspired Thomas Kinsella's poem 'King John's Castle'.)

Several centuries later, in 1690 King James II and William of Orange fought their battle for the throne of England along the banks of the Boyne, and the action is marked out there on signposts. The defeat of James was a turning-point in Irish history which we have not yet been able to put behind us.

It is no small wonder that the writers who grew up among these tumultuous memories wrote mainly of small people and gentle ways.

'If you go to Tara', wrote Francis Ledwidge to Katharine Tynan from the muddy trenches of Flanders, 'go to Rath-na-Rí and look all around you from the hills of Drumconrath in the north to the plains of Enfield in the south, where Allen Bog begins, and remember me to every hill and wood and ruin, for my heart is there. If it is a clear day you will see Slane blue and distant. Say I will come back again surely, and maybe you will hear pipes in the grass or a fairy horn and the hounds of Finn — I have heard them often from Tara.'

Francis Ledwidge holds a special place in the affections of this traveller, as it was a poem of his that first opened the consciousness of a child's mind to the music of poetry. It was the 'Lament for Thomas McDonagh'. The child had no idea what it was about. The title meant

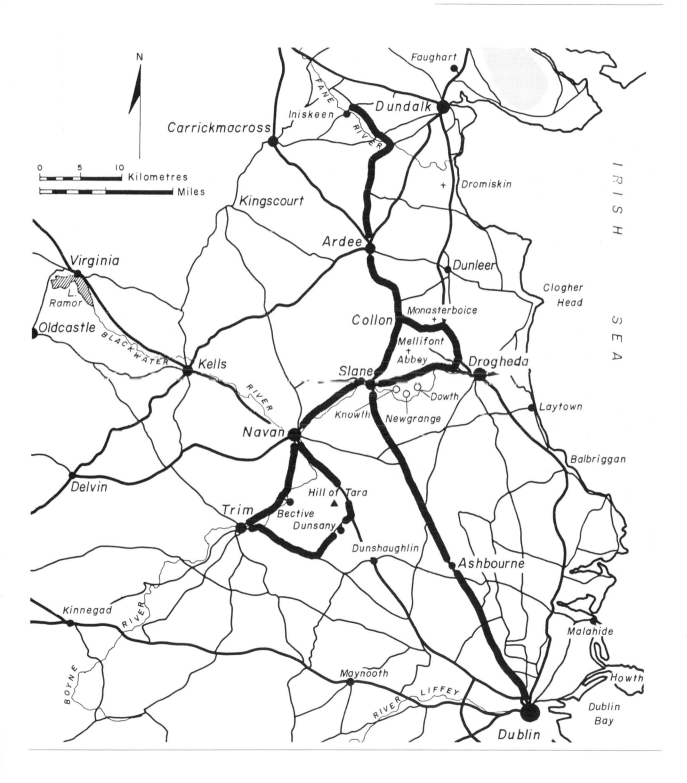

nothing. But the sonorousness of the lines, the mystery of its images, resonated deep and unforgettably in the child's soul, so that the response evoked by any poetry forever after was measured by it. Let us hear it again, just for the sheer pleasure:

He shall not hear the bittern cry
In the wild sky, where he is lain,
Nor voices of the sweeter birds
Above the wailing of the rain.

Nor shall he know when loud March blows
Thro' slanting snows her fanfare shrill,
Blowing to flame the golden cup
Of many an upset daffodil.

But when the Dark Cow leaves the moor,
And pastures poor with greedy weeds,
Perhaps he'll hear her low at morn
Lifting her horn in pleasant meads.

Years later one learned to appreciate the anguish that inspired it: the execution of McDonagh along with the other leaders in the aftermath of the Easter Rising of 1916, at a time when Ledwidge himself was serving in the British army. His decision to follow Redmond and join that army must have been difficult enough. Some blame the decision on an unhappy love affair; others blame the influence of his patron Lord Dunsany, and some say it was just for the sake of 'a steady job' for a while. Maybe we should just accept his own explanation:

I joined the British Army because she stood between Ireland and an enemy common to our civilization and I would not have her say that she defended us while we did nothing at home but pass resolutions.

The decision cost him his life. He was blown to pieces at Liège, near Ypres, on 31 July 1917, not quite thirty years old. His lament for his friend McDonagh can serve for himself, in whatever grave he lies at Boesinghe, far away from the rich pastures of Meath. The Ledwidge cottage is found just outside Slane, on the main road to Drogheda. It is one of the small local authority houses which used to be called 'labourer's cottages', and it is maintained nowadays as a memorial to him. He was the second youngest of a large family. His father died when he was four, and his mother laboured in service and in the fields well into Francis's young manhood. His own schooling finished when he was twelve, when he went to work on the roads. When he was sixteen he was sent by his mother to be apprenticed to a grocer in Rathfarnham in Dublin. There he found himself writing 'Behind the Closed Eye':

I walk the old frequented ways
    That wind around the tangled braes,
I live again the sunny days
    Ere I the city knew ...

I hear him* and I feel the lure
    Drawing me back to the homely moor,
I'll go and close the mountains' door
    On the city's strife and din.   (* the blackbird)

Which is what he did, literally. Sick with loneliness for where 'Five

Opposite: Enigmatic symbols decorate huge stones at Newgrange, Knowth and Dowth, and as shown here, at Lough Crew cairn.

Francis Ledwidge cottage, Co. Meath

roads meet on the hill of Skreen' and where 'The kingfisher comes down to drink/Like rainbow jewels falling down,' he sneaked out of the sleeping house and walked away from the city and his job. He walked the thirty miles back to Slane, in the dark, resting on every milestone.

His poems were all about the fields and hedges, the birds and flowers. And he wrote beautifully about the seasons. His poem to June begins:

> Broom out the floor now, lay the fender by,
> And plant this bee-sucked bough of woodbine there,
> And let the window down. The butterfly
> Floats in upon the sunbeam, and the fair
> Tanned face of June, the nomad gipsy, laughs
> Above her widespread wares, the while she tells
> The farmers' fortunes in the fields, and quaffs
> The water from the spider-peopled wells.

Among his last poems is one he calls 'A Soldier's Grave', which ends

> And where the earth was soft for flowers we made
> A grave for him that he might better rest.
> So, Spring shall come and leave it sweet arrayed,
> And there the lark shall turn her dewy nest.

Lord Dunsany (Edward John Moreton
Drax Plunkett) at home in 1952

Lord Dunsany (1878-1957)

The turrets of Dunsany Castle rise above the trees a mile (1.5 km) south of Tara. Lord Dunsany befriended Ledwidge after the younger writer sent him some of his youthful poems. He gave him encouragement and advice, and helped to get the poems published. He also introduced him to some of the prominent figures of the day, including Thomas McDonagh.

Dunsany himself published nearly fifty books, most of them pretty well forgotten. But at his best he had a vivid poetic imagination, and often a splendidly comic wit. In the latter mode, he gives us the marvellous character of Dean Spanley who, when adequately primed with tokay, reverts to a previous life as a spaniel and behaves accordingly. Most of his plays and tales were of gods and myths — eastern

192

Above: Royal Tara, seat of the High Kings.
Right: The kerbstone at Knowth

(Above) Lough Key on the upper reaches of the Shannon. Yeats thought to set up a contemplative centre for poets and mystics on Castle Island, in the middle distance.

(Opposite page) Row upon row of human heads: echoes of the old Celtic head cult in a twelfth-century Christian cathedral. Clonfert was founded originally by St Brendan the Navigator in 563 AD. A medieval dynasty of poets, the O'Daly's, is also associated with Clonfert.

(Right) A mermaid, complete with comb and mirror, appropriately adorns the chancel arch of Clonfert Cathedral.

(Previous page overleaf) 'St Kieran's City Fair'. Clonmacnois, founded by St Kieran in 545, was one of the greatest of the monastic centres. It was ravaged and plundered over and over until finally, in 1552, it was completely destroyed by an English garrison from Athlone. Its situation on the winding banks of the Shannon adds to the air of peace and serenity of its several churches, cathedral, round tower and collection of very early grave-slabs.

(Above) Inniskeen, Co Monaghan, Patrick Kavanagh
country. He was born nearby in the townland of
Mucker. The church near the stump of a round tower
has been made into a folk museum.

(Right) The cows are gathered — in curiosity or
homage? — around Cloghfarmore, the Stone of the
Big Man, which according to legend is the stone to
which the hero Cúchulainn tied himself when mortally
wounded. It is near the village of Knockbridge, off the
Dundalk-Louth road.

Sandycove, Co Dublin, with Joyce's Tower on the right, where one June morning in 1904, 'Stately, plump Buck Mulligan came from the stairhead, bearing a bowl of lather on which a mirror and razor lay crossed.' (Ulysses)
June 16th is commemorated as 'Bloomsday' every year with celebrations, recitals and readings from Joyce. Edwardian garb optional.

Two denizens of Dublin: (above) George Bernard Shaw,
his statue outside the National Gallery in Merrion
Square, and (above, right) Patrick Kavanagh,
commemorated on the canal bank, close to Baggot Street
Bridge.

(Right) Killiney Bay from the summit of Killiney Hill, looking southwards to Bray Head and the Sugarloaf mountain along the line of the DART, Dublin's local railway.

(Below) Dublin at night, looking down-river from a spot close to Guinness's Brewery.

Anna Livia Plurabelle. The river Liffey, at its source high in the Wicklow hills.
'That's where. First. We pass through grass behush the bush to.'

ones usually, rather than the local variety, and with a philosophical twist. His most autobiographical work is, hardly surprisingly, the most Irish. It is *The Curse of the Wise Woman*. In it he describes a house which could well be his own:

It was built by a forbear of ours who was a historical character, but it is just about that time that the history of Ireland begins to be fabulous, so that it is truer to tell you merely that the house was very old. Of the period of its furniture and its fixtures I can tell you at once: it was no period at all. As chairs and such things wore out they were replaced in different generations, and the only thing that they all had in common was that they were all bought by the same family. There is a right and a wrong place for antiquity; it is right in walls, wrong in carpets; wrong too in curtains and wall-paper and hearthrugs. We had antiquity everywhere.

'The Curse of the Wise Woman' is the story of a boy and his relationship with a gamekeeper, Marlin, and Marlin's mother, the Wise Woman who lived on the edge of the Bog of Allen and was imbued with strange powers. The story could be regarded as ahead of its time insofar as it was about these people's passionate determination to preserve the bog. The curse of the old woman was called down on the syndicate that planned to drain it. She won in the end: there is a tremendous description of a mighty storm and the bog moving, slipping off the mountain in a great wave, devouring all before it, including the syndicate's huts and all the machinery. David Bellamy could hardly have done better.

Dunsany had a genuine affection for Ledwidge, and always regretted that he didn't find some way of getting him out of the army when the young man discovered that he hated it all. Despite his addiction to the usual pursuits of his class at that time, shooting and hunting and cricket, Dunsany appears to have been what one would call 'a lovely man' — kindly, charming, untidy, boisterous, with a kind of innocence about him. Up to the end he wrote with a quill pen, often a feather from a goose he had shot himself. Best of all he liked a swan's feather, and as late as February of 1956, in one of his last letters, he asked 'If ever you know a boy or a swan who have a swan's feather to spare I should be glad of one or two ...' He died before that year was out. He was buried in Kent, and as the family returned to Dunsany after a memorial service at Kilmessan, it is said that four wild swans rose from the water in the park and flew in formation over the Castle.

From Tara you can look down also towards Mary Lavin's Bective, close by its western edge. 'Do you know Bective?' she writes in one of her short stories, 'A Likely Story'. 'Like a bird in the nest, it presses close to the soft green mound of the river bank, its handful of houses no more significant by day than the sheep that dot the far fields. But at night, when all its little lamps are lit, house by house, it is marked

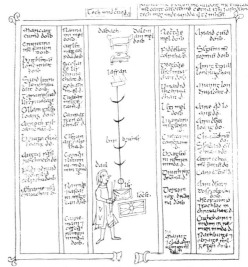

Plan of the banquet hall at Tara, from the Book of Leinster

Mary Lavin (1912–1996)

EDITOR'S NOTE:
Mary Lavin died in 1996.

out on the hillside as clearly as the Great Bear is marked out in the sky. And on a still night it throws its shape in glitter on the water.'

Mary Lavin is one of Ireland's finest storytellers. She wrote two novels, but the short story is where her genius lies, and where her deep understanding of the complex ways of seemingly simple people is demonstrated. Lord Dunsany became her patron also in her youth, and wrote the introduction to her first collection, *Tales from Bective Bridge*. 'I have had the good fortune to have many stories and poems sent to me by young writers' he says, '... but in only two of them have I felt sure that I was reading the work of a master. And these two great writers, as I believe them both to be, both wrote to me by a strange coincidence from the same bank of the same river, the left bank of the Boyne.' They were, of course, Ledwidge and Mary Lavin, though separated by a couple of decades. Her home for the greater part of her life has been in a deeply rural setting, an old farmhouse close to Bective Abbey. The fifteenth-century Cistercian abbey stands beside a triple-arched stone bridge over the curving Boyne among a network of little roads, and peace literally drips from the trees. In this quiet spot she seems to have grown wise and absorbed the secrets of the human heart.

Living in the aura of the Abbey, it is hardly surprising that one of

Mary Lavin with fellow writers Benedict Kiely and Jennifer Johnston

her stories, 'Brother Boniface', is set in such a place. Resting by its stone arches, we can see the scene as she describes it:

Brother Boniface sat in the sun. The sun shone full on the monastery wall, and brightened the gold coins of its ancient lichen. It fell full on the rough stone seat where Brother Boniface sat smiling. It fell through the leaves of the elm trees and littered the grass with its yellow petals. It splattered the green and white palings that shut off the kitchen garden from the blazing flower beds on the lawn.

There was no one to be seen out under the hot midday sun but Brother Boniface and the monastery cats ...

The dreamy young man had entered the monastery thinking it was the one place there was quiet and time enough for him to be able to look at the stars, and finds himself at eighty, put to sit in the sun after a lifetime of work and tasks, lauds and matins, only now at last with time to look at the sky. Except he couldn't, because now he had to keep his attention on the cats, and stop them from breaking the flowers in the flowerbed which were needed for Corpus Christi.

It is a gentle story, but it is a theme which crops up in a few of her stories, sometimes with a harsher background. In 'Lilacs' for instance, Phelim Molloy's daughters live in rage and resentment at the farmyard dunghill outside the kitchen window which is sold for manure, and dream of having a lilac tree in its place. After Phelim eventually dies, the eldest of the girls plans to plant the lilac trees. 'Where?' Jasper asks.

'There!' said Stacy, pointing out of the back window. 'There where the dunghill is now.' She drew a brave breath. 'I'm getting rid of the dunghill, you see,' she said.

Jasper stayed looking out of the window at the dunghill. Then he looked at Stacy. He was an old man.

'But what will you live on, Miss Stacy?' he said.

Patrick Kavanagh knew all about dungheaps, and what he saw as the material, cultural, emotional and spiritual deprivation of living in the country. Coming in the generation of poets immediately succeeding Yeats, sharing, in fact, with Austin Clarke the mantle of Yeats, Kavanagh rejected and mocked at Yeats' romantic view of the 'noble peasant' and asserted a literally more down to earth version. But then, was he himself, as an eminent poet, not one? His personality, certainly, did not present itself as 'noble', but his poetic genius did, and in spite of anger and anguish, he wrote with exquisite tenderness of the plough-turned sod, and the prickly sow thistle, the stony grey soil, a primrose, of spraying the potatoes:

> The barrels of blue potato-spray
> Stood on a headland of July
> Beside an orchard wall where roses
> Were young girls hanging from the sky ...

Cover of Patrick Kavanagh's By Night Unstarred, *courtesy of Goldsmith Press*

Patrick Kavanagh (1906-1967)

He wrote also of Christmas morning:

My father played the melodeon
Outside at our gate;
There were stars in the morning east
And they danced to his music.....

My father played the melodeon,
My mother milked the cows,
And I had a prayer like a white rose pinned
On the Virgin Mary's blouse.

Paddy's birthplace, and last resting-place, the townland of Mucker by the village of **Inniskeen**, County Monaghan is found among a maze of small roads a couple of kilometres north of the Dundalk-Carrick-macross road. His father was a shoemaker, and Paddy was apprenticed to the trade but already was writing furiously on any old copybooks he could get his hands on. The Kavanagh home is sign-posted, and various landmarks associated with his poetry — Shancoduff, Cassidy's Hill — are nearby, and the school to which he first went in a pink bib. A small church next to an old round tower has been turned into a museum. His 'black hills' rise all around:

> The sleety winds fondle the rushy beards of Shancoduff
> While the cattle-drovers sheltering in the Featherna Bush
> Look up and say: 'Who owns them hungry hills
> That the water-hen and snipe must have forgotten?
> A poet? Then by heaven he must be poor.'
> I hear and is my heart not badly shaken?

His two novels, *The Green Fool* and *Tarry Flynn*, are largely autobiographical, and are wonderful reading, like when he is describing a passionate encounter on a boreen:

'I wasn't expecting you,' he said ... 'I was just thinking of going up this old road when you came —'

They walked, threading their way among the bushes and briars and over rabbit burrows and the greasy stumps of long-felled trees.

'Marvellous weather,' said he with all the passion of a lover.

'Terrific,' she said.

'Look at the rabbit,' he said, continuing his love talk. 'Give me your hand and I'll give you a pull over that gripe.'

He pulled on her hand and having landed her over the soaking trench let go of her hand. He felt that it was up to him as an honourable man not to get a set-in in that way. Afterwards he was mad with himself. It would be much harder to make a second attempt ...

'Aren't them nettles very vicious looking?' she said...

He thought he was dragging himself out of the bog by walking to Dublin, but he found Dublin life a bad let-down. He raged at the pretension and the insincerity. He railed too at the Church, which he saw in its Irish version as stifling of life and joy, with little real spirituality, and in his long poems 'The Great Hunger' and 'Lough Derg' he castigates its deadening hand.

His disappointment, and probably something inherent anyway in his character, turned him bitter and resentful, and to give vent to his anger and his satirical invective he invented a newspaper for himself, *Kavanagh's Weekly*, which had a brief existence in the 1950s. Copies of it are now collector's items. He became something of a 'character' around Dublin: he had not 'been trained in the technique of reserve and restraint' as he says himself. Unfortunately, this personality tended to overshadow the quality of his work in the popular mind.

John Ryan, editor of the literary magazine *Envoy* was an ardent admirer, and remembers him in those days (in *Remembering How We Stood*) when Paddy lived in Baggot Street, and their first meeting.

With not a little trepidation, I broached the subject of *Envoy*, asking him would he care to contribute a poem or something. He looked at me in utter loathing, let out a dying roar, and took off down the street under full rig. O'Sullivan, who (as it happened) liked me, gave chase and in his own equally intimidating voice demanded why the so-and-so he couldn't have the civility to answer (me) his friend. Paddy at last relented and it was agreed that we go into the nearest pub. It was the beginning of a friendship that was to last for the rest of his life — twenty turbulent years.

He remembers their last meeting too, less than a year after Paddy's wedding to Kathleen Maloney:

A week before his death the Abbey players were giving a performance of 'Tarry Flynn' in the town of Dundalk. He asked me to drive him up there, which I did. We took the same road that the young man had walked over forty years before. He told me again how as a boy he had walked to Dublin from Inniskeen, yet only crossed the lands of three men ... We dropped into Dan MacNello's pub in Inniskeen — an old friend. The pub is the social centre of Inniskeen. Not far from it is the bridge over the lovely Fane river 'one of the best trout rivers in Ireland,' where Paddy as a boy had helped to poach the great salmon. We had a drink or two there with some of the actors. Pat Laffan had a camera, so that there is for posterity a photograph of us all in MacNello's. In the last picture, Paddy looks like Moses; and did he not, like the patriarch, show us the promised land? And, like the prophet, fail to attain it himself?'

It is good to take the time to wander in the countryside around Inniskeen with a book of Kavanagh's poems. He wrote about small things, but for him they were imbued with profound meaning.

> I have lived in important places, times
> When great events were decided, who owned
> That half a rood of rock, a no-man's land
> Surrounded by our pitchfork-armed claims.
> I heard the Duffys shouting 'Damn your soul'
> And old McCabe stripped to the waist, seen
> Step the plot defying blue cast-steel —
> 'Here is the march along these iron stones'
> That was the year of the Munich bother. Which
> Was more important? I inclined
> To lose my faith in Ballyrush and Gortin
> Till Homer's ghost came whispering to my mind
> He said: I made the Iliad from such
> A local row. Gods make their own importance. ('Epic')

For Peter Fallon, please see *Crossing the Millennium*, page 261.

17. THE TÁIN

'Aren't you the lucky woman to be married to a fine wealthy man like me,' or words to that effect, said Ailill to Medb (Maeve). They were chatting in bed. 'What do you mean?' said Medb, indignant. 'I was just as well off without you.' Medb was Queen of Connacht, daughter of the High King of Ireland. Ailill, her consort, was younger brother of two kings, those of Tara and of Leinster. So they counted and compared: their ancestry, their retainers and their retinues, their household goods, their jewels, their clothes, and they were equal in all things. Then they matched their sheep, pigs, horses, cattle. Ah, cattle. These were matched and counted and noted also, and found to be the same. Until they came to Ailill's great bull, Finnbennach or the White

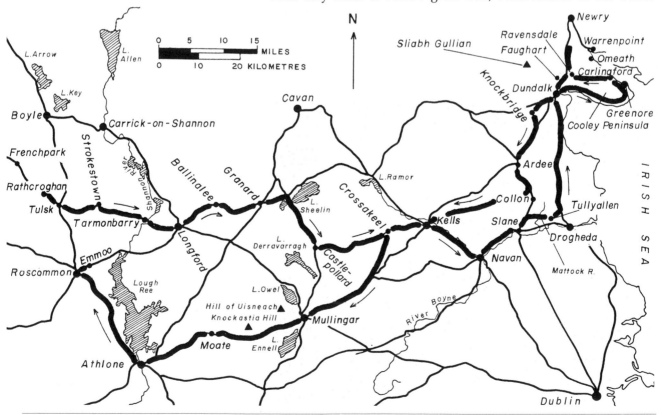

Horned. 'Match that,' said Ailill. And that started the trouble which led to the Táin Bó Cuailnge, or the Cattle Raid of Cooley, one of the great epic cycles of ancient Irish literature.

Cruachan, or Rathcroghan, in the plains of Roscommon, was the royal seat of the kings of Connacht. It seems no more than a crossroads on the road between Frenchpark and Tulsk. But that crossroads is in the centre of about a hundred square kilometres of ancient mounds and other earthworks. They have barely been touched by excavation, so nobody knows what secrets they conceal. But stand on one of those mounds, and let your imagination follow the chariots and the massed troops with shields and spears, and the war-like Queen marching them towards Ulster to steal the Brown Bull of Cooley, for pride.

For that is the basis of the story. It is the earliest vernacular epic in western literature, first written down more than twelve centuries ago, and nobody knows how old it was before that. It comes down to us in a few medieval manuscripts which have survived, almost miraculously, the ravages of Irish history. The translation by poet Thomas Kinsella (first published by Dolmen Press in 1969 in association with Oxford University Press, with illustrations by Louis le Brocquy) was greeted as 'the book of the decade.' Kinsella worked mainly from the eighth-century manuscript, *Lebor na hUidre*, or The Book of the Dun Cow (now in the Royal Irish Academy) and the late fourteenth-century Yellow Book of Lecan, now in Trinity College Library, backed up, where necessary, with the twelfth-century version in the Book of Leinster, as the earlier, and in Kinsella's view finer, versions were not complete.

Fifty mounds, I assert
are in the Assembly-place of Cruachu
Fifty keen truly honourable men
Are beneath each of these mounds.

The three heathen cemeteries are they
The cemetery of Tailtiu for choosing
The cemetery of ever-pure Cruachu
And the cemetery of the Bruig.
(Leabhar na hUidhre/Book of the Dun Cow)

Thomas Kinsella (1928-   )

Celtic cult stone, Castlestrange, Co Roscommon

Literary Tour of Ireland

Michael Harding
Patrick McCabe
See *Crossing the Millennium,* page 260

It is a remarkable fact that, twelve centuries or more after the tale was first written down by monks, the route followed by Maeve's armies can still be followed with fair certainty on the ground over modern roads, and the sites of particular incidents located. In 1975 Kinsella charted the journey for the journal *Ireland of the Welcomes,* and we gratefully acknowledge our dependence on the consequent article for the information in this chapter. To follow the route of the Táin, reading from the book as you travel, is a powerful experience.

As the story goes, Medb sent out to find where in Ireland there was a bull to match her husband's. Such a bull was located in Ulster. It was Donn Cuailnge, the Brown Bull of Cooley, owned by Daire Mac Fiachna. So Medb sent a deputation to Daire at Cooley to ask for a loan of the bull for one year, in order to breed a matching animal from it, offering such inducements as 'a portion of the fine Plain of Ai equal to his own lands, and a chariot worth thrice seven bondmaids, and my own friendly thighs on top of that.' What man who was a man could refuse such an offer? Not only would he loan the bull, announced Daire, but he would come with it himself!

But that night, in their cups — for they were extended the normal lavish hospitality of the time — one of the messengers boastfully let slip that if the request had been refused, they would have taken the bull anyway. Upon hearing which, Daire flew into a rage. He swore that because of this incivility, Medb would never have the bull. Medb, of course, in her turn, swore she would. The Cattle-Raid was on.

It was a great army that Medb assembled at Cruachan, with companies from the three other provinces, including exiled troops from Ulster itself. And magnificent. Cormac led three companies. The first had speckled cloaks over knee-length tunics and carried stabbing-spears with full-length shields. The second had red embroidered tunics and carried five-pronged spears. The third, with Cormac himself in their midst, wore purple cloaks over red-embroidered tunics, and each carried 'a spear like a palace pillar'.

The armies set out in the direction of Strokestown, and make their first camp at Ardakillan Lake (Carrcin) near Kilcooley (Cuil Silinne) which is two miles (3 km) south-east of Tulsk. Here Medb distributes the Leinster warriors among the rest of the army, as she is uneasy at their great prowess together. They cross the Shannon near **Tarmonbarry** (Moin Coltna) and are assaulted by the War-Spirit Nemain during the night spent on the Plain of Spears (Trego) between here and Longford town. On to Granard (Granaird) via pretty **Ballinalee**, and via **Castlepollard** to **Crossakeel** in Co. Meath (Iraird Cuillenn).

At this point in the story Fergus, out of old loyalty, has secretly sent a warning to Ulster. For reasons given in another story, the Ulstermen are incapacitated for five days, all except the youthful Cúchulainn.

Cúchulainn was a young warrior, but more than that. He was also imbued with more-than-mortal powers and prowess, with bravery and cruelty, with strength and tenderness, with savagery and personal comeliness. His home was the fort of Dealgan, at the place called Dundalk today. Cúchulainn, accompanied by his father, had come to observe the armies at Iraird Cuillenn, and leaves a challenge and a warning. Maeve's army avoids the challenge by turning southwards through a forest and proceeding via Crossakeel to **Kells** (Cuil Sibrille/Cenannos), where Cuchulainn makes a reckoning of the army.

On now to **Slane**, northwards for about 3 miles (5 km), then eastward to the Mattock river. Here Cúchulainn stuck a branch in the middle of the stream (Ath Gabla, the Ford of the Forked Branch) with a new challenge. He killed two warriors, with their charioteers, who came on him, and stuck their heads on the forked branch. 'Do these heads belong to us?' asked Medb. 'Yes they do, and to the very best among them.' Ailill said. Then Fergus, to explain what kind of youth they were contending with, tells stories of his awe-inspiring Boyhood Deeds.

Maeve dismissed the stories, saying he was still only a youth, and not beyond being taken.

Just how wrong she was, Medb had still to find out.

On they went through **Tullyallen**, and northwards, to 'the Pig-keeper's Plain', a district about 3 miles (5 km) north-west of **Drogheda**. Here there was another challenge from Cúchulainn, and many of Medb's warriors fell.

There are various other encounters with Cúchulainn as the army continues its march, until it reaches **Dundalk Bay** (Ath Lethan). It would have crossed the bay at low tide (possible up to the turn of this century) to Cooley, which is the Carlingford peninsula, to a point near **Rockmarshall**, under Slievenaglough hill (Sliabh Cuinciu). We will drive around through Dundalk, and follow the signpost to Carlingford and Greenore after two miles. (We should take time to render homage to the builders of Proleek Dolmen, one of Ireland's most noble tombs, in the grounds of the Ballymascanlon Hotel, and later to look around Carlingford, which is a most interesting Norman town, with a welcoming Village Inn.)

Here at last on Cooley, the army splits up and spread out to search for the bull. After various failures, it was discovered that the bull had been hidden in 'Glenn Gat of the Osiers,' which is the valley above Ballymakellett, on the road going north-westwards from Rockmarshall to Ravensdale.

So they encircled the animal and drove him towards the crossroads called 'The Bush' on the Carlingford road, but he attacked the herding heroes and vanished back into the fastnesses.

This is where the route comes closest to Brugh na Bóinne, the celebrated Bronze Age Cemetery which is described in Chapter 16. A detour to visit it, and the monastic site of Clonmacnois, will enrich this journey even more. The passage-graves belong to a race much older than the Celtic warrior-race of the Táin.

So the armies headed for **Slieve Gullion** 'ravishing Cuailnge as they went' but couldn't find the bull there. We don't need to follow them on their fruitless detour. (Slieve Gullion, or Cuilinn, is west of the main Dundalk-Newry road). They returned to Cooley to camp by Big River, which is the main river which flows down from **Windy Gap**.

Next day they went over the Windy Gap, which we can follow by road to great satisfaction. Instead of continuing down to **Omeath**, however, which is what the road does, Medb's army crosses westwards over the mountain ridge above Tullaghomeath. Anyone prepared to abandon transport here and ascend the mountainside to follow in their footsteps will be highly rewarded by an exhilarating excursion. From close to the summit, a grass-grown track follows an ancient trail downwards on the southern slopes to **Ravensdale** by the Flurry River, which is identified with the Belat Aliuin of the march.

The more mundane option is to drive back around to Ravensdale and pick up the next part of the route from there.

A marked walking route called 'The Táin Trail' has been laid out around the peninsula. It does not in fact follow the Táin route but does enter the territory, and is a fine walking route giving a magnificent viewpoint for the imagined action.

Medb, in her continuing search, moved northwards 'along the Midluachair road', that is the road from Dundalk to Newry, part of one of the great roads of ancient Ireland. Meanwhile, a troop of Ailill's men had finally located the bull in Slieve Gullion.

Strangely enough, the story, as told, does not deal with the capture of the bull in any dramatic fashion, compared with the graphic way in which it describes each individual single combat engagement between the warriors. It is almost as if the purpose of the conflict had been forgotten in the bitterness of it — as we have often seen happen. Anyway, Cúchulainn caught sight of them. He killed the leader, Buide mac Bain, at Ath Buide, Buide's Ford, on the Flurry River a mile west of Trumpet Hill, and several others of the troop.

Then, the story tells us, the Connacht army gathered together at **Faughart**, the hill to the west of the main road, across from Ravensdale. From the old churchyard on the hilltop, there is a wide view of Dundalk Bay and the surrounding countryside, including the Plain of Muirthemne to the south. Meanwhile Cúchulainn turned toward that plain 'to defend his beloved home' — he was, after all, 'Cúchulainn of Muirtheimne.'

Cúchulainn continues to defend the territory, but is weakening. Medb arranges a meeting, to ask for a truce, at Faughart Hill. But it is a ruse. She treacherously sets fourteen men against him, but he survives them, and continues to harass the army.

The four provinces of Ireland settled down and camped on

An incident here throws an interesting light on the nature of aristocratic and military life in this culture. Ailill, the king, had his own satirist as part of his retinue. Not being a warrior, and presumably because of the immunity normally extended to such as he, he was sent to take Cúchulainn's javelin from him.

He went to Cúchulainn and demanded the javelin. Cúchulainn could not refuse the satirist without losing face, honour and good name. So he gave it to him — through the head.

Muirtheimne Plain. Cúchulainn is faint from his wounds, but a warrior from the *sidhe* comes to his aid, heals his wounds, and gives him rest for three nights. When he departs, Cúchulainn, refreshed, rises up and prepares for a great battle. In a wonderful descriptive passage, full of high heroic drama, he summons up his war-rage with terrible contortions, convulsions and tremblings.

And he hurled himself upon his enemies, and wreaked terrible slaughter. The retreat of the 'army of the four provinces' was begun. But all was not over yet. One of the most moving episodes of the entire Táin occurs at the place now named Ardee, which is Ath Fhirdia, Ferdia's Ford.

When Medb thought about who should be sent to protect their retreat from the Ulster warrior, her mind fell on Ferdia. Ferdia, though part of Medb's army, was 'Cúchulainn's own ardent and adored foster-brother.' He would not go against his friend. But he was tricked and bribed and lied to, and told that Cúchulainn had belittled him. And he was plied with wine. He was brought to Medb's and Ailill's tent. 'Their daughter Finnabair was put beside him. She handed him the goblets and cups, with three kisses for every cup. And at the neck-opening of her shirt she offered him certain fragrant sweet apples, saying that Ferdia was her darling and her chosen beloved of the whole world.' In the end he agreed. Cúchulainn and Ferdia met at the ford, they bitterly reproached each other, and they broke off their friendship. They fought terribly for three days. At the end of the first and second days' battling, they came up to each other and each put his arm round the other's neck and gave him three kisses, and each through the night sent healing plants and herbs to the other. When, on the third day, Cúchulainn struck the final blow on his beloved friend, he ran towards him and clasped his two arms around him and carried him across the ford, so that Ferdia would have the honour of having crossed the river where they fought. And he chants a bitter lament:

> O Ferdia, you were betrayed to your death;
> Your last end was sorrowful;
> You to die, I to be living,
> Our parting is an everlasting grief.

Now at last Ulster rises from its pains, the curse having run its designated time. The troops gather and begin their march southwards, 'great heroes thronging in might and violence' hot for battle.

And the men of Ulster held the day. Medb's army retreated across Ireland, with pitched battles near **Collon**, and **Teltown**, and **Crossakeel**, and near **Mullingar**. One of the major camps of the Ulster army, Slemain Midi, has been identified as Slanemore, four miles west of Mullingar. Slanemore Hill has on its summit three Bronze-Age

Cúchulainn died eventually on Muirthemne Plain, though not during the Táin. It is a different story, and versions of how he met his death are told by Yeats, by Lady Gregory and others. Mortally wounded, he tied himself to a pillar-stone so that he would die still facing his enemies. Even then they would not approach too near, fearing him to be still alive, until they saw a raven alight on his shoulder.

A tall standing stone known as Cloghfarmore, the Stone of the Big Man, in a field close to the village of **Knockbridge** just off the Dundalk-Louth road, is traditionally pointed out as the Pillarstone on which the hero died. A statue by Oliver Sheppard commemorating this incident stands in the General Post Office in Dublin as a memorial to the 1916 Rising.

Navan Fort

A visit to Emain Macha, which is Navan Fort near Armagh city fills in the experience of the Táin territory. Emain Macha was the great Royal Site of the Ulster kings, and it was from here that the Ulster troops marched southwards under King Conchobor, or Connor. See Armagh, Chapter 14.

mounds. The important ritual site of **Uisneach** is close by and, on the southern side of the Mullingar-Ballymore road, Knockastia Hill bears a Bronze Age cemetery on top. So history, archaeology and legend merge when we read that the last great battle took place at what in the Táin is called Gaireach, which has been identified as Garhy hill, on the south side of the Mullingar/Moate road. Medb's army was demolished.

But that is not quite the end of the story. Medb had taken the precaution of sending the Brown Bull off towards Cruachan by a roundabout route. At the place called in the story Tarbga, which means Bull-strife, thought to be the hill at **Emmoo**, 3 miles (5 km) north-east of Roscommon town, the Brown Bull met Finnbennach, the White-horned, coming against him. They locked their horns, and in their ferocious battle they circled all of Ireland. When morning came, the men of Ireland saw the Donn Cuailnge coming westward past Cruachan with the mangled remains of Finnbennach hanging from his horns. He flung pieces of the White-horned to the four corners of Ireland, until he fell dead himself with his face towards Ulster.

The battle was over. Medb and Fergus (one of her captains) surveyed the carnage. Maeve said they had been shamed and vanquished. Fergus observed bitterly that they had followed a misguiding woman, that it was usual for a herd led by a mare to be lost and destroyed.

It is a mighty tale from a barbaric and heroic age. It is interesting that in the translated version, one can feel a tremendous ebb and flow of energy in the telling. It would have been a monastic scribe, for few others could write, who first took down the story from a story-teller. It is a wearisome task for both teller and scribe, and it would be difficult for the teller to maintain the pace and colour of the tale over a lengthy period, at the scribe's pace, and probably without the accustomed audience and their reactions. So sometimes it seems to run out of steam, and then again recovers to build an almost overpowering torrent of words and images, at its most dramatic moments rising to an incantatory verse, obscure and complex. And the scribe is not even likely to have been a sympathetic listener to this pagan story.

In the Book of Leinster version, which would have been copied from older manuscripts in about the twelfth century, in old Irish, the monkish scribe makes it clear that he neither enjoyed his job nor approved of it. He adds his own comment, at the end, in Latin which translates roughly as:

I who have written down this story or, rather, fantasy, don't believe a word of it. It is full of wicked lies and poetical fancies. Some bits are possible, others not. Most are just for the entertainment of idiots.

18. DARTING AROUND DUBLIN BAY

... from swerve of shore to bend of bay...

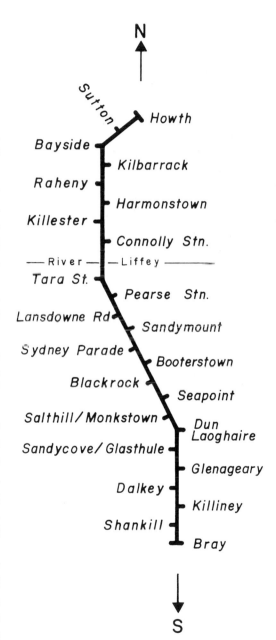

riverrun, past Eve and Adam's, from swerve of shore to bend of bay, brings us by a commodius vicus of recirculation back to Howth Castle and Environs ...

Joyce's writings have given rise to such an immense literary industry that even to enter into that vast field is presumptuous, and superfluous. We will, however, encounter Joyce's characters, and Joyce himself, here and there as we explore Dublin and its surroundings, as well as other great personalities such as Yeats, Synge, O'Casey, Behan and Beckett.

As a preliminary to an exploration of the city, however, we should explore its setting. Writing four centuries ago, Richard Stanihurst described it in these terms:

The seat of this citie is of all sides pleasant, comfortable and wholesome. If you would traverse hills, they are not far off. If champaign ground, it lieth of all parts. If you be delited with fresh water, the famous river called the Liffie runneth fast by. If you will take the view of the sea, it is at hand.

Dublin has changed in many ways since 1577, but its situation has not. The wind from the bay can be felt in the heart of the city, and as we noticed in the beginning, the slopes of the Wicklow hills seem to rise at the end of every street in the southern suburbs. The Liffey, Anna Livia Plurabelle, burbles into life high among those hills and in a long loop makes its way around the hills and down through the city, and into Dublin Bay which stretches in a sweeping curve to the Hill of Howth.

We have a wonderful way provided for us to get that preliminary overview of Dublin and its setting. We can travel, 'from swerve of shore to bend of bay' by the neat little green train, the Dublin Area Rapid Transport system, or DART, from its southern terminus, the seaside town of Bray with its esplanade and bandstand, first along the crescent edge of Killiney Bay, then by Dublin Bay into the heart of the city, and out through its northern fringes to hug the shore again and

The DART

James Joyce (1882-1941)

finish up by, literally, Howth Castle and environs.

A modestly-priced day-ticket from Iarnród Éireann allows you to alight and re-embark at as many points as please you along the way. A week's ticket doesn't cost much more, and makes it possible to spread the journey over several days, which is worth doing as there is so much to explore. We meet Joyce at both ends, and many other literary figures in between, apart from which it is a grand journey on a fine day, encompassing the wildness of bird-haunted cliffs, wide sweeps of sand, rocks and harbours and seaside villas. Swishing its way through the heart of the city, the DART overlooks the streets and backyards of deepest Dublin, and the suburban gardens, conservatories and tennis courts of the rather grander outer suburbs. To give the journey an elegantly circular character, we suggest you take the 45a bus from the city centre to Bray, and from Howth a bus will bring you back to your starting point.

At **Bray** there is a house that draws us even before we get on the DART. Stand at the station and look northwards along the shoreline. Two hundred yards away there is a nice dignified terrace, painted assorted pastel shades and encircled by a white wrought-iron balcony. This is Martello Terrace and at No. 1, the one nearest to the sea, the Joyce family lived for five years, during John Joyce's (Pappie's) more affluent days. Pappie was a drinker and profligate and slowly dragged the family down, but he was good company, was a great story-teller, and James adored him. The move to Bray from town was really in order to move farther away from his wife's relatives — 'the train fare would keep them away'. There were to be a dozen or more changes of address by the time James was twenty, each of them a notch further down the social scale as Pappie drank his way through the income from his Cork property.

But here life was good — mostly. Pappie fished, swam, rowed and entertained his cronies, and the sea crashed over the sea wall on stormy days. On Sundays friends would come to join in singing in the upstairs drawing-room to Mrs Joyce's accompaniment on the piano. It was while they lived here by the sea that the family was joined by Mrs Herne Conway to act as governess to the children (there were now five of them). She came to be known as Dante, (probably a scrambling of 'the auntie') though she was never referred to by Pappie as anything but 'that old bitch upstairs.' And it was here that the famous Christmas dinner took place in *A Portrait of the Artist as a Young Man* when the bitter row broke out over the church's part in bringing about Parnell's downfall, with Dante taking the church's side. And the row getting more and more heated over the turkey and gravy, Dante fiercely defending the clergy, the guest Mr Casey finally in his anger shouting No God for Ireland, Dante running from the room screaming Blasphemer! Devil! and Mr Casey, bowing his head on his hands to weep for Parnell.

Let's leave them there, with their passion and grief, and step aboard our DART. As it moves away you can glimpse first a Martello Tower (we will be talking about these towers later) and then Martello Terrace to the right, and notice that most of the garden space has been taken over by a store yard since the Joyces' time. **Shankill** station comes next, then **Killiney**. As the DART moves away, look back to see Killiney Bay curving southwards with Bray Head and the graceful points of the two Sugar Loaf mountains framing it. Ahead the curve is closed by Dalkey Island. Killiney Hill rises steeply above, a rocky eminence clothed with trees and gorse and crowned with an obelisk. It is a remarkably unspoilt scenic parkland considering its closeness to Dublin, and a walk on it is rewarded with a view of Mediterranean splendour.

Torca Cottage, where George Bernard Shaw spent the happiest days of his youth, is on the slopes of Killiney Hill. He was born in 1856

George Bernard Shaw (1856-1950)

Vandaleur Lee (centre) with George Bernard Shaw's mother on his right and father behind on his left.

Maeve Binchy
Dermot Bolger
Neil Jordan
See *Crossing the Millennium*
page 260–261

at No. 3 (now 33) Synge Street off Dublin's South Circular Road (the house is now a Shaw Museum), and one can imagine the sense of euphoria with which young 'Sonny' (or 'Ginger' — he was called by various names, all of which he hated) embraced his new summer residence, surrounded by sea and sky and affluent villas tucked discreetly behind high walls. It was no thanks to his father, the boozy and inadequate George Carr Shaw, that they had this splendid retreat, but to his mother's singing teacher and patron, George John Vandaleur Lee, who provided it. In this rather unconventional set-up, Mrs Shaw lived a life of musical absorption and healthy vegetarian eating, largely ignoring the existence of her son, who was left to the tender mercies of a series of servant girls and so-called governesses, and her husband, whom she eventually abandoned, along with G.B., to follow her singing teacher to London, accompanied by her two musical daughters.

Torca Cottage is about half way between Killiney and **Dalkey** stations. The approach from Killiney is by far the more rewarding, because of the views. Just follow the coast road until it turns uphill, then keep right and continue along the Vico Road until the houses begin on the seaward side. Here a flight of steps on the left lead to Torca Hill. Shaw's cottage is the third from the blind end of the road: a small almost illegible plaque announces that he lived there from 1866 to 1874.

Sean O'Faolain lived on the other side of Killiney Hill, in the house named 'Knockaderry'. Poet Richard Murphy also lives nearby, and in his collection *The Price of Stone* celebrates some of the local landmarks.

If your enthusiasm, or your energy, allow, you could descend the steps again and continue the walk into Dalkey village and the next station. Before you re-embark, you could walk through to the other end of the village, and ascend the steep and narrow Dalkey Avenue to find the location of Clifton School where Stephen Dedalus, and also his creator, Joyce, taught a boys' class, and Stephen talks with the headmaster, Mr Deasy, about nationalism and foot-and-mouth disease. It is the large house on the right just before the turn with the sign Old Quarry. The house has since been divided into two private residences. Rather than disturb their owners, we suggest you peer through the small gate with the openwork cast-iron panels just under the giant beech tree. You might be lucky, and catch it on a day when, 'through the checkerwork of leaves, the sun flings spangles, dancing coins'. To reach Torca Cottage from this end, you should continue up Dalkey Avenue, turn left into Ardbrugh Road, and follow it to where it ends in a cul-de-sac.

As if all this was not enough, there is *The Dalkey Archive* to consider. In it we learn that the cranky and reticent barman in a Dalkey hotel is really a certain world-famous author who repudiates 'the filthy books' ascribed to him. The mad scientist de Selby lives near White Rock by the Vico Road and strange experiments are carried out at the Vico swimming place. Flann O'Brien, author of *The Dalkey Archive*, of *At Swim-Two-Birds*, *The Third Policeman* and a number of other wickedly inventive novels was also Myles na Gopaleen of the *Irish Times* column 'Cruiskeen Lawn'. This was for years the most popular of all Irish newspaper columns, and his caustic pen deflated all pretension and parodied all clichés both of thought and language. As critic Anne Clune observed, he had 'an incurable habit of immediately undercutting any even semi-serious thought by inventing and exaggerating it until it became nonsense'.

His real name was Brian O'Nolan but most people called him Myles. He was born in Strabane in County Tyrone, in 1911, in an Irish-speaking household, and spent most of his career as a civil servant in Dublin. It was his bad luck that his best literary output was during and immediately after the war years, when Irish-published material sank without trace in the wider English-speaking world, and it was not until after his death in 1966 that he became almost a cult figure, and his books, and compilations of the 'Cruiskeen Lawn', began to be published repeatedly.

Flann O'Brien (1911-1966)

Are we quite finished with Dalkey? No, not altogether. Because there is still Hugh Leonard, one of our best-known and most commercially successful playwrights, who was born in Dalkey in 1926, and lives there now again after a spell abroad. The play he called *Da*, which won the Play of the Year award on Broadway in 1978, is a dramatised version of his years growing up in Dalkey, focusing on the, to him, infuriatingly modest and selfless character of his foster father. Events in various of his writings, in *A Life* and *Home before Night*, happen in and around the locality. Leonard still writes a witty and usually biting column for the *Sunday Independent*.

Hugh Leonard (1926-   )

Glenageary, next stop. (Our DART is now, and for a handful of stations, sunk between high walls, so we lose the view until emerging at Dun Laoghaire.) J.M. Synge lived with his family quite close to Glenageary station, at Glendalough House. They moved here to be near the Stephens (that is, Synge's sister Annie and her husband Harry Stephens) who had moved in 1906 to the much grander Silchester House, immediately next to St Paul's Church where Silchester and Adelaide Roads meet. When his mother was away he often stayed at the Stephens' house, though he wrote to Molly that he felt like a poor relation there, and felt they despised him as a man of letters and therefore not a serious person.

52 Upper Clanbrassil St, birthplace of Leopold Bloom, according to Joyce

James Joyce (1882-1941)

5 Parnell Square

Oliver St John Gogarty (1878-1957)

Sandycove/Glasthule

'Stately, plump Buck Mulligan came from the stairhead, bearing a bowl of lather on which a mirror and a razor lay crossed. A yellow dressing-gown, ungirdled, was sustained gently behind him by the mild morning air. He held the bowl aloft and intoned
-*Introibo ad altare Dei*

The words will be familiar as the opening lines of James Joyce's *Ulysses*. The action took place at the Martello Tower at Sandycove on 16 June 1904, the day that has since come to be called Bloomsday. From the DART station, the Tower is a nice ten-minute walk along the seafront.

The stately Buck Mulligan of the novel was based on the character of Oliver St John Gogarty, on-and-off friend of Joyce's, who was the real leassee of the Tower, though in the novel Joyce claims to be paying the rent. Gogarty had leased it from the British War Office at a yearly rent of £8. Joyce, impecunious as ever, was glad to take up the offer of a space, and moved in on a wet September day. Four or five nights later Trench, one of the three occupants, had a nightmare about a black panther, and cried out in his sleep. Gogarty, in typical mock-gallant style having a pistol to hand, shot at the imaginary panther, the shot bringing a collection of pots and pans down around Joyce's head where he slept. Enraged, he quit the tower, and shortly after Ireland, for good.

A string of these Martello Towers lies along Ireland's east coast: there are seven of them along our DART journey, mostly abandoned, though one is a fashionable residence, another a tea-shop. They were built in 1804 when the British administration had visions of Napoleon sailing across the Irish Sea to incorporate Ireland into his Empire. A hundred years later, as the authorities were not able to think of any better use for them, some of them were put out for rent. This one was opened as a Museum devoted to the writer in 1962, and Gogarty's tower became known as Joyce's Tower ever after.

Billy Pitt had them built, Buck Mulligan said, when the French were on the sea. But ours is the *omphalos. (Ulysses)*

From the gun emplacements on the parapet you can look out over the snotgreen sea, taking in, close to the foot of the Tower, the Forty-foot Men's Bathing Place, where Haines and Stephen accompany Mulligan for his plunge after their greasy breakfast, and Stephen walks on, and away, and into literary history.

'Bloomsday,' 16 June, is celebrated every year by assorted Dubliners, visiting scholars and general enthusiasts, starting with what might be called an organic breakfast at a hostelry in the vicinity of the Tower which opens at 6 a.m. for the convenience of patrons. The Tower opens

Bloomsday 1954 — 'Our pilgrimage' departed from the Martello Tower — celebrating were A.S. Levanthal, Anthony Cronin, Flann O'Brien, Patrick Kavanagh, Tom Joyce

at 8 a.m. There are readings, Edwardian music and other entertainments. It is not obligatory to arrive in Edwardian clothing, but many do. Celebrations move by stages towards the city as the day progresses, to Davy Byrne's pub, the Ormond Hotel and other venues. The James Joyce Centre in North Great George's Street in the city has its own programme.

It is worth quoting the whole story of the first Bloomsday commemoration, as told by John Ryan in his nostalgic book *Remembering How We Stood*.

On 16 June 1954, the fiftieth anniversary of the day on which the events of Joyce's *Ulysses* took place, we [i.e Ryan and Myles na gCopaleen] decided to commemorate it by covering as much of the original ground as the book had charted.

James Joyce Museum

Better known as Joyce's Tower, this is the focus of more literary pilgrimages than any other spot in Ireland. It was opened as a museum by Sylvia Beach, Joyce's friend, guardian angel and first publisher of *Ulysses*, in 1962. It has an interesting collection of Joyceana — letters, manuscripts, photographs and, naturally, some rare editions of his works. Among the personal items are Joyce's piano and guitar, waistcoat and tie and, most moving of all, Joyce's death-mask, which seems to have the semblance of a smile on the face. But the most important exhibit is the tower itself, with its massive granite walls and view over the sea:

'Thalatta! Thalatta! She is our great sweet mother. Come and look.'

The tower is open to the public daily from May to September, or by arrangement at other times (Tel. 01- 872 2077 or 280 9265)

There were still a few horse cabs plying the streets for hire in those days (the one-horse 'brougham' was as peculiar to Dublin in Joyce's day as the hansom cab was to London in Conan Doyle's); so we chartered two splendidly decrepit examples, all black and verdigris, straw stuffing bursting through the upholstery and the indispensable 'jarveys' with watery eyes and noses that they had spent a lot of time and money colouring.

We agreed that the company should consist of ourselves A.J. (Con) Levanthal, Anthony Cronin, Patrick Kavanagh and Tom Joyce. Con Levanthal, being Jewish, was to symbolize Bloom; Cronin, the young poet, his surrogate offspring Stephen; Myles enjoined Simon Dedalus and Martin Cunningham; I was Myles Crawford (for I had been an editor), Kavanagh — the muse, and Tom Joyce, The Family; for he was a cousin of James — a dentist who had, in fact, never read *Ulysses*!

Our 'pilgrimage' ... departed from the Martello Tower, from the parapet of which Buck Mulligan presides over the opening ceremonies of the book. This is the 'Telenachus' chapter. Our plan thereafter was to take in the 'Nestor' episode in nearby Dalkey, proceed directly to the 'Proteus' section of Sandymount Strand, thus to Eccles Street (the beginning of the 'Calypso' chapter) and then in one broad swathe, take in the 'Lotus Eater' (Westland Row and environs), 'Hades' (Glasnevin cemetery), 'Aeolus' (the *Freeman's Journal* office — we proposed to substitute the *Irish Times* for that defunct organ), pausing for lunch and liquid refreshments at 'Lestrygonians' (Davy Byrnes, the Bailey).

Our leisurely afternoon would be taken up with 'Scylla and Charybdis' (The National Library), 'The Wandering Rocks' (no fixed abode — so our plan for that was to ascend Nelson's Pillar and drink toasts in Cork whiskey to the four quadrants of Dublin), afterwards to the Ormond Hotel for the interlude of the 'Sirens', and then to the nearest extant pub in the vicinity of that dried up well, Barney Kiernan's 'Court of Appeal' for the explosive 'Cyclops' scene — back quickly to Sandymount for 'Nausicaa', then onwards to Holles Street Hospital (a passing glance only) for the 'Oxen of the Sun', thence to Mabbot and Mecklenburg Streets — Dublin's vanished nighttown' — for a moment's silence for Bella Cohen, then for 'Eumaeus' — a late-night cup of coffee at some stall (the cabmen's shelter is also gone) and finally to number seven Eccles Street for conviviality and to celebrate the return to 'Ithaca' and 'Penelope', thus ending our Odyssey.

Well, it was a good try ... From the Martello tower our two-carriage progress soon became a cavalcade as numerous other vehicles tagged on behind. More pubs were visited *en route* than even the most faithful adherence to the Joycean master-plan demanded. By the time we reached the purlieus of Duke Street ('Lestrygonians'), communications became unreliable, transport broke down and the strict order of procedure was permitted to lapse. If we could have delayed this ossification to the 'Circe' eposode it would have been more in accordance with the structure of *Ulysses* ... The early part of our progress was, as I say, a reasonably stately affair and while, in retrospect, it is somewhat lazy, I clearly remember the dulcet tones of Cronin as he warbled the melodies of Tom Moore — the great *Believe Me If* and the sublime *Ah-ja-Pay-ill Muene* to mention but two. All agreed that these were the songs that Joyce himself would have liked sung, for indeed were they not the songs he sang so well with that fine, light, Irish tenor voice of his (a present from the da) ... Somewhere around Blackrock, on the main funeral route from Dublin to Dean's Grange Cemetery, lies a tavern, and there we had cause to pause for yet further refreshment. Perhaps it was the sound of our horses and carriages without, or just the sombre appearance of Myles (for he was wearing one of those black homburg hats he dubbed 'County Manager'), or merely the fact that he usually had funeral parties at about this time, that caused the landlord to approach us. He took Myles' hand to offer condolence. 'Nobody too close, I trust?' he queried hopefully. 'Just a friend,' replied Myles quietly, 'fellow by the name of Joyce — James Joyce ...' meanwhile ordering another hurler of malt. 'James Joyce, ...' murmured the publican thoughtfully, setting the glass on the counter, 'not the plastering contractor from Wolfe Tone Square?' 'Naaahh ...' grunted Myles impatiently, 'the writer.' 'Ah! the *sign* writer,' cried the publican cheerfully, glad and relieved to have got to the bottom of this mystery so quickly, 'little Jimmy Joyce from Newtown Park Avenue, the sign writer, sure wasn't he only sitting on that stool there on Wednesday last week — wait, no, I'm a liar, it was on a Tuesday.'

'No!' Myles thundered, 'the *writer*, The wan that wrut the famous buke "Useless"'. 'Ah, I see,' said the bewildered publican, and then more resignedly, 'I suppose we all have to go one day,' and resumed the drawing of my pint. 'Aye,' said Paddy Kavanagh, 'that's the way it is with some; more with others...'

Back to the Sandycove/Glasthule station. What a contrast for the young Pádraic Colum, born in the workhouse at Longford, to come to this affluent and leisured locality by the sea, where rich families had their yachts and garden-parties, and parasolled ladies strolled in the summer. His father had got the job of stationmaster at Sandycove station. They came to live in the wee cottage standing flush with the footpath on Eden Road, reached by a laneway next to the station, and young Pádraic attended the Glasthule National School, delivering packages with his father after school hours. A five-year scholarship from a wealthy American philanthropist later allowed Colum to devote himself full-time to his writing, and to become such an eminent man of letters, poet, novelist, playwright and essayist. He wrote three of the Abbey Theatre's earliest plays, *The Fiddler's House*, *The Land* and *Thomas Muskerry*. His poetry, evocative of a kind of idyllic Ireland, was popular with all levels of readers, as were his children's stories. He lived long and had an immense output. Though he and his wife Mary spent much of their later life in America, his work has its lifespring in the Irish soil. His book of reminiscences *Our Friend James Joyce* is a thoroughly enjoyable portrait of that artist. Padraic and Mary are buried in St Fintan's Cemetery in Sutton, close to the end of our DART journey.

Dún Laoghaire. Large residential town, shopping area and holiday resort; terminus of the car-ferry from Holyhead. Sailing boats seem to bob about perpetually in and beyond its fine harbour. The town still

Pádraic Colum (1881-1972)

84 Merrion Square

Samuel Beckett (1906-1989)

AE (George Russell) (1867-1935)
James Joyce (1882-1941)

manages to maintain some of its old air of an elegant watering-place. For those not familiar with the origins of its name, it derives from a fifth-century king and his 'dún' or fort. Dún Laoghaire was renamed Kingstown in 1821 by the civic dignitaries, with a rush of loyalism to their collective head. They were expecting King George IV to set first foot there on his Irish visit. In fact His Royal Majesty stepped ashore at Howth instead, speechlessly drunk, a condition in which he remained during the better part of the visit. However, he embarked for home from 'Kingstown', after a brief acknowledgment of the cheers of the populace. A later generation of civic dignitaries thought better of it, and renamed it back again. The Corporation managed to restrain itself from any such dramatic gestures for a later royal visit, that of Edward VII in 1907, but the occasion provided the opening chapter of James Plunkett's novel *Strumpet City*. The most memorable event of that visit was the theft of the Crown Jewels from Dublin Castle. They have never turned up since.

On one of Samuel Beckett's reluctant visits home after the war, he had a moment of revelation as he walked the East Pier one windy March night: 'great granite rocks the foam flying up in the light of the lighthouse and the wind gauge spinning like a propellor, clear to me at last ...' the new direction for his writing. *Molloy*, *Malone Dies*, *Waiting for Godot* and *The Unnamable* followed. Incidentally, the macabre climax of *Malone Dies* is played out when a party of lunatics take a boat trip to Dalkey Island.

Back again between high tunnelled walls to **Salthill** and **Seapoint**, where the view of the bay opens up, with Howth in the distance and the twin chimneys of the Electricity Supply Board at Ringsend pointing skywards in between. At Seapoint, a popular bathing place, another Martello Tower perches above the water and the butterfly wings of windsurfers are constantly a-flutter. AE (George Russell) often spent time at his parents' home near the Seapoint station, No. 5 Seapoint Avenue, a red-brick cottage-style residence near the Dublin end.

Blackrock. Joyce again: a picture from *A Portrait of the Artist as a Young Man*. The picture is of Uncle Charles in his 'arbour' at the end of a garden, his hair brushed scrupulously and his tall hat on his head, happily smoking the foul-smelling tobacco which he found so 'very cool and mollifying'. The garden is that of 'Leoville', which is 23 Carysfort Avenue, Blackrock, a five-minute walk from the station. The Joyces had moved back nearer to town from Bray, to this slightly smaller house. Nowadays it bears the name Leoville and a small plaque announcing tersely 'In this house lived James Joyce.' It is the last house at the bottom of the road, in an area which has changed enormously since his time, the cosy village having disappeared between sprawling shopping arcades separated by a wide highway. In those days Blackrock was a genteel place of old residences and gardens full of roses and apple trees. Immediately behind the Joyce home was Frascati Lodge, the summer home of young Lord Edward Fitzgerald, and the place to which he brought his beautiful young bride Pamela in 1793. He is remembered fondly as the romantic hero who, inspired by the ideals of the French Revolution (but not sufficiently horrified by its realities) joined the United Irishmen in their Insurrection of 1798, for which he forfeited his life. The house, with its spacious gardens and lawns, was swept away in the early eighties, amid loud and widespread protests, to make way for a supermarket complex.

But to get back to our Artist as a Young Man. Young James loved living here, and enjoyed running errands around the village with his uncle and practising long-distance running in the park. In the real life story, however, not told in the *Portrait*, he did not enjoy the sight which met his gaze one day of his father, well on in his cups, playing a barrel organ in the main street and singing 'The Boys of Wexford', having elbowed out of the way the Italian organ-grinder who owned it. It wasn't long after that episode that, barely ahead of their creditors, the Joyces left Blackrock for the city centre.

Booterstown. The journey is along the sea-front where thousands of sea-birds and waders feed and roost, some rarer specimens congregating along the marshy pools on the inland side of the railway, a little bird sanctuary which runs along the main road. This is the Booterstown Marsh of Frank McGuinness's play *The Bird Sanctuary*. In the play, a large decaying Georgian house owned by a family called Henryson looks out over 'every watery inch reed and rush all the wildness of the bird sanctuary that is truly God's blessing on this boundary.' One of that family has spent three years desperately painting it as if by doing so she is ensuring that it is maintained in existence. She makes a strange bargain with another member of the family in order to prevent the house being sold: the implication is that the marsh and all it symbolised would then be lost too.

Frank McGuiness (1953-   )

On that same road, look out for one of those charming slightly daft Victorian houses of which there are so many in this area. The one sporting a cone-topped turret at the corner and ornamental steps up to the front door is named Glena. It was for some time the home of John McCormack, Ireland's most celebrated tenor, with whom James Joyce on at least one occasion shared a concert stage. Joyce actually won a bronze medal at the Feis Ceoil of 1905, but threw it away because it wasn't the first prize — although Gogarty claimed it was because he couldn't pawn it. Gogarty sums up his views of Joyce's singing thus:

> There is a young fellow named Joyce,
> Possessed of a sweet tenor voice.
> He goes down to the kips

James Joyce

Oliver St John Gogarty (1878-1959)

With a song on his lips
And biddeth the harlots rejoice.

Sydney Parade comes next. Readers of Joyce's *Dubliners* stories will remember it as the scene of the tragic accident in 'A Painful Case'. In the story, a news item in the daily paper reads:

DEATH OF A LADY AT SYDNEY PARADE: A Painful Case
Today at the City of Dublin Hospital the Deputy Coroner (in the absence of Mr. Leverett) held an inquest on the body of Mrs Emily Sinico, aged forty-three years, who was killed at Sydney Parade Station yesterday evening. The evidence showed that the deceased lady, while attempting to cross the line, was knocked down by the engine of the ten o'clock slow train from Kingstown, thereby sustaining injuries of the head and right side which led to her death.

The news item goes on to recount evidence that the lady, a highly respectable one, had taken to 'intemperate habits' over the last two years. And reading it, one Mr James Duffy of Chapelizod, cashier of a private bank in Baggot Street, and a man of *very* temperate habits, is racked by remorse at having spurned her, after an increasingly close — one might almost say intimate — relationship, because once in an excess of enthusiasm at his discourse, she had caught up his hand and pressed it to her cheek.

Leaving Mr Duffy to reflect on his cold aloneness, we look across the endless sand uncovered by the retreating tide: 'Ineluctable modality of the visible: at least that if no more, though through my eyes. Signatures of all things I am here to read, seaspawn and seawrack, the nearing tide, that rusty boot. Snot-green, bluesilver, rust: coloured signs. Limits of the diaphane.'

It is Stephen Dedalus musing as he walks into infinity along Sandymount Strand. You might like to alight at Sandymount Station, not only to walk to the sea's edge (the DART has moved slightly inland at this point) and join Stephen on the ridgy sand, but also to pay a visit to Sandymount Village Green. Here, a bust of W.B. Yeats acknowledges the fact that he was born at 1 George's Ville, which is the same as 5 Sandymount Avenue, near the Ballsbridge end of the latter road (that is, the farthest from the village Green). Though he lived there for only three years before the family moved to London, he could write later: 'my earliest memory is of looking out of an Irish window at a wall covered with cracked and falling plaster'. That doesn't sound like a description of the pleasant villa nowadays, but gardens have many lives.

At **Lansdowne Road**, dominated by the towering stand of the Rugby Stadium, we are close to Ringsend, once a quite separate fishing community, separated from Dublin by the broad estuary of the River Dodder. The irrepressible St John Gogarty paid it his own typical back-handed kind of tribute:

I will live in Ringsend
With a red-headed whore,
And the fan-light gone in
Where it lights the hall door;
And listen each night
For her querulous shout,
As at last she streels in
And the pubs empty out.
To soothe that wild breast
With my old-fangled songs,
Till she feels it redressed
From inordinate wrongs,
Imagined, outrageous,
Preposterous wrongs,
Till peace at last comes,
Shall be all I will do,
Where the little lamp blooms
Like a rose in the stew;
And up the back garden
The sound comes to me
Of the lapsing, unsoilable,
Whispering sea.   (*Others to Adorn*)

Shelbourne Hotel

Oscar Wilde (1854-1900)

The last lines are worthy of the master wordsmith, Joyce himself.

From **Lansdowne Road**, through **Pearse Station**, **Tara Street**, **Connolly Station**, we are travelling through Dublin city, past gardens and backyards, conservatories and pigeon-lofts, office blocks, factories, warehouses and apartment blocks. Even as this is being written, the great Gasometer, one of Dublin's landmarks for several generations, is being dismantled, having been granted a few years' remission because a pair of peregrine falcons had chosen to nest on its parapet. We sail across the Liffey on the loop-line bridge, being afforded a superb bird's eye view of the Custom House, Dublin's finest architectural masterpiece, on our right, and on the other side Liberty Hall, the city's nearest approach to a 'skyscraper'. That tower replaces the building where Constance Gore-Booth of Sligo, beloved of Yeats but by then the Countess Markievicz, manned (womanned?) the soup-kitchen to feed the children and wives of strikers in the great 1913 lock-out. James Plunkett tells the story of that great confrontation, and of the labour leader James Larkin, in his novel *Strumpet City*.

Clontarf Road, the next station, practically overlooks Marino Crescent, a graceful curved terrace of modestly dignified houses. Here, at No. 1, lived the lovely young Florence Balcombe with whom the twenty-year-old Oscar Wilde fell in love. He was a frequent caller to her house, and together they would go to Evensong, sometimes all the way to Christ Church. Alas, his love was unrequited. Her heart belonged to another — a young man who lived farther along the terrace, at No. 15. When Wilde heard of his Florence's (or Eleanor's, which was the name he called her) marriage to her neighbour, he wrote and asked her to return a gold cross he had given her as a token of his affection. He was gracious enough to add: 'Though you have not thought it worthwhile to let me know of your marriage, still I cannot leave Ireland without sending you my wishes that you may be happy; whatever happens I at least cannot be indifferent to your welfare; the currents of our lives flowed too long beside one another for that.' Before his homosexuality manifested itself publicly, with such tragic consequences, he met and married Constance Lloyd of London.

Bram Stoker (1847-1912)

Above: Bram Stoker 1906
Below: Marino Crescent today

But his rival for the hand of Florence Balcombe? It was Bram Stoker, master of the horror story and creator of the best-known of all spectres, one that has maintained its hold on the popular imagination for nearly a century — the vampire, Dracula.

Stoker was sickly as a child, but became quite an athlete in later years at Trinity College, a big red-bearded man who might well have had a more manly appeal for a lady than the foppish Oscar. He also had a great love for the theatre. He paved the way for the Irish visit of the great actor Henry Irving, in 1876. He then gave up his job to join Irving in London, becoming his manager and tour organiser, and staying with him until the actor's death. But he wrote all the while. His mother, a Sligo woman, was a great teller of stories, and she had a penchant for horror-filled ones from having lived through the cholera epidemic of 1832, when coffin-makers made the rounds knocking at doors touting for business. These stories obviously had their effect on young Bram. He wrote eighteen novels in all, most of them thoroughly forgotten. *Dracula*, however, is not only regarded as a Gothic master-piece but is as popular today as it was when it first appeared in 1897. Literally hundreds of films have been based on the story. There are Dracula fan clubs all over the world, Dracula museums, Dracula newsletters, and tours to Transylvania. Nowadays the cult extends itself to T-shirts and iced lollies. And many, many Dracula fans have never heard of Bram Stoker.

The Terrace, directly by Clontarf Station, is also halfway between Connolly and Killester stations, a twelve-to-fifteen minute walk from either. The walk from Killester is the more pleasant, and has the added advantage that it passes en route Harry Byrne's pub on the Howth Road, which, you will be assured, was a haunt of Bram Stoker's.

From Marino Crescent, a 10-minute walk up the Malahide Road is recommended to visit the Casino, which was Lord Charlemont's summer house, a miniature masterpiece built about 1760. Its appearance is that of a small classic pavilion, a most deceptive impression as in reality it is a three-storey villa with fine reception rooms, bedrooms and spacious kitchens. It is exquisitely detailed — a workman was recorded as remarking that each of the carved stones which went into its building was worth a townland. Though Maurice Craig, architectural historian, says it is 'one of the most beautiful buildings of its kind anywhere', it is now, crassly, surrounded by housing estates. It is open to the public at appointed times from June to mid-September. There has always been a story that Marino Crescent was built out of spite by the developer Ffoliott, to block Lord Charlemont's view after the two had a falling-out.

Killester, Harmonstown, Raheny, Kilbarrack: we are now travelling through the territory of *The Commitments* and *Paddy Clarke Ha Ha Ha*, *The Van*, *The Snapper*, all of Roddy Doyle's unforgettable characters with lives so full of vigour, warmth, pathos, cruelty and love. *The Commitments*, from which a prize-winning film was made, is the story of the type of music group or rock band of which Dublin is reckoned to have more than two thousand — yes, thousand — at any one time. *The Snapper* made another lively film. *Paddy Clarke Ha Ha Ha*, the story of a ten-year-old tough little urchin watching his parents' disintegrating marriage, brought Roddy Doyle the coveted Booker Prize. There is hardly a descriptive word in any of these books, yet the background asserts itself vividly in the imagination. It is a vast and sprawling conurbation of new and newish housing estates of mixed social levels. It is Roddy Doyle's own home territory and he writes about his people with great affection and insight. He taught English and geography for a dozen years in Greendale Community School at Kilbarrack. This is not the one you see to the left from the station, but another which is

Darting around Dublin Bay

Roddy Doyle (1958-   )

Scene from a film of Roddy Doyle's novel The Snapper — *Sharon and friends on a night out*

just hidden but close by on the right.

Howth Junction, **Bayside**, **Sutton**, our DART takes us along the isthmus which connects to the rugged cliff-bound headland of Howth. The end of our journey is at Howth Castle (and environs) with its rhododendron gardens and cliff walks, wildness, gorse and heather, completing the journey from swerve of shore to bend of bay, the lines which open *Finnegans Wake*, to the place that ends it.

Howth Castle and Environs, looking over at Ireland's Eye

19. DUBLIN CITY

And here we are by (what else but) a 'commodius vicus of recirculation' back in Dublin where we began, a city where, to James Joyce at any rate, 'the air without is impregnated with rainbow moisture, life essence celestial, glistering on Dublin stone there under starshiny *coelum*. God's air, the Allfather's air, scintillant circumambient cessile air. Breathe it deep into thee.' (*Ulysses*).

Dublin is regarded as the most literary city in the world, and was so even before Joyce dissected its body and soul and presented it in virtual reality to an astonished audience. Stand on any street corner and the ghosts beckon — writers and poets, playwrights and novelists. (Patriots too, but we'll try to avoid being side-tracked by these, though, as in life, it is not always possible).

> Dublin is splendid beyond my expectations. I can go round its walls and number its palaces, until I am grilled almost into a fever. They tell me the city is desolate ... of which I can see no appearance, but the deprivation caused by the retreat of the most noble and opulent inhabitants must be felt in a manner a stranger cannot conceive.
>
> *(Sir Walter Scott in a letter to Richard Lovell Edgeworth after a visit to Dublin in 1825).*

PLAYWRIGHTS AND PLAYERS

As the Liffey divides Dublin north from south, so O'Connell Street divides it east from west. Parnell Square is at the northern end of O'Connell Street, and on the northern side of Parnell Square is the Dublin Writers Museum (it seems, like *Finnegans Wake*, to eschew apostrophes). It is the logical place to begin an exploration of the city.

Parnell Square, formerly Rutland Square, was one of the earliest and grandest of Dublin's eighteenth century squares, the tone having been set by Charlemont House which now houses the Hugh Lane Gallery of Modern Art. Though converting it to the Gallery entailed several alterations to the house that Sir William Chambers designed for Lord Charlemont, it conveys a sense of the aspirations of the time. The Museum and Writers' Centre, Nos. 18 and 19, have been well restored, and it is interesting to compare the relatively restrained decorative plasterwork in the Adams style, in the entrance hall of No. 18, with the later excessively ornate and gilded decoration in the magnificent salon on the first floor (and, after that if you are sufficiently interested in such things, with the full-blooded baroque in the Chapel of the Rotunda Hospital on the opposite side of the square — enquire at the Matron's Office).

Sean O'Casey (1880-1964)

After the Act of Union of Ireland with Great Britain was passed in 1800, and Ireland lost its independent Parliament, many of the wealthy families moved to London, and Dublin's great houses gradually fell into decay and were converted into tenements. And it was these decayed houses of the gentry, the crowded dwellings of Dublin's poor, that were the inspiration and setting for the plays of Sean O'Casey.

The horrific tenements of the nineteenth century, and even later, have, God be praised, disappeared, but there is enough left of those streets and squares that have been salvaged and made more habitable, to get a sense of O'Casey's world. A block away to the north from Parnell Square is Upper Dorset Street, where he was born at No. 85, in the year 1880 — a plaque marks the house. It is now the Bank of Ireland, an ironic transformation for the home of one of the have-nots. He describes his childhood in these surroundings in *I Knock at the Door*, the first volume of his autobiography. He was 'the shake of the bag,' insofar as his mother knew she would never have another child: he was the thirteenth, and one of only five to survive into adulthood. His father was fiercely Protestant, with a knowledge of Latin, and considered by his neighbours to be a scholar. His mother was gentle and enduring. Father regarded the teachings of Bishop Berkeley as too dangerous to leave on the bookshelves. The sensible Mrs O'Casey said that it 'was all about nothing being real, and that all things we saw were only images of our own ideas, and that such books were only to be read and thought of by minds big enough to understand that they were rubbish.'

BRENDAN BEHAN

Dublin in many ways belongs as much to Brendan Behan (1923-1964) as it does to O'Casey or Joyce. Not just because he reputedly drank in every one of its pubs (a wild exaggeration: he had his half dozen favourites) but because he was that rare thing, 'a real Dubbalin-man,' without a single trace of 'culchie' (rural) blood in his ancestry. Furthermore, he was a north-sider, which he considered even more superior in that category. He was born at 14 Russell Street (now demolished) — 'less than an ass's roar from Nelson's Pillar' he said himself, and the same area as Sean O'Casey. It was a tenement street, and in the mid-1930s his family, with many others, were offered houses across the Liffey in Kimmage (his was at 70 Kildare Road), which seemed so far off that it could be inhabited by cannibals.

He chose to set *The Hostage*, the play which brought him highest international acclamation, in Nelson Street, off Eccles Street and close to his first home. It is close, too, to his occasional home from home, Mountjoy Jail, where his republican activities landed him, and from which 'that auld triangle/went jingle-jangle/along the banks of the Royal Canal,' in the words of his song which now every Dubliner knows. Detention in Borstal and Mountjoy provided material for the books that made his fame, and the fame, encouraged by drink, created the out-of-control character that created turbulence in London, Paris, Stockholm, New York and home, and that finally destroyed him at the early age of 41. Although he lived much of his married life in the despised (to the northsider) Dublin 4, it was honouring his true background that he was buried in Glasnevin on his own side of the city, with half of Dublin following.

In spite of his rumbunctiousness, he inspired great affection and loyalty. In the 'Catacombs' days — when the hedonistic gathering-place for an assortment of intellectuals, artists and students was a basement complex in Fitzwilliam Square — he was said to be the best-read of all of them, the best mimic, the best singer, and the best story-teller.

Sean O'Casey was baptised at St Mary's on the corner of Mary and Jervis Streets, a block south from Parnell Street and west from King's Inn Street. School was St Mary's National School, at No. 20 Dominick Street, four blocks to the south. (The house, which is now the head-quarters of the National Youth Federation, has some of Dublin's finest stuccowork, in the flamboyant high relief style of Robert West.) How-ever, because of the painful eye problems that dogged him all his life, his attendance at school was only sporadic and he was largely self-taught. In fact, the boy who was to become the celebrated playwright learned to read only in his teens.

There is still enough of that old Dublin left in this area to be able to follow young Sean (or Johnny as he was known then) with his mother on her weekly shopping trip to Lipton's of Dame Street as he describes it himself, a miserable, half-blind, wretched child, lagging behind and hanging out of his mother's arm.

Brendan Behan

They'd pass through an avenue formed by tiers on tiers of cabbages an' cauliflowers, bushels of turnips, bins of spuds, hanks of onions, an' bunches of carrots, ready to be plucked, weighed, scooped out, or handed over to anyone who needed them ... through an alley of butchers' benches piled high with cutlets, chops, beef for boiling and beef for roasting; with the butchers in their blue and white overalls, bawling, buy away, buy away ... on from Dorset Street into Bolton Street, where his mother popped into a chandler's shop, and filled the can with half a gallon of oil, and her basket with quarter a stone of washing-soda, a bar of yellow soap, two candles, a penny box of Colman's starch, and some bundles of firewood, bought to fulfil what was spoken by the prophet, saying, Wash ye, make ye clean; to keep the hearth aglow, and to be a light to them that sit in darkness.

And Johnny slips a conveniently-knocked lump of bacon into his carrying-bag, and snatches up an egg as they pass by, continuing (like one of Joyce's Dublin journeys) into the dark and gloomy King's Inn Street, through Liffey Street, up the quay, across Essex Bridge, 'into Dame Street and, at last, into the warm, brightly lighted busy big shop of Lipton's' — now gone, of course, with many a family grocer from the city centre. (*I Knock at the Door*).

On the way down Bolton Street, and just before turning left into King's Inn Street, they would have passed Henrietta Street on the right. This was once the finest of all north Dublin's great streets, built on almost palatial scale, and home of such personages as the Earls of Kingston and Thomond and the Archbishop of Armagh. By O'Casey's time each of its great salons had been divided and sub-divided, and each house could have contained up to thirty families. Such was the setting for his first three masterpieces, *The Shadow of a Gunman, Juno and the Paycock* and *The Plough and The Stars*. And such were the grim prisons where valiant women like Juno Boyle, Minnie Powell, Bessie

Dublin Writers Museum

At No. 18 Parnell Square, the Dublin Writers Museum was established in 1991. It houses a collection of memora-bilia relating to the writers, an interest-ing collection of portraits, some manuscripts and rare editions, and a display giving the history of Irish litera-ture. Its audio-tape provides a good overall outline of Irish writing from the early bards and poets, up to Behan and Beckett. It takes about 30 minutes to follow its guidance through the various rooms and displays, and at the end of it you will be glad of its welcoming Coffee Shop to sit and rest, or reflect. It is open every day. Tel. 01-872 2077.

The Irish Writers' Centre adjoining the museum is a resource centre for the use of writers.

Abbey Theatre

*Above: Sean O'Casey by Dublin cartoonist 'Mac'
Below: The old Abbey theatre*

Burgess, and his own widowed mother, overcame poverty and deprivation with the gift of richness of spirit.

By then he was living at 422 North Circular Road, the house most closely associated with his name nowadays. Much of his education he owed to the Gaelic League, which he joined as a young man. He worked as a manual labourer and even his successful plays didn't bring him anything worthwhile. Under the influence of Jim Larkin O'Casey became a committed socialist, a view of the world that directed the rest of his life and his work.

At its first production in the Abbey Theatre, *The Plough and The Stars* caused the kind of hostile sensation that Synge's plays had a short time earlier. On the fifth night Yeats faced the cat-calling audience: 'Is this going to be a recurring celebration of Irish genius? Synge first, and then O'Casey. Dublin has once more rocked the cradle of a reputation.' It was after that that O'Casey left Ireland for London — but, as with Joyce, Dublin stayed with him. His marriage to Eileen, whom he met after only a few weeks there, created the most constant and stable anchor for his formidable and difficult personality.

The scene of all that dramatic furore, the Abbey Theatre in Lower Abbey Street close to the bottom of O'Connell Street, burned to the ground in 1951 — ironically, after a performance of *The Plough and The Stars*, which ends with Easter Week and Dublin city in flames. The rebuilt theatre has in recent years been rising from the flames in other ways too, with new playwrights approaching the stature of Synge and O'Casey, chief among them Tom Murphy, Frank McGuinness, Brian Friel, and others still emerging. Ireland is in the throes of a new literary resurgence.

The history of the Abbey riots is well known. Yeats' own earliest play, *The Countess Cathleen* (produced not in the Abbey but in its forerunner, the Antient Concert Rooms) produced the first uproar. To suggest that any Irish person would sell their soul to the devil as Cathleen did, even as a bargain to prevent their tenants starving, was sheer blasphemy. That was in 1899. Eight years later the genius of Synge had emerged, with his power, as Micheál MacLiammóir put it, 'of moulding out of the wild earth that had borne them, characters that seemed half human, half titanic; big, laughing, voluble creatures who ride towards us, as it were, out of some distant elemental tumult, live out their lives in a brief hour or so, and are gone.' The tamed, urbanised, respectabilised Dubliners of the time could not look at their own real nature as it was shown to them. *The Playboy of the Western World*, with a hero who boasted of having murdered his da, and which referred to girls in their shifts, drew such fury and indignation that police had to intervene. And in 1926, with the war for independence still a raw wound, *The Plough and The Stars* was taken to be a mockery of all that had been fought for, never mind the suggestion that there were actually prostitutes in the Dublin of the time. Unthinkable!

The theatre that had nourished playwrights like Yeats, Synge, O'Casey, Shaw, George Moore, and Lord Dunsany gradually ran down in creative energy. The building had once been the City Morgue, and at one stage Frank O'Connor remarked that it had been 'fully restored to its original purpose.'

Into that temporary lull stepped the partnership of Hilton Edwards and Micheál MacLiammóir, and the Gate Theatre, in the old Rotunda building on the corner of Parnell Square, became the new focus of exciting drama. Edwards and MacLiammóir shared the theatre with Lord Longford's company, Longford Productions, and between them they opened windows on a wider world. They brought Shakespeare, Tolstoy, Ibsen, Cocteau and Strindberg, Aeschylus and Sophocles to an audience hitherto used only to the kitchen comedies that followed Synge and O'Casey. It was in the Gate that MacLiammóir perfected his perhaps most famous one-man show, *The Importance of Being Oscar*, based on the life and writings of Oscar Wilde, with which he toured the world.

Dorset Street and its neighbourhood was the childhood territory too of Austin Clarke, Ireland's major poet after Yeats. He was born in

Gate Theatre

Austin Clarke (1896-1974)

PUBBALIN

The pub has traditionally been the omphalos of Irish literary life. Benedict Kiely, in his small anthology *Dublin*, says that you went to pubs if you wanted to find out what Irish literature was currently about. 'You could also have read books, but going to the pubs was easier and much more fun.' Patrick Kavanagh wrote about meeting a man in London who dreamed about returning to Dublin

'Where among the failures he would pass unnoticed,
Happy in pubs talking about yesterday's wits,
And George Moore's use of the semi-colon.'

Though the dark and smoky interiors that saw the birth — and death — of so much inspiration have largely given way to chrome and bright leather, the pub is still the centre of Dublin's social, and therefore literary, life, and the talk still goes on, ceaseless, circular, all-embracing.

Several of the hostelries in the city centre were — some still are — regarded as specifically 'literary' pubs. Mac-Daid's in Harry Street, for instance, the particular haunt of Kavanagh among others, where Behan often produced his rackety typewriter to finish off a story while cursing anyone tending to spill his pint on it; Neary's and Sinnott's in nearby Chatham Street, patronised by actors and patrons of the Gaiety Theatre; the Fleet and Palace Bars, where the

Irish Times journalists used to gather. Then there is, of course, the Bailey Restaurant in Duke Street, where the doorway of Leopold Bloom's vanished home in Eccles Street was once enshrined (at the installation ceremony, Patrick Kavanagh formally declared it 'Now Shut') and Davy Byrne's across the road from it, the 'moral pub' which Bloom found more to his taste: Madigan's in Moore Street to match wit and repartee with the market stall-holders. Any Dubliner will have his own list. Nowadays the scene shifts and flows with the younger generation more than it used to, but something of the flavour of the old intense days still lingers. There are pubs for talk and pubs for singing, pubs for music and pubs for silence. And pubs for 'the best pint'.

A Dublin Literary Pub Crawl is conducted every evening in summer, at weekends through the winter, starting from The Bailey on Duke Street at 7.30 pm. Colm Quilligan and one or more of his merry men, acting not only as guides but as players and minstrels, give renditions of verse, drama and song along the way — with built-in time for 'refreshment'. Booking recommended. Tel. 01-4540228 — or tickets may be bought at the Tourist Information Office.

JAMES JOYCE CENTRE

35 North Great George's St. The Centre is open every day. There is a programme of talks and audio-visual events, and conducted walks to places nearby of interest to Joyce scholars. Ken Monaghan, a nephew of Joyce's, is usually in attendance, sometimes aided by artist Paul Joyce, a grandnephew of the master.

A reading room, lecture room, library, bookshop and coffee shop are provided.

1896 at No. 83 Manor Street, several blocks away towards the west. Manor Street was reached from the quays by Stonybatter, and young Clarke was proudly conscious of the fact that it was in ancient times part of the highway between royal Tara and royal Cuala. The family moved to Mountjoy Street off Dominick Street, close to St Mary's Chapel of Ease, a bizarre vaulted and buttressed black edifice never known as anything but the Black Church. It gave him the title for his book of early reminiscences, *Twice round the Black Church*, in which he tells of risking eternal damnation by attending a Protestant service there with two small girls of his acquaintance. And other recollections:

I was in the kitchen of our house in Mountjoy Street near the window which I had known so well. Every day from that window, I could see the concrete yard and shed, the tall swing, the elder bushes in the small garden, and beyond them the backyards of the cottages in St. Mary's Place. Paradise Lane was hidden by the walls and I could only see near the sky the backs of the tenements in Dorset Street, gay with washing hung from poles stuck out from the broken and patched windows ... I knew that (my father) had left the Waste Water Department in Castle Street, near the City Hall, and was cycling down Parliament Street, across Capel Street Bridge, up Bolton Street, past the Fire Brigade Station, and, at any moment, I would hear his latchkey turn in the hall-door lock.

So much the streets of O'Casey's and Clarke's childhood overlapped. Clarke went on to Belvedere College and University College, Dublin, where he learned Irish from Douglas Hyde and studied English with the poet and patriot Thomas MacDonagh, whose lectureship he inherited after MacDonagh was executed in the aftermath of the 1916 Rising.

Unlike O'Casey, Clarke turned to the Irish tradition for inspiration, and became fascinated with the melodic and assonantal systems of the Irish poetic forms. 'Assonance,' he explained, 'takes the clapper from the bell of rhyme.' In his long and distinguished career he overcame, though with difficulty, the legacy of his strictly puritan upbringing to evolve a relaxed and humorous sensuality. The struggle can be followed in the journey from *Night and Morning* (1938), through *Ancient Lights*, to the poems of *Flight to Africa* (1963). He died in his home at Templeogue Bridge in March 1974 attended by his wife Nora. It had been his mother's house, and she allowed him only a life interest, the property to pass to the church after his death. It is ironic that the house was swept away subsequently in a bridge-widening scheme.

> He heard Aretes
> Calling him.
> Gentle hand was touching his elbow.
> 'Come in, dear
> Friend, for the purple-robed hours pass by. Luna has led her
> Star-flocks home — and your cup of hot milk waits on the table.' ('Tirsias')

PORTRAIT OF THE CITY BY A YOUNG ARTIST

In following O'Casey, we have been exploring mainly the streets to the west of the dividing line of O'Connell Street. For the other great Dublin portraitist, Joyce, we look in the other direction.

From the Dublin Writers Centre let us walk eastwards, across Great Denmark Street, and turn right into North Great George's Street and the James Joyce Cultural Centre, at No. 35. In the Wandering Rocks chapter of *Ulysses*, we meet 'Mr. Dennis J. Maginni, professor of dancing, etc., in silk hat, slate frockcoat with silk facings, white kerchief tie, tight lavender trousers, canary gloves and pointed patent boots,' setting out from the dancing academy where he teaches at 35 North Great George's Street and walking with grave deportment towards the city centre.

Originally this had been a very fine house, lived in in the late 1700s by the Earl of Kenmare, but like all such houses it fell on hard times. In Joyce's time it could have been relatively well maintained, but it was in a sad way by 1950 when it was acquired by Dublin Corporation. In 1990 a group of enthusiasts which included Ken Monaghan, a nephew of Joyce's (Ken's mother was Joyce's sister May), with the welcome support of Guinness, took it over in its derelict state and with great courage and determination set out to make it into a fitting Joyce memorial place in Dublin. And they have succeeded magnificently. The wide finely-proportioned hallway and two complete floors have been beautifully restored to something like their original grandeur, with Stapleton's delicate plasterwork rescued from under layers of paint and worse. The dark-red Maginni room on the ground floor is particularly appealing, because in the cleaning process a series of amusingly naive paintings of rustic dancing scenes, obviously introduced in Maginni's time, surfaced in the classic eighteenth-century plaster roundels, which originally may well have borne paintings by such as Angelica Kaufmann.

Ken Monaghan will tell you that this is the heart of Joyce's Dublin territory. Belvedere College, which he attended as a day pupil for some years before he moved on to University College Dublin, closes the view at the top of the street, on Great Denmark Street. For a while the Joyces lived at No. 14 Fitzgibbon Street, reached by continuing along Great Denmark Street, Gardiner Place and the north side of Mountjoy Square. Much of the street, including No. 14, has been demolished. From Great Denmark Street again, Temple Street leads to Eccles Street; No. 7, near the Dorset Street end is perhaps the most famous Joycean address of all. Sadly, nothing of the old red-brick house is to be seen. Its space has been subsumed into a hospital extension. Only the door was rescued, and it is now happily enshrined in the Joyce Centre.

Peter Sheridan
See *Crossing the Millennium*, page 261

> My mother would spare me sixpence and say,
> 'Hurry up now and don't be talking to strange
> men on the way.' I'd dash from the ghosts
> on the stairs where the bulb had blown
> out into Gardiner Street, all relief.
> A bonus if the moon was in the strip of sky
> between the tall houses, or stars out,
> but even in rain I was happy — the winkles
> would be wet and glisten blue like little
> night skies themselves. I'd hold the tanner
> tight
> and jump every crack in the pavement,
> I'd wave up to women at sills or those
> lingering in doorways and weave a glad path
> through
> men heading out for the night ...
>   Paula Meehan ('Buying Winkles')

But if we stand quietly we might see the ghost of Mr Leopold Bloom step out on the doorstep as he did on the morning of 16 June 1904, drawing the door softly closed behind him in order not to disturb his sleeping wife; noticing the morning sun nearing the steeple of Saint George's Church nearby and deciding it was going to be a warm day.

On one of Joyce's return visits to Dublin an acquaintance called Cosgrave implied that he had had an affair with Nora while Joyce was courting her. Joyce was distraught, and it took his old friend F. J. Byrne, then living at 7 Eccles Street, to calm him and convince him it was just a malicious lie. So in a way it was the address at which he re-found her, and so it joined Bloomsday, 16 June 1904 which was the day on which he first met her, to mark and celebrate the woman of his life.

The constantly moving Joyce family took up temporary abode at several other addresses in this neighbourhood. They include 29 Hardwicke Street, which runs behind Belvedere College (now demolished); 17 North Richmond Street, a cul-de-sac across the North Circular Road from Fitzgibbon Street — turn right and then left; and 32 Glengarriff Parade, also off the North Circular road, near the back of Mountjoy Jail. 'Monto', Dublin's then-notorious red-light district, which the young artist began to explore in his teens, was centred around what is now Railway Street, towards the Liffey end of Gardiner Street.

ACROSS THE RIVER: Lord and Ladies, and old gods

As we have seen, in the eighteenth century the Dublin houses of the rich and fashionable, the titled and the landed gentry, which later became the slum settings for Sean O'Casey's plays, were clustered around a relatively small area north of the river. When in 1745 young

---

From the south-east corner of Mountjoy Square, Great Charles Street extends to the North Circular Road. At No. 21, the home of the artist and Gaelic scholar George Petrie, the work of the Ordnance Survey was carried on in the middle of the nineteenth century. In line with the new enthusiasm for native culture and Irish themes, the Six-Inch Survey, first in these islands, was planned to concern itself with far more than the actual mapping of territory: it was to survey all the antiquities, investigate the folklore, analyse the place-names and the proper meaning of their Irish forms and formalise English designations for them. The remarkable group of people gathered together for this purpose included John O'Donovan, Eugene O'Curry and the poet James Clarence Mangan, as well as Petrie himself. A. P. Graves has described 'O'Curry with his hungry horse-face, tall, lean figure, and long unkempt white hair;

O'Donovan, a plump, dapper, pleasant-faced man, as he stood shaking his snuff-box or taking a pinch from it, while he paused from his beautiful Gaelic script to answer our ... questions,' the wild-looking Mangan, with his tattered cloak, his noble head, badly-fitting false teeth and dark green spectacles, sipping at his bottle of tar-water. This bunch of somewhat bizarre people produced work of lasting importance and fine scholarship, which is now part of the treasure-trove held mostly at the National Archive on Bishop Street near St Stephen's Green; more of it is held at the Ordnance Survey Office in the Phoenix Park. Unfortunately, the authorities decided to withdraw funding for the work before it was completed. John O'Donovan's researches on the meaning and translation of place-names provided the basis for the theme of Brian Friel's play *Translations*.

Lord Kildare, who later became the Duke of Leinster, decided to build a new residence for himself across the river among the open fields, there was consternation: nobody, just *nobody*, lived out there. 'They will follow me,' he retorted. And of course he was right. It was not long before the grazing sheep and cattle were moved off the pastures and Merrion and Fitzwilliam Squares began to rise from the fields as fashion gradually moved south. Leinster House, as the Duke's house on what is now Kildare Street was called, in time became the seat of the Dáil and Senate.

Walking from O'Connell Street towards Kildare Street, you come to the front gate of Trinity College, flanked by statues of two of its many illustrious alumni, Edmund Burke and Oliver Goldsmith — though, truth to tell, Goldsmith never distinguished himself while he was there. On an island close by outside the gates stands a figure of Henry Grattan, one of the greatest speakers of the Irish Parliament. All three statues are by John Foley. Beyond Grattan is a modern sculpture by Edward Delaney of which the dominant figure is Thomas Davis, the poet, leader of the Young Ireland revolutionary movement in the 1840s.

Walking through the cobbled courtyard you are walking in the footsteps of Swift and Berkeley, Congreve and Farquhar, Synge and Beckett, as well as the aforementioned Burke and Goldsmith. The famous library — the Long Room — has three million books and journals, thousands of ancient papyri and manuscripts, including the very early Book of Durrow, the Book of Armagh, and the twelfth-century Book of Leinster. Here also is the show-case for the most prized item of all, the Book of Kells.

Following the railings of the college around into Nassau Street and along Leinster Street, lift your eyes to the gable of the first building you meet on that (the left-hand) side. There, still faintly to be seen, though leaf-shaded, are the words *Finn's Hotel*. No longer such — a vegetable shop occupies the ground floor — but still a reminder to the rest of the world of what was imperishable in the memory of Joyce: here Nora Barnacle laboured as a chambermaid when he first met her. Was its name echoed also in the last work, *Finnegans Wake*?

Around the corner is Lincoln Place, where poor Belacqua of Beckett's *Dream of Fair to Middling Women* gets sick 'quietly and abundantly mainly on the boots and trousers of the Guard' who had accosted him.

But let us go back to the eighteenth-century theme we were pursuing. We are on our way to Kildare Street, in the wake of the Duke of Leinster. Just spare a thought in passing (and keep perhaps for a visit later) for the Royal Irish Academy with its remarkable library on Dawson Street.

Leinster House, home of the Irish parliament and sporadically busy

The Royal Irish Academy

19 Dawson St, Dublin 2. Tel 676 2570
The library of the Royal Irish Academy houses perhaps the finest collection of ancient manuscripts held anywhere in Ireland. One of the most precious is St Columcille's psalter, the famous 'Cathach' of the O'Donnells, the story of which is told in Chapter 13. Its highly ornamented shrine is in the National Museum. Also housed here is one of the original autographed copies of the *Annals of the Four Masters* compiled by the monks of Donegal Abbey and discussed in the same chapter. A different manuscript is on display every week.

The Library is open weekdays from 10.30 am to 5.15 pm. Groups should make arrangements ahead.

Oliver St John Gogarty was born at No. 5 Rutland (now Parnell) Square which, he said, 'looked out east at the backs of the houses in North Great George's Street which, though not as good an address as Rutland Square, held many distinguished persons including the great Sir John Pentland Mahaffy, afterwards Provost of Dublin University or Trinity College as it is also called. John Dillon, the patriot, had a house there and there dwelt Sir Samuel Ferguson whose poems and influence are responsible for the so-called Irish Renaissance.' Ferguson's house on North Great George's Street was No. 20, across the road from the James Joyce Cultural Centre. He was a Belfastman and according to Yeats, the 'most Irish' of the poets of his time, 'truly bardic, appealing to all natures alike, to the great concourse of the people.' His was a most gregarious and sociable personality. So lively were the dances and musical evenings at his home and so expansive the hospitality that the house became known among his friends as The Ferguson Arms.

Lady Morgan (1776?-1859)

with the comings and goings of politicians and Government ministers, is flanked by on one side the National Library, on the other the National Museum of Ireland, both of which are an essential part of any cultural tour of the capital.

The Library shares with Trinity College the privilege of being entitled by law to a copy of every book published in the State and has, in addition, a vast collection of manuscript, picture and photo archives. It is unlikely that there is any Irish writer who hasn't spent hours in its Reading Room. James Joyce used it regularly. His favourite desk was up front near the entrance. Near the end of the *Portrait of the Artist* Stephen notes in his diary that he went to the library and tried to read three reviews, but couldn't because his mind was on a woman. And in *Ulysses*, Bloom, the 'wandering Jew,' wanders between Stephen and Buck Mulligan as they discuss Shakespeare on the steps of the Library. If you would like to visit the panelled curvilinear Reading Room, you must leave your coat and purse below-stairs. To touch a book, you need a Reader's Ticket, with photo, issued on the spot: too many precious documents disappeared in times of less strict security.

If the Library stores the words of the nation, the National Museum, directly across the small strip of lawn, stores its artefacts. Cramped and inadequate in practically every way you could think of, it is still capable of rendering visitors awestruck with its collection of prehistoric gold ornaments and the products of the Early Christian churches: the barbaric beauty of, for instance, the Bronze-Age Broighter collar, contrasted with the exquisite and tender workmanship of the Derrynaflan chalice and paten, created twelve centuries back and dug out of a bog in the 1980s.

As to Leinster House itself, it didn't bring the Fitzgeralds much happiness. The Duke and his family found it a gloomy place, and the later occupant, the romantic young Lord Edward Fitzgerald, was killed in the Rising of 1798. It was sold to the Dublin Society (which became the Royal Dublin Society) in 1815, just about the time when the soirées of Lady Morgan, across the street, were beginning to get into their stride.

Kildare Street had become a lively and fashionable one by Victorian times and the liveliest house was that vivacious lady's at No. 39 (which was No. 35 when she lived there). A plaque now marks Kildare House, an office block which incorporates Nos. 36-42.

> Oh, Dublin City, there is no doubtin',
> Is the finest city upon the sea —
> 'Tis there you may see O'Connell spoutin'
> And Lady Morgan making tea.   (anonymous street-ballad)

Her ladyship was born Sydney Owenson sometime around 1780 (a lady doesn't always tell) and by all accounts she was a delightfully out-going and entertaining personality, the life and soul of the several distinguished households where she worked, as governess or companion, before she married the staid English Sir Charles Morgan and persuaded him to live in Dublin. Her several novels, particularly *The Wild Irish Girl* had great popular appeal, but they were rather looked down on by the intellectuals, and resented by the establishment because of their liberal and nationalist viewpoint. Whatever they thought of her literary output, they all came to her parties and musical evenings — Thomas Moore, Sheridan le Fanu, Samuel Lover, even Paganini during a Dublin visit. She records in 1835, 'My soirée was very fine, learned, scientific and *tiresome*. Fifty philosophers passed through my rooms last night.'

Kildare Street leads upwards to St Stephen's Green where Dublin's office population sit in the sun (it does shine sometimes), eat their luncheon sandwiches and feed the ducks. The Green provides a nice setting for a scattering of monuments. One, a graceful Henry Moore sculpture on a raised rockery on the west side, honours the great William Butler Yeats (his Dublin home was at 82 Merrion Square, which we will come to later). Near the bandstand a bronze head of James Joyce displays on its plinth the words: 'Crossing Stephen's, that is, my green ...' — words given to Stephen in the *Portrait*.

Outside the railings close by, a bench bears a small black plaque, erected on the occasion of the sixth International James Joyce Symposium in 1977:

> In memory of James Joyce, Dubliner, and
> his father John Stanislaus Joyce, Corkman.

(Trust a Corkman to always have to get himself into the limelight, Dubliners say). The bench and memorial are well placed, looking across the road at Newman House, where John Henry Newman founded a Catholic University in 1853 which became University College, Dublin. UCD has largely been transplanted to a spacious campus at Belfield, on the south side of the city, and Newman House is used for 'cultural and literary occasions'. In its recently restored glory, the public is asked to pay a small donation to view it. Its basement is given over to a fine restaurant named, appropriately, The Commons.

Joyce was a great admirer of Ibsen, and read a paper 'Drama and Life', in defence of the dramatist, to the Literary and Historical Society in Newman House. And Stephen Dedalus, hero of the *Portrait*, spent much time there with his fellow students, discussing the eternal questions of thinking youth, the nature of beauty, the rights of the individual — even those of women — questions of war and peace and a better world. The discussion he had with the Dean of Studies, the

Lady Morgan — Sydney Owenson author of The Wild Irish Girl

Above: 12 Aungier Street
Below: Newman House, St Stephen's Green

Gerard Manley Hopkins (1844-1889)

George Moore (1852-1933)
Oliver St John Gogarty (1878-1957)

'English convert' Fr Joseph Darlington, is thought to be the beginning of his explorations of language.

A more notable 'English convert' who lived and taught at Newman House was Gerard Manley Hopkins who was Professor of Greek from 1884 to 1889. The small claustrophobic room which was Hopkins' bedroom, livingroom and study for the last five years of his life has been furnished as it would have been in his time, close enough to a traditional monastic cell with its little iron bedstead, small cupboard, a writing-desk and little more: it may be visited at appointed times, like the rest of the house, between June and September or at other times by arrangement. In Dublin he was miserable most of the time; his time of academic drudgery were to him 'five wasted years' relieved only by occasional forays to the hospitable home of his friends the Cassidys at Monasterevin, Co Kildare. Born into a prosperous Protestant family in Essex, he became not only a Catholic but, to the total dismay of his family and friends, a Jesuit. His misery arose partly from his disposition (he was inclined to melancholia, or what he called world-sorrow), partly because he felt himself in exile from his own English milieu, partly from his feeling of alienation from the other Jesuits among whom he worked. He was agonisingly conscious that some of his colleagues gave emotional if not actual practical support to the nationalist movement, and he was beset by spiritual conflicts. Despite all that, he wrote some of his loveliest poetry during those years, including that wonderful work 'That Nature is a Heraclitean Fire,' which ends on such a note of ecstasy:

> In a flash, at a trumpet crash,
> I am all at once what Christ is, since he was what I am, and
> This Jack, joke, poor potsherd, patch, matchwood, immortal diamond,
> Is immortal diamond.

Proceeding eastwards (by the corner closest to the Shelbourne Hotel) along Merrion Row we come to Ely Place, on our right. Ely Place is even now a comparatively quiet cul-de-sac. At the turn of the century it was a sequestered place, cut off from the main thoroughfare by its own gateway. But its air of quiet respectability was not always what it seemed, especially when George Moore lived at No. 4 near the far end of the street, Oliver St John Gogarty lived opposite, in a Victorian-style house where the Royal Hibernian Academy Gallagher Art Gallery now stands, and Sir Thornley Stoker, surgeon and brother to Bram Stoker, lived in Ely House, which is No. 8. They were all challenging, high-spirited and temperamental people, who caused each other great entertainment and great provocation. George Moore in particular annoyed practically everybody who lived there — incidentally, he said his greatest delight in living there was the fact that he could enjoy the view of the Loreto Convent garden and the nuns' underwear hanging out to dry. Because the other tenants objected strenuously to the loud colour he painted his front door, he rattled his stick loudly along the railings every night, awakening all the neighbourhood dogs. The neighbours, in turn, hired an organ-grinder to play outside his window just as Moore was settling down to write.

Gogarty, in *As I was Going Down Sackville Street*, very uncharitably recounts a scandalous story of a dinner-party at Stoker's house, when the host's unfortunate mentally-disturbed wife burst into the room, unclothed and followed by two nurses. The mortified Stoker begged his guests for their discretion, appealing especially to Moore, as the only one he was unsure of. 'But it was charming, Sir Thornley,' said Moore. 'I demand an encore.' Stoker got his revenge some time later when Moore was bitten by what he decided was a mad dog. He rushed to the nearest medical — Sir Thornley of course — for a defence against hydrophobia. The surgeon found two small scratches on Moore's leg, enlarged them and screwed caustic into the wound.

Ely Place

Stoker's home, incidentally, was famous for its distinguished furnishings and *objets d'art*: he referred to them as his 'museum pieces'. Typically, Gogarty put it about that each represented the proceeds of a surgical operation.

Ely Place had over the years many distinguished residents. No. 4, which Moore occupied, had been the home of John Philpot Curran, the most famous member of the Irish bar, before he moved to 80 St Stephen's Green. The great advocate Charles Kendal Bushe lived at No. 5, and John Fitzgibbon, Earl of Clare, at No. 6. Of the latter it was said that his career displayed 'dauntless courage, the highest intellect, the utmost selfishness and unrestrained arrogance.' John Wilson Croker, editor of Boswell's *Life of Johnson*, lived for a while at No. 25.

AE (George Russell 1867-1935)

No. 3 was occupied for a period by a small residential community of Theosophists who lived a celibate life of monastic simplicity and apparent harmony. In the 1890s AE (George Russell), already attracted towards mysticism, joined them as a young man and stayed for seven years. 'The seven years I lived there were the happiest in my life. How fortunate I was to be drawn into companionship with six or seven others, all as I think wiser and stronger than I was then.' He afterwards married one of them, Violet North, from England.

Merrion Street, directly north from Ely Place (cross over Merrion Row), leads to Merrion Square, the west side of which is taken up mainly by Government Buildings and the other face of Leinster House, which straddles the block between here and Kildare Street. At the far end of Leinster Lawn (on the left) is the National Gallery, which has a far finer collection than could be expected of a gallery its size. The gallery's masterpieces gave power to the imagination of the youthful George Bernard Shaw, compensating for his rather haphazard educa-

George Bernard Shaw (1856-1950)

Dublin's cartoonist 'Mac' depicts a haughty Yeats, head in clouds, and a contemplative AE, head bowed, passing each other by unnoticed on route between their houses at 82 and 84 Merrion Square.

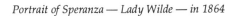
Portrait of Speranza — Lady Wilde — in 1864

Merrion Square, always one of Dublin's most fashionable addresses. Yeats, AE Oscar Wilde and Speranza provide a literary context

tion. In gratitude and recognition of its enrichment of his life, he bequeathed some of the royalties from his plays to the National Gallery, for which it is eternally grateful (particularly for the proceeds of the film *My Fair Lady*, which was based on his play *Pygmalion*).

Merrion Square was always one of Dublin's most fashionable addresses; here were the most eminent doctors, lawyers, MPs, a handful of peers. No. 1, the corner house nearest the Gallery, was the wild home of the Wildes. It has been pointed out that many a talented son has been overshadowed by a famous father. Here was the opposite: Surgeon-Oculist, archaeologist and Celtic antiquarian Sir William Wilde (whom we encountered at his other home, Moytura House in Co. Mayo), for all his many accomplishments was outclassed, in fame at any rate, by his extraordinary son Oscar.

Oscar Fingal O'Flahertie Wills Wilde was born in 1854 at 21 Westland Row, close by, and moved to 1 Merrion Square shortly after. Here the flamboyant Lady Wilde, who wrote patriotic verse for *The Nation* under the pen-name Speranza, held court, and to the spacious corner house thronged all the intellectuals of the day. To avoid any harsh light, her salons were conducted only by shaded oil-lamp or candle-light, even if it was daylight outside, when the windows were heavily shuttered. Meanwhile the learned Sir William tried his luck with various of the ladies. So the childhood of Oscar and his brother Willie was studded with celebrities. These included Sheridan le Fanu, who lived at what was then No. 15 and is now No. 70, headquarters of the Arts Council.

Le Fanu was a grand-nephew of the celebrated playwright, Richard Brinsley Sheridan (who was born on the other side of the city at No. 12 Dorset Street, the same street as Sean O'Casey). Though born in Dublin, his youth was spent in Abington near Limerick, his father having been appointed Dean of Emly. In Dublin, he spurned the Bar, to which he was called in 1839, to devote himself to journalism and writing. After the publication of his *Ghost Stories and Tales of Mystery* in 1851, he became more and more preoccupied with the supernatural and macabre. After his wife's death he became as strange as any of the characters in his books. He withdrew from society and took to his bed, where he did most of his writing between midnight and dawn, by the light of two candles. When he did sleep, he was tormented by nightmares and it was perhaps out of these nightmares that *Carmilla* was born. Carmilla was a beautiful 'young' vampire who liked to make her victims fall in love with her before she killed them. Le Fanu's vampire was a forerunner to that of Bram Stoker (who, until he left for London in his thirties, lived at 15 Marino Crescent at Clontarf and at 30 Kildare Street). The Gothic tradition out of which stories such as Le Fanu's

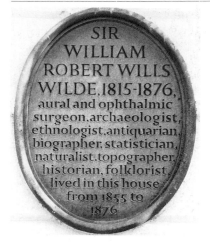

Sir William Wilde (1815-1876)
Jane Francesca Wilde (Speranza) (1826?-1896)
Oscar Wilde (1854-1900)

Sheridan Le Fanu (1814-1873)

Above: 16 Herbert Street
Below: 8 Anglesea Road

Eavan Boland (1944-   )

Carmilla, Uncle Silas and *The House by the Churchyard* emerged had already been established by the equally eccentric Rev Charles Robert Maturin, who lived at York Street, west of St Stephen's Green.

At one period W.B. Yeats lived at 82 Merrion Square, and AE (George Russell) had his offices second next door, at 84 Plunkett House, headquarters of the Irish Agricultural Organisation Society, of which AE was organiser. There is a famous cartoon, reproduced above, of the two deciding to visit each other and passing on the way without seeing each other, Yeats with his gaze aloft at the clouds, AE's head bowed ruminatively on his chest.

As well as being organiser of the IAOS, AE was editor of its paper, *The Irish Homestead* which later became *The Irish Statesman*, and in that capacity he encouraged and helped many aspiring writers including James Joyce, Frank O'Connor and Patrick Kavanagh. This most remarkable man, who travelled the countryside spreading the gospel of co-operation among small farmers, was on the face of it the last person on earth one could imagine for such a job. He was a poet, playwright, painter, editor, brilliant conversationalist and mystic. He painted fairies and mystical beings. He was almost universally loved, and regarded as something of a saint: 'His flame has always burnt upward clearly. There is no room in him for any of the small meannesses of humanity,' wrote the poet Katharine Tynan. 'AE was the nearest to a saint you or I will ever meet. You are a better poet but no saint,' Mrs Yeats told her husband. 'He was a tribunal before which the ignoble dwindles,' said Con Curran.

In an age of salons and 'at homes' — it was said one could attend a different one every night of the week in the Dublin of the 1920s — the Russell home at 17 Rathgar Avenue was the favourite and best attended. Sooner or later every literary figure gravitated there to overflow the chairs and couches, and share cushions on the floor. He believed absolutely in the power of the imagination. 'The poetic nature is like the weathercock on the spire, it catches the first breath of a changing wind. Tell me what the poets are saying today and we will know what the mass will be dreaming of in the next generation.'

The National Maternity Hospital at Holles Street in the north-eastern corner of the Square is where, in *Ulysses*, Leopold Bloom keeps vigil while Mrs Purefoy gives birth upstairs. This may be why the hospital has taken the interesting step of appointing a poet in residence: appropriately, Eavan Boland, who writes so beautifully about 'the quiet barbarities of the suburbs.' And childbirth:

> It was the dark month
> when ice delivers from the earth
> crocus by quick crocus
> snow's afterbirth.

I wove under the lights
my lace of sweat.
Lifted, I looked down
at the snaky wet

my legs beheaded,
the slick, forked tongues
of your head
and for a glance

I petrified with the season.
Little gorgon
how you marrowed stone
into me,

the bitter truth
that giving birth
was our division.
A skull cap

of forceps cauled
the python stings,
the ringlet coils.
I lay back

to a cluck of nuns,
to a stone knowing:
from now our meetings
would be mere re-unions.

('The Gorgon Child')

Above: 47 Percy Place.
Below: 62 Pembroke Road

The view from South Merrion Square along Upper Mount Street offers a particularly fine Georgian perspective, closed by St Stephen's Church, popularly known as the Peppercanister for obvious reasons. Behind the church flows the Grand Canal, offering a quiet tree-lined haven from the worst noise of city traffic.

By the canal bridge Stephen Dedalus makes his statement about art and beauty to his friend Lynch: 'To speak about these things and to try to understand their nature, and having understood it, to try slowly and humbly and constantly to express, to press out again, from the gross earth or what it brings forth, from sound and shape and colour which are the prison gates of our soul, an image of the beauty we have come to understand — that is art.'

For a while in the 1960s, a cluster of major writers — a small constellation — lived in this neighbourhood, much as at an earlier period they grouped around Merrion Square and the Green. There was the somewhat reclusive Thomas Kinsella, first on Baggot Street and later at 47 Percy Place, John Montague at 6 Herbert Street, Brendan Behan at 18 Waterloo Road, then at 15 Herbert Street and later at 5 Anglesea Road, and Patrick Kavanagh at 62 Pembroke Road. Parson's bookshop on the bridge corner acted as a kind of fulcrum, where they all met up or assiduously managed to avoid each other, and where Mary O'Flaherty held court and little Miss King (she was never anything but *Miss* King), shy but endlessly knowledgeable, hid in the corner behind piles of books. The 'Parsons' valued and encouraged and mothered their temperamental neighbours and in time the shop became something of a gathering-place for writers from all parts. The shop's demise as a bookshop in the 1980s was a loss to all literary pilgrims.

Kavanagh is the one who has left the most obvious mark on the area.

> O commemorate me where there is water,
> ·Canal water preferably, so stilly
> Greeny at the heart of summer ...
> O commemorate me with no hero-courageous
> Tomb — just a canal-bank seat for the passer-by.

Patrick Kavanagh (1904-1967)

he wrote in 'Lines Written on a Seat on the Grand Canal'. And that is what his friends did: built a stone bench there, where you, a passer-by, may sit and rest, and watch the mallard play their mating games. Later, a bronze statue of Patrick by John Coll claimed a place on the opposite bank.

Other poems found birth here too. Kinsella reflects on the nature of reality in 'Baggot Street Deserta,' and John Montague writes of 'Herbert Street Revisited':

John Montague (1929-   )

> A light is burning late
> in this Georgian Dublin street:
> someone is leading our old lives!
>
> And our black cat scampers again
> through the wet grass of the convent garden
> upon his masculine errands.
> The pubs shut: a released bull,
> Behan shoulders up the street,
> topples into our basement, roaring 'John!'

Elizabeth Bowen was born at 15 Herbert Place, and wrote of her 'Seven Winters' there. Liam O'Flaherty lived his later years in Mespil Flats by Baggot Street Bridge. So did Frank O'Connor, queueing up at Parsons with office workers from the Irish Tourist Board and the clerks from the Bank of Ireland for his daily paper or a copy of the latest literary sensation. Was this bespectacled professional-looking gentleman with the immaculate polished shoes and obvious air of distinction the same as the angry little boy in Cork who helped his drunken father home so often? After his death, Brendan Kennelly wrote for him:

Frank O'Connor (1903-1966)

> LIGHT DYING
> In memoriam Frank O'Connor (Michael O'Donovan)
>
> Climbing the last steps to your house, I knew
> That I would find you in your chair
> Watching the light die along the canal,
> Recalling the glad creators, all
> Who'd played a part in the miracle:
> A silver-haired remembering king, superb there
> In dying light, all ghosts being at your beck and call ...

The associations of this Baggot Street area seem endless. One of the most appealing ghosts, if such a thing there be, must surely be that of Thomas Davis, leading light of the Young Irelanders, a group of mainly

Thomas Davis (1814-1845)

Protestant young nationalists who urged the leaders of society to the rediscovery of the Gaelic past. In a very short life, through his accomplishments, idealism and personal charm he exerted an enormous influence on his contemporaries, and on political thought and action up to the present day. His death in 1845, at the early age of thirty, profoundly shocked the nation and his funeral jammed the streets. Sadly and to our shame, his vision of a union embracing 'Protestant, Catholic and Dissenter — Milesian and Cromwellian — the Irishman of a hundred generations and the stranger who is within our gates' is still a pious aspiration.

One of Davis's most important actions was to found the weekly newspaper *The Nation* as a platform of ardent national reawakening. It became the vehicle for highly-charged nationalistic prose and poetry, both his own and that of several aspiring writers such as Oscar Wilde's mother, writing as 'Speranza'. Davis's own ballads, 'The West's Awake' and 'A Nation Once Again', though regarded as overflowery and over-romantic by modern literary critics, keep his memory fresh in the popular mind to this day.

An only child, he was born at Mallow in Co. Cork after the death of his army doctor father. He was brought to Dublin when he was four and lived at 67 Baggot Street with his family for most of his short life. To Arthur Griffith, leader of the Free State Government, he was 'the prophet I followed, throughout my life, the man whose words and teaching I tried to translate into practice in politics ...' To Samuel Ferguson, in his bitter 'Lament for the Death of Thomas Davis', he was the 'young salmon of the flood-time of freedom'. There is a beautiful head, in marble, of his beloved Anna Hutton in the National Gallery in Merrion Square.

Other echoes too. The Red Swan Hotel of Flann O'Brien's brilliantly comic novel *At-Swim-Two-Birds* is located by the banks of the Grand Canal: in it the unfortunate author Mr Dermot Trellis is hijacked by his characters, who decide they want to write their own story. And in Samuel Beckett's *More Pricks than Kicks*, Belacqua Shuah finds relief for his belly-ache at one of the canal bridges, 'not Baggot Street, not Leeson Street, but another nearer the sea'.

Flann O'Brien (1911-1966)

Samuel Beckett (1906-1989)

Before we leave this neighbourhood, let us look southwards again towards the hills, as we did at the beginning of the book. And even at this distance we can see, with the eye of our imagination, that there is a strange light on Kilmashogue, moving down the hill.

The mountains, as everybody knows, are the homes of the gods, so that the light must be — yes, it is the light around Aengus Óg, the god of love, coming with Caitilin, his loved one, and the hosts of the shee, marching and dancing and leaping and tripping and singing down to Dublin, the Town of the Ford of Hurdles, coming to liberate the

James Stephens (1880?-1950)

Top: Stephens with Joyce and tenor John Sullivan in Paris.
Below: Caricature captioned 'James Crock of Gold Stephens' by Dublin cartoonist 'Mac' in 1925

Right: 'He saw Caitilin Ní Murrachu walking a little way in front with a small vessel in her hand.' A Thomas MacKenzie illustration (1926) for James Stephens' The Crock of Gold.

Philosopher from the prison of the ignorant, and the Intellect of Man 'from the hands of the doctors and lawyers, from the sly priests, from the professors whose mouths are gorged with sawdust, and the merchants who sell blades of grass — the awful people of the Fomor.'

Whether they succeeded in liberating them is for yourself to judge. This is the ending of James Stephens's wonderful novel — fable, allegory, call it what you like — *The Crock of Gold*. In it gods and men mix freely and equally. Caitilin, daughter of the humble peasant Meehawl MacMurrachu, is a fit companion of the gods, and the two

Wise Women who hated the two philosophers because of their superior wisdom married them in order to be able to pinch them in bed. It is wonderfully comic in its interweave of the profane and divine, of realism and fantasy, and in its use of the characters and style of old mythologies, but its intent is in deadly earnest, and it is in that ending quoted above: Ireland needed to be liberated from the suffocating narrow-mindedness and intellectual poverty of the time, and to move towards a higher consciousness and vision of life.

James Stephens liked to keep a bit of mystery about himself, and his fiction spilled over into anything he offered by way of autobiography. We know neither where (except that it was Dublin) nor when (except that it was in or around the year 1880) he was born. If that date is correct (and there are arguments for 1882) it makes him just six years old when he was found begging in the street, for which offence he was committed to the Meath Protestant Industrial School for Boys in Blackrock, Co. Dublin — not the worst of fates, indeed, because he got a good education there, good enough to get him a series of jobs as clerk in various solicitors' offices around Dublin, and later as registrar of the National Gallery in Merrion Square. There *may* have been intervals before that as a jarvey and as a clown in a circus. His appearance would, in fact, support the latter possibility: he was tiny, with an enormous forehead and dark liquid eyes — he reminded people of a leprechaun. We can believe him, however, when he states, 'The Dublin I was born to was poor and Protestant and athletic. While very young, I extended my range and entered a Dublin that was poor and Catholic and Gaelic — a very underworld. Then as a young writer, I further extended to a Dublin that was poor, and artistic, and political. Then I made a Dublin for myself, my Dublin.' It was sad that Dublin lost him in his later years, to London, the BBC, and the lecture round.

GHOULS and savage indignation: Gothic Writers and the Dean

We should wander into the Green again — it is always a pleasure — and look at more of its offerings.

Another of the Green's monuments, to the left (that is, west) of the fountain, is one to James Clarence Mangan. His work is largely neglected now, as it was during his unhappy lifetime, though he is regarded by many as the greatest poet before Yeats. The fine bust of Mangan is by Oliver Sheppard. A small marble head set into a niche in the pedestal represents Róisín Dubh, that is Dark Rosaleen; it is the last work of Pádraic Pearse's sculptor brother, Willie, who was also executed in 1916. The verses of Mangan's poem 'My Dark Rosaleen' are familiar to many to whom his name means nothing. He was born in 1803 at No. 3 Fishamble Street (which is now gone) and lived for some

James Clarence Mangan (1803-1849)

Charles Maturin (1780-1824)

Huband Bridge

Thomas Moore (1779-1852)

time at No. 6 York Street (also gone) which opens off West St Stephen's Green — behind the back of his pedestal. Poor Mangan, living at all times in dire poverty, haunted and melancholic, alcoholic, opium-addicted, on the verge of madness, and dying of cholera aided by self-neglect in 1849. The sense of awful desolation summoned up in 'O'Hussey's Ode to Maguire' is a true reflection of the torment of his soul:

> Where is my Chief, my Master, this bleak night, *mavrone!*
> O, cold, cold, miserably cold is this bleak night for Hugh,
> Its showery, arrowy, speary sleet pierceth one through and through,
> Pierceth one to the very bone! ...

> An awful, a tremendous night is this, meseems!
> The flood-gates of the rivers of heaven, I think, have been burst wide -
> Down from the overcharged clouds, like unto headlong ocean's tide,
> Descendeth grey rain in roaring streams ...

A neighbour, and hero, of Mangan's was the Rev Charles Maturin, curate of St Peter's Church in Aungier Street, who lived at No. 37 York Street (now demolished). It was Maturin, who with lurid horror novels like *Women* and *Melmoth the Wanderer*, established the genre of the Gothic novel in Ireland, to be followed by Le Fanu and Bram Stoker. He was liked and respected, but he was every bit as eccentric as either Mangan or Le Fanu, perhaps even more so. His passion was dancing. He organised morning and afternoon dancing parties, keeping the shutters closed and the candles lit to keep out the daylight — a habit taken up later by his niece, Lady Wilde, for her parties at Merrion Square. It is ironic to read Mangan's description of Maturin walking along York Street in a treble-caped rug of an old garment, a boot on one foot and a shoe on the other, considering that Mangan assumed a style and a cloak in imitation of the older writer, and would certainly have been more disreputable-looking.

York Street leads to Aungier Street where used to stand St Peter's Church that Charles Maturin administered — another victim of redevelopment. The street has, however, a better claim to fame. Thomas Moore, Ireland's best-loved songster, was born at No. 12, which is now a pub. No. 12 was another of Dublin's lively and hospitable households, with supper parties and musical evenings presided over by Thomas's mother. When his friendship with the patriot Robert Emmett looked likely to lead him into dangerous ways, he was packed off to London at the end of his teens. His mother's musical evenings had served him well, because he soon became a favourite in the fashionable drawing-rooms of London. Lady Morgan commented that 'he was the guest of princes and the friend of peers.' He did not, however, lose touch with his background, and many of his songs were strongly patriotic, even if romantically so. 'The Harp that Once', 'The Minstrel

Boy', 'Let Erin Remember', were on everyone's lips in Ireland. He was feted as pop-stars are today; everywhere he travelled people lined the roads. On his last visit to Ireland, which was in 1852, he had his coach stop outside the old house on Aungier Street. 'I am looking,' he explained to his companion, George Petrie, 'for the little gable window by which I penned my earliest verses, the Melodies.'

Maybe it is carping to mention that many of the 'melodies' were adapted — without acknowledgement — from airs collected by the northern musician, Edward Bunting, from traditional sources. Better to remember the words of Lord Byron: 'Moore had a peculiarity of talent, or rather talents — poetry, music, voice, all his own; and an expression in each, which never was, and never will be, possessed by another.'

The narrow street opening almost directly across from Moore's birthplace leads to the inappropriately named Golden Lane, which extends from the Old Chinaman pub to the railings of Saint Patrick's

Charles Maturin

THE SHAW BIRTHPLACE 33 Synge Street

Aungier Street leads upwards via Wexford Street and Camden Street to the South Circular Road, meeting the latter at a portion named Harrington Street. Turn right into Harrington Street, and the first *left* leads to Shaw's house. (The fact that Synge Street crosses South Circular Road often causes confusion).

The house where George Bernard Shaw was born is No. 33, though it was No. 3 when the Shaws lived there. It is now a museum dedicated to the writer. The interior has been carefully furnished to reproduce the authentic claustrophobic atmosphere of his dismal childhood there. You find exactly what he describes himself: 'It had, in the basement, kitchen, servant's bedroom and pantry; on the *rez de chaussée*, parlour (diningroom), nursery and return room (my bedroom and my father's dressing room, over the pantry) and on the first (top) floor, drawingroom and best bedroom. My sisters slept in the nursery when we grew out of it.'

The tour of the house begins in the kitchen where, though the atmosphere was somewhat less cheerless to the young 'Sonny' than that upstairs, meals were 'stewed beef...badly cooked potatoes ... and much tea out of brown delft left to draw on the hob until it was pure tannin.'

Mother was a singer, and the only pleasure in the household was created by music. Shaw later declared that he owed what education he had to the Musical Society and the National Gallery. The family was rescued from the dingy respectability of the house in Synge Street by mother's music-teacher and patron, George John Vandaleur Lee, who transplanted them to a much finer house at No. 1 Hatch Street, close to St Stephen's Green South. 'The arrangement was economical, for we could not afford to live in a fashionable house and Lee could not afford to live in an unfashionable one' commented Shaw. Later Lee provided the house at Torca Hill in Dalkey, and later again a home for Mrs Shaw and her two daughters, *sans* husband and son, in London.

The Shaw Birthplace is open from May through September Mon to Sat 10 am to 5 pm, on Sundays and Bank Holidays 2pm to 6pm. Tel. 01-875 0854 (May-Sept), or 01-872 2077. Fax 01-872 2231.

Illustration by Robert Gibbings for Swift's Poems

Park. It is an area of apartment blocks and much rebuilding but in its day it had the distinction of being the birthplace of John Field, the child prodigy that the musical impresario Clementini paraded around Europe until they parted company acrimoniously in Russia. The inventor of the nocturne, which Chopin later made so much his own, lived a high old life of fame and dissipation in Moscow until his death in 1837. The house no longer exists, but a monument to the composer stands at the end of Golden Lane, on the left.

Bride Street, leading to Werburgh Street towards the right, crosses the end of Golden Lane. Mangan lived at No. 2 Bride Street for a while, in a derelict shell of a house where a hole in the wall served as door and window. John Field was baptised in Saint Werburgh's Church, near the end of that street, on 5 September 1782, as a plaque on the church announces. Christ Church Cathedral is just beyond, but let us leave that for the moment and give our attention to Saint Patrick's Cathedral.

Saint Patrick's is the locus of one of the great literary forces of Dublin or elsewhere — its dean, Jonathan Swift. In the history of Dublin, Swift is a giant figure. His satiric novels and his poems, his pamphlets and his charities, his loves, his rages have become the stuff of myth and folklore.

If you back-track along Golden Lane you come to Ship Street on the left. It runs down to the back gate of Dublin Castle, the Ship Street Gate, where a plaque announces, guardedly, that Jonathan Swift was 'reputedly' born at No. 7 Hoey's Court in 1667. Hoey's Court is demolished, but the plaque marks the spot. Swift's father was already dead when he was born, so he was brought up by a bunch of doting women, until an uncle insisted on sending him, at the tender age of six, to Kilkenny College. It could be that the shock of displacement accounts for the fact that neither there, nor at Trinity College which he entered eight years later, did he distinguish himself.

This was the youth that was to become the brooding Dean, the scourge of the Establishment, the cleric full of furious indignation. Contemptuous of his fellow countrymen, he nonetheless spent his energies in attacking England's policies in Ireland. He aligned himself with the poor and the dispossessed in a period of increasing hardship. He railed against corruption, pretension and hypocrisy in both countries. As the pamphleteer 'M. B. Drapier', he fought the circulation in Ireland of copper coins minted in England as a favour to the king's mistress. He proposed the eating of every fourth child of the poor to stop them being a burden on the state. He wrote a savage satire on the foolishness of man called *Gulliver's Travels* and saw it stupidly bowdlerized into a children's tale. And he wrote the tenderest, most moving, most delicate love-letters and poetry to two women who worshipped

Left: St Patrick's Cathedral

Marsh's Library

MARSH'S LIBRARY

Marsh's Library, immediately adjoining St Patrick's Cathedral, was founded in 1720, the first public library in Ireland. Entering it is suddenly to step into the past. The interior, with its dark oak bookcases and wired cages into which readers were locked, has been kept virtually unchanged since its foundation over three centuries ago. Some of the more valuable books are still chained to the wall. There are about 25,000 rare and wonderfully bound volumes, mainly of the sixteenth, seventeenth and early eighteenth centuries, and some important manuscripts. Swift made use of the library, and his own personal collection of books resides there now. In a fashion that would be deplored nowadays (may well have been then, for all we know) he copiously annotated the margins of some of them. The Library is open to the public on weekdays, except Tuesdays, from 10 am to 5 pm, though closed from 1 to 2 pm. The excellent curator, Ms Muriel MacCarthy, is usually on hand to guide or answer questions. Tel 4543511. The library's own bindery carries on the age-old craft of conservation of its precious collection.

Jonathan Swift (1667-1745)

him, 'Stella' (Esther Johnson) and 'Vanessa', Esther van Homrigh, who came from England to be near him.

In between his clerical duties and his writing, and his sharing of time with his two women, Swift was an obsessive gardener. He leased some land near the deanery, where the Meath Hospital now stands, to establish one. He called it Naboth's Vineyard and grew peaches and nectarines in that unlikely clime. He drove his friends too to gardening excesses, particularly the Delanys at Delville in Glasnevin (the house is gone) and the Achesons at Market Hill in Co. Armagh. But then, he was given to excesses in all things. The onset in his later years of Meniere's disease, which was not understood at the time, led to his being thought insane by everybody including himself. He lies within the Cathedral, 'where savage indignation can no longer lacerate his breast', at the west end of the nave. Close by, a bronze plaque marks the grave of Stella. Poor Vanessa, separated in death from her master, as in life, is buried in St Andrew's Church (in St Andrew's Street, close to the bottom of Grafton Street), which has recently suffered the indignity of becoming a Tourist Information Office.

Swift's last gesture to the country of his love/hatred was to leave his entire legacy for the foundation of St Patrick's Mental Hospital:

> He gave the little Wealth he had,
> To build a House for Fools and Mad:
> And shew'd by one satiric touch,
> No Nation wanted it so much ...

That fine institution is reached from here — it's a good twenty minutes' walk — via Patrick's Street, turning left into High Street,

SAMUEL LOVER 1797-1868

Amongst the plaques and monuments in St Patrick's is one dedicated to Samuel Lover. It describes him as:
'Poet, painter, novelist and composer, who, in the exercise of a genius as distinguished in its versatility as in its power, by his pen and pencil illustrated so happily the characteristics of the peasantry of his country that his name will ever be honourably identified with Ireland.'
Rather over-fulsome praise, surely, particularly in the company of the mighty Dean. He was, however, immensely popular in his time, despite the fact that his depiction of 'the characteristics of the peasantry' offended the more sensitive nationalist souls. He produced a ceaseless flow of novels, ballads, songs and paintings — he thought of himself as primarily an artist. *Handy Andy* and *Rory O'More* are the books best remembered. We can thank Lover also for the invention of the 'Irish Evenings,' that sometimes enjoyable but more often squirm-inducing form of entertainment.
'Lover and Lever' was a kind of humorous shorthand at their time for himself and Charles Lever, his contemporary and friend, a doctor turned writer, who moved in the world of London literary society and the expatriate English literary and artistic circles of La Spezia and Trieste. Like Lover, needing a wider readership than Ireland provided, Lever responded to the English demand for stage-Irish stories. The fact that these were frequently illustrated by the comic artist 'Phiz,' who had a pretty savage pen, gave them a sharper edge than their author intended. Thackeray was a great admirer of his, and dedicated to him his *Irish Sketch Book*. Lever was an inveterate traveller, and died in Trieste in 1872.

continuing along Cornmarket and Thomas Street to where James's Street, Bow Lane and Steevens Lane meet. The hospital is bounded by Bow Lane and Steevens Lane. Swift's will, plans for the buildings and such personal items as his watch and snuffbox are kept there. These items are not normally on view, but exceptions can sometimes be made for serious enquirers, who should write to the Secretary.

Before leaving the precincts of St Patrick's Cathedral, however, it is worth proceeding down the hill to the neighbouring cathedral, Christchurch. The explanation for two medieval cathedrals almost side by side is that Christchurch was within the city walls, while St Patrick's was just outside and therefore less subject to officialdom. Christchurch stands on the oldest part of the old city. Below the ridge on which it stands, the Black Pool which gave Dublin its name (dubhlinn, literally the black pool) was formed by the confluence of the Liffey and the Poddle. Around its feet the Viking origins of the original settlement have been uncovered, layers of overlapping centuries of building and living. A good picture of the Dublin that Swift was born into can be had from the multi-media re-creation of Dublin's formative period which is offered at the Synod Hall adjoining the cathedral. Though it relates primarily to the period up to 1540, Dublin was still very much a medieval city a century later, when Swift was born.

When Handel came to Dublin to present the first ever performance of *The Messiah,* the venue for the occasion was the Musick Hall which stood on the site now occupied by Kennan's ironworks on Fishamble Street. The date was 13 April 1742. The Dean had very reluctantly lent some of his choirboys and musicians for the occasion, but he vigorously denied he gave them licence to consort with 'fiddlers, pipers, trumpeters, drummers, drum-majors or in any sonal quality' at a club of fiddlers in Fishamble Street, or presume to sing and fiddle there 'at the instance of some obscure persons unknown.' He may have been alluding to Handel's concert, or he may have been confusing the rehearsals with activities at the hostelry called The Brazen Head on Bridge Street close by, which is still dispensing refreshment today. His illness and confusion was by then at an advanced stage, and his wits had almost deserted him.

The dean no doubt disapproved too of the famous Smock Alley Theatre, first opened in 1660. It was located close to Fishamble Street, on what is now Essex Street West, under the shadow of Christchurch. Its players included Peg Woffington, the Dublin street urchin who went on to take London by storm, and George Farquhar who was useless as an actor but turned out to be a brilliant playwright. It was regarded as a moral judgment on such goings-on when the gallery collapsed and killed many of the audience. But playgoing continued unabated. Crowe Street Theatre opened nearby under the same man-

Swift's Vanessa' — Hester van Homrigh, and below 'Stella' — Esther Johnson

POETRY IRELAND

The organisation Poetry Ireland Ltd publishes *Poetry Ireland Review*, a quarterly of new poetry, reviews and criticism. It also organises readings by Irish and visiting poets and acts as Irish partner, with the Tyrone Guthrie Centre, in the European Translation Network. Its extensive library is open to the public by arrangement.
Tel. 01-6714632, Fax 01-6714634.

THE GREAT BOOK OF IRELAND

The Great Book of Ireland is a kind of time-capsule reflecting and celebrating the wealth of contemporary Irish art, poetry and craftsmanship in the two decades, the 1980s and 90s. Its hand-made vellum pages have been inscribed and decorated by 140 of Ireland's fore-most poets, 120 painters and 9 compos-ers to create what has been described as the modern equivalent of the Book of Kells. Many of the pages are individu-ally priceless. Samuel Beckett has con-tributed his hand-written comment. Thomas Kinsella, John Montague, Seamus Heaney, Derek Mahon have written in some of their work. Painters Louis le Brocquy, Patrick Scott, Tony O'Malley, Imogen Stuart, have illumi-nated the pages.

The Great Book of Ireland is a joint venture between Poetry Ireland Ltd and Clashganna Mills Trust, an enabling or-ganisation for disabled people.

George Farquhar (1677-1707)
Richard Brinsley Sheridan (1751-1816)

agement. Audiences were what might be called participative. Manager Thomas Sheridan warned his customers to refrain from turning the place into a bear-garden and the stage and green-rooms into brothels. The audiences were responding to productions such as *The School for Scandal* and *The Rivals* by Thomas's son, Richard Brinsley Sheridan, and Goldsmith's *Good Natur'd Man* and *She Stoops to Conquer*, all very modern and up-to-the-minute.

The towers — 'bunkers' Dubliners call them — of the new Corpo-ration offices form an incongruous background to all this history.

Right: Richard Brinsley Sheridan
Below: Smock Abbey Theatre

Overleaf: Samuel Beckett

AND WHAT OF BECKETT?

Samuel Beckett, dramatist of the absurd and chief contemporary chronicler of the more or less daft, slipped on stage to the world in a house in Foxrock in the south Dublin suburbs. 'Cooldrinagh' it is called. The 63 bus from Fleet Street runs close to its quiet location at the junction of Brighton Road and Kerrymount Avenue. It is a pleasant, comfortable house, green-lawned about and scented with climbing verbena, and overlooking Leopardstown Racecourse — a house such as Moran in *Molloy* inhabits, or Mr Knott in *Watt*, but without the sinister bits of the latter. The date was Good Friday, 13 April 1906 (though his birth certificate records the date as 13 May).

He was educated at Royal Portora School in Enniskillen, Co Fermanagh, where Oscar Wilde had also spent a few terms, and later studied modern languages at Trinity College, Dublin. He lived for a while on the top floor of No. 6 Clare Street (opposite Greene's bookshop and close to Finn's Hotel where Nora Barnacle worked) while he taught at his old school. He left Ireland more or less permanently in the 1930s; after that, his infrequent visits were so stressful that he usually became ill — possibly because of his frayed relationship with his widowed mother. He wrote for the rest of his life in French, translating his work into English himself. He acted as unpaid secretary to James Joyce for a period and became involved, just a little, with Joyce's daughter Lucia. His service in the French underground during the war was awarded with the Croix de Guerre and with his wife Suzanne Dumesnil, a fellow member of the Maquis.

Like Joyce, Beckett carried Dublin into his self-imposed exile. But Beckett's Dublin and environs are usually hazy and insubstantial. They are always more surreal or tangential than Joyce's.

The image of Foxrock railway station emerges in *Watt* and *All That Fall*. Belacqua can be followed easily enough around Dublin's streets in *More Pricks than Kicks* and *Dream of Fair to Middling Women*. The characters admire the view from the Dublin mountains, after Belacqua has driven furiously to pick up his friend Ruby in Irishtown. Beckett felt drawn to tramps and cripples and lunatics: Mácmann, in *Malone Dies*, finds himself in St John o' God's in Stillorgan (it isn't far from Cooldrinagh) and Belacqua and Winnie in 'Fingal' stroll about Portrane Lunatic Asylum which is at a small seaside village near Malahide on the north Dublin coast, about ten miles (16 km) from the city. The Magdalen Mental Mercyseat, MMM, is Beckett's own invention.

The macabre climax to *Malone Dies* takes place when a boatload of lunatics is taken by a kindly lady for a trip to Dalkey Island from Coliemore Harbour. And on Dún Laoghaire's east pier, Beckett himself had the blinding revelation of the course of writing he would henceforth pursue. 'What he had recorded over years, he would now play back.'

The Irish locations in Beckett's work have been chronicled minutely by Eoin O'Brien in his magnificent illustrated book *The Beckett Country*. They grow more subtle and diffuse in the later writings: it seems pointless, for instance, to try to locate Estragon and Vladimir in the Dublin rather than any other lonely hills. The territory of the playwright's youth does hang around — 'a ghostly presence more profound than reality' according to one critic. But it seems a pity to impose too much literaliness on the surreal mindscape of a writer who deliberately retreats into greater and greater obscurity, until we have *Come and Go* in which the same action is repeated three times — in silence, and *Breath* in which one action takes place once, and again in reverse.

Someone asked Brendan Behan once if he understood Beckett, 'No,' he replied, 'I don't understand the sea but I love an auld swim.'

20. THE RIVER LIFFEY
Anna Livia Plurabelle

O
tell me all about
Anna Livia! I want to hear all
about Anna Livia. Well, you know Anna Livia? Yes, of course,
we all know Anna Livia. Tell me all. Tell me now.

There is one more journey to make. It is a pilgrimage following the
Liffey river from its source to the sea. For the purpose, we need the
Ordnance Survey half inch sheet No. 16. *The Book of the Liffey*, published
by Wolfhound Press in 1988, will make a good companion for the road.

No river anywhere has been so commemorated as the Liffey has
been by James Joyce in *Finnegans Wake*. The river is the idea and the
subject and the heroine of the best known chapter. The name Anna
Livia springs from the Irish *Abha an Liphe* — the river of Liphe, Liphe
being the plain between Dublin and the Curragh of Kildare through
which it flows before making its way to the sea. Joyce added the
'Plurabelle', making it, or her, 'the loveliest'. In the book Anna Livia is
the wife or lover of Finn: 'Was her banns never loosened in Adam and
Eve's or were him and her but captain spliced?' Two washerwomen
gossip at length about her ways and her doings, while she herself
dreams of her youth on the slopes of Kippure mountain. In the
contorted words and sentences we find all the landmarks of her course,
and the names of half the rivers of the world hidden beneath the flow
of language, like weeds or fishes below the surface of the flowing
water, half-seen, half-heard, half understood.

As we intend to follow her life's journey until she moves out at last
to meet her 'cold, mad feary father the sea', so we should be present
at her birth. The Liffey rises in the Dublin mountains. We passed the
place in the first chapter. From the village of Glencree, reached either
from the larger village of Enniskerry or over the Featherbed Mountain
from Rathfarnham in the Dublin suburbs, we proceed southwards more
deeply into the mountains, past the cottage at Lough Bray where J.M.
Synge so often rested, then steeply upwards to pass, one and a half
miles later, the gateway to the Kippure television mast on a bleak
but majestic plateau. Another half-mile and we reach what looks like

a small pile of boulders on each side of the road. It is easy to miss, so watch carefully. This uninspiring structure is Liffey Head Bridge. And since this, after all, is Ireland, you have of course your wellies in the boot. Don them, and follow the infant stream leftwards between the rushes and the heather, leaping over a mossy tussock or two, disturbing the odd frog. Maybe five hundred yards. Its womb is a deep black pool in the black heather-topped peat, appropriately counterpointing the Black Pool, the Dubh Linn, which is Dublin at the end of her journey.

Here we are just about ten miles from the sea. But perversely, the infant river Liffey turns her back to the sea, faces inland and sets out on a wandering 80-mile (128 km) journey through three counties before becoming the calm and stately river of Dublin, remembering perhaps the freedom of her spreading banks of old as she flows between the quays which now confine her old untidy sprawl.

But up here in the mountains 'she was just a young thin pale soft shy slim slip of a thing then, sauntering, by silvamoonlake' before the 'ages behind that when nullahs were nowhere, in county Wickenlow, garden of Erin, before she ever dreamt she'd lave Kilbride and go foaming under Horsepass bridge, with the great southwestern wind-storming her traces and the midland's grain-waster asarch for her track, to wend her ways byandby, robecca or worse, to spin and to grind, to swab and to thrash, for all her golden lifey in the barleyfields and pennylotts of Humphrey's fordofhurdlestown ...' — the latter being, of course, Dublin under its other name, Baile Átha Cliath, the ford of the hurdles. Other landmarks are here too. Wicklow is 'the Garden of Ireland', Kilbride is on the lower slopes of the mountains, Horsepass Bridge has been since Joyce's time submerged under Blessington lake, and we hear an echo too of Golden Falls beyond the lake, which we will come to later.

Anna Liffey is temperamental and moody. At times she is open and beguiling, but at other times she is shy and hides herself away so that it is difficult to follow her course closely all the way. But while she is still high among the 'meadowgrass and riverflags, the bulrush and waterweed, and of fallen griefs of weeping willow' it is easy to stay close to her by continuing westward and turning right at the crossroads that is called the Sally Gap, to Kilbride. These are some of her loveliest stretches. Continue past Kilbride until meeting the T-junction of the main road, and turn left for Blessington.

Here at Blessington Anna Livia is at her most generous and kind. At the behest of man, and helped by a couple of dams, she has spread herself benevolently to fill a valley with a wide and complex lake, to supply Dublin with sweet water to drink and with her great energy to send power to light its streets and homes. And incidentally to provide a great playground on and around which to play and sail and ski and wander and make love and sandcastles.

The main road continues past Blessington to Pollaphuca, the home of the Pooka, a fearsome monster who takes many shapes, its favourite being that of a frightful Black Horse who will toss the unwary traveller — particularly an inebriated one — on to his back and ride him to exhaustion. Here the river plunges down from the highlands of Wicklow towards the plains of Kildare, partly over the power station's Golden Falls, partly in the remains of an old cascade now difficult to observe beneath the road bridge.

Ballymore Eustace is where Liffey water is purified for the pleasure and to the satisfaction of Dubliners. It is also a pretty village, with a beautiful six-arched bridge. It is reached by a by-road a little way back on the Dublin side of Pollaphuca. The river is now flowing down into the plain of Kildare, where it hides frequently among private demesnes and between high walls, sometimes being contactable only at the occasional bridge where road and river meet briefly. But the journey is nonetheless a pleasure, because it goes along little winding roads and leafy lanes, through old country with little traffic.

Between here and Dublin there are many stately homes, some of them occasionally open to the public. Up a driveway such as one of these might Freddie Montgomery have gone to steal the painting and murder the maid, in Wexford-born John Banville's *The Book of Evidence*, portrait of an aimless and dissolute anti-hero attempting to find any reason for himself in a marvellously-written story which is a blend of farce and tragedy In *Birchwood* by the same author, the slow disintegration of such a house and its owning family are chillingly recounted. And in a similar 'Big House', now decayed, the sisters Imogen and Helen are exploited and betrayed by their German guest in Aidan Higgins' novel *Langrishe, Go Down*. A whole genre of Anglo-Irish novels share such a setting.

The road onward to Droichead Nua (Newbridge) will keep you fairly close to the river. From there, instead of following the main road to Naas, stay on the left bank of the river and depend on your map-work to bring you first to Victoria Bridge, then Caragh Bridge and then the remarkable Leinster Aqueduct, where the road and the Grand Canal together bridge the river, some 26 feet (8 metres) above its burbling ripples.

To the left (north) of Clane a wooded cluster hides the spires and mock battlements of Clongowes Wood College. In this Jesuit establishment the young James Joyce was enrolled, in the autumn of 1888, at the tender age of six years, and survived there, not too unhappily it seems, until the state of the family finances forced his father to withdraw him three years later. In one of its classrooms

He turned to the flyleaf of the geography and read what he had written there: himself, his name and where he was.

> Stephen Dedalus
> Class of Elements
> Clongowes Wood College
> Sallins
> County Kildare
> Ireland
> Europe
> The World
> The Universe

That was in his writing: and Fleming one night for a cod had written on the opposite page:

> Stephen Dedalus is my name,
> Ireland is my nation.
> Clongowes is my dwelling place
> And heaven my expectation.

He read the verses backwards but then they were not poetry.

There Stephen Dedalus (but not Joyce) got beaten for breaking his spectacles, and is vindicated when he appeals to higher authority. His fellow-students carried him on their shoulders and cheered. 'And they gave three groans for Baldyhead Dolan and three cheers for Conmee and they said he was the decentest rector that was ever in Clongowes.' The quiet peace Stephen experiences at the end of this incident brings us back to our watery theme. He was listening to the sounds of the cricket practice, 'and from here and from there through the quiet air the sound of the cricket bats: pick, pack, pock, puck: like drops of water in a fountain falling softly in the brimming bowl.'

And does the pick, pack, pock, puck, also sound like falling tears? They might well, for we are nearing Celbridge, and Celbridge Abbey, where Swift's Vanessa waited patiently for her master's hurried visits.

'I ever feared the tattle of this nasty town, and told you so, and that is the reason I said to you long ago that I would see you seldom while you were in Ireland,' he wrote impatiently in 1720. So different from an earlier letter: 'you are the only person on earth who has ever been loved, honoured, esteemed, adored by your friend.'

Esther van Homrigh, his 'Vanessa,' was the daughter of a rich Dutch merchant who became Lord Mayor of Dublin. After van Homrigh died, his wife took her four children to London, and it was here that the strange relationship began between Esther and the author of *Gulliver's Travels*, a man more than twice her age. He was aware of the disparity:

> Vanessa not in years a score
> Dreams of a gown of forty four,
> Imaginary charms can find
> In eyes with reading almost blind.

When Swift moved from London to Dublin to take up the Deanship of St. Patrick's they continued to correspond in loving terms: 'I was born with violent passions,' she wrote to him, 'which terminate all in one — that inexpressible passion I have for you.' Then Esther inherited the riverside house called Celbridge Abbey, and she moved to Ireland to be near him. She lived for his occasional secret visits. She built a bower near the water's edge where they could commune unobserved. But his attentions were by now divided. In Dublin there was 'Stella,' Esther Johnson, whom he had known since she was a child and who was his constant companion. There were rumours that they had been secretly married. Vanessa in a distracted fit of jealousy wrote to Stella and demanded to know the nature of her claim on the Dean. Stella apparently showed Swift the letter, whereupon he left the house, rode hard in a towering rage to Celbridge, flung the letter down in front of the hapless Vanessa and left without a word spoken.

Three weeks later, the woman to whom he once had written 'Believe me, if anything in the world is believable ... that all your desires will always be obeyed as commandments that would be impossible to violate,' was dead. Of a broken heart it was said. Anna Livia, in her endless cycle of renewal, would have observed it all. The Abbey, now St Raphael's School for boys with special needs, is owned by the Brothers of St John of God. They are happy to allow visitors, but ask that notice be given in advance.

At the other end of Celbridge rises the gateway to Castletown, the

Fresco in Dublin's City Hall — On behalf of the King of Cornwall, Tristan asks the Irish king (standing on right, his queen seated by him) for the hand of Iseult (on the left, with her maid).

finest noble house along the Liffey, and the largest in Ireland. No fewer than eighty windows look out from the front of the house. The grounds, by which the river flows, are open at all times; there is a small admission charge to the house

Through Leixlip now (the Danish Lax-hlaup, salmon leap) and Lucan, and for a while we have lost contact with our river, though it is not far away, just hidden. We are approaching the city and soon we meet a swirling complexity of new 'by-pass' roads. Try to steer a course through them to the village of Chapelizod, by the riverside.

Chapelizod: Seipeal Iseult — Iseult's, or Isolde's, Chapel. Tristan, a Norman knight, came over the water to ask for the hand of Isolde on behalf of King Mark of Cornwall. Tristan was young and handsome; Isolde was young and beautiful. Inevitably, and with the help of a love potion administered by Isolde's maid, they fall in love before he has brought her to Cornwall to the king. King Mark discovers them at a secret meeting: Tristan is mortally wounded, Isolde's heart breaks. As in all tragic love-stories, they are reunited in death.

The story gave Wagner his theme for a suitably dolorous opera, which had its first public performance in Munich in the year 1865. If the world had forgotten the story for all those hundreds of years, it had not been forgotten along the banks of the Liffey. For wasn't Isolde the daughter of King Aengus? And didn't Aengus's chapel-royal stand where the old Church of St Mary is now, in Palmerstown? And isn't part of the original sixth-century 'Chapel of Iseult' built into the fabric of St Laurence's, the present parish church of Chapelizod? And isn't a mound in Phoenix Park that the Magazine Fort was later built on, always known as Isolde's Fort, and a spring there also named after the princess, as was a tower near Capel Street Bridge in the city?

Another momentous event, in a more recent century, takes place in Chapelizod. One Saturday night, H.C. Earwicker, proprietor of the Mullingar House pub, retires. He dreams he is a wild Viking. He is also Tristan, Brian Ború, Finn McCool, Parnell — in fact he becomes Dublin, with his head forming the hill of Howth and his feet at Castleknock. And lying beside him Anna Livia Plurabelle, in her own dream, has now become a woman, mature and calm. 'Anna was, Livia is, Plurabelle's to be.' She has left behind the old wild ways when 'lyne aringarouma she pattered and swung and sidled, dribbling her bounder through narrowa mosses'. The gossiping washerwomen have grown old. The dusk is growing. Anna Livia goes 'home slowly now by own way' to the sea in Dublin Bay.

Sounds are getting fainter and fainter. 'Can't hear the waters of. The chittering waters of ... Night night! Tell me tale of stem or stone. Beside the rivering waters of, hitherandthithering waters of. Night!'

Opposite: James Joyce and family in Paris

CROSSING THE MILLENNIUM

A lot has happened in the field of Irish writing since this book was first published. Seamus Heaney received the Nobel Prize for Literature and, it seems, practically every other literary award including, for the second time, the Whitbread Book of the Year. This was for his translation, or re-working, of the eighth-century Anglo-Saxon epic *Beowulf*, an undertaking reminiscent of Thomas Kinsella's fine rendering of *The Táin* in 1969.

John Montague was elected to the first Ireland Chair of Poetry, a post he will occupy for three years at Queen's University Belfast, Trinity College Dublin and University College Dublin consecutively. Meanwhile, Paul Muldoon was honoured with appointment to the Chair of Poetry at Oxford.

New Irish plays have received glowing audience and critical acclaim in London and New York, new volumes of Irish poetry regularly fill booksellers' shelves, and first-time Irish novelists have been offered five-figure advances by enthusiastic publishers.

It is not the intention of this book to offer a survey of contemporary writing in Ireland. Apart from the volatility of reputations, younger writers have yet to become associated, among the general readership, with particular locations. This book is, after all, a tour of places rather than an appraisal of national literary output. There are, however, some literary events that have drawn so much international attention that they deserve a mention, and their 'place' associations merit inclusion in the appropriate tour route.

First, to Cork. The untimely death of Sean Dunne may not have attracted world-wide attention, but in Ireland it was felt with particular sadness. Dunne was not quite forty years of age when he died in 1995. He was born in Waterford, but most of his working life was spent in Cork, and it is with this city that he is mainly identified because of his years as Literary Editor of *The Cork Examiner* (now *The Examiner*). Dunne was a poet, writer and broadcaster. Apart from his own poetry collections, he edited *The Cork Anthology*, which he did not live to see published. He was also responsible for another anthology entitled *Poets of Munster*, a group amongst whom he is securely counted. 'The Road to Silence' told of his own spiritual quest.

Although in Dunne's time the great literary names associated with Cork, such as O'Connor, O'Faolain and Corkery, had already passed on, the literary tradition did not die with them. John Montague was inspiring young writers in Cork University and Thomas McCarthy (b. 1954 in Cappoquin) was working as librarian. Poets included Seán Ó Riordáin, Paul Durcan (living at that stage in Montenotte) and Patrick Galvin (whose off-beat poem, or incantation, 'I am the Mad Woman of Cork' has become almost a local anthem). There was David Marcus, the publisher of many of

Ireland's talented young poets and Theo Dorgan who became Director of *Poetry Ireland*, based in Dublin. Eiléan Ní Chuilleanáin named one of her poetry collections simply *Cork* after her native city. Water is a frequent theme of her work, perhaps as a result of the river channels above which Cork is built. Áine Miller is another Corkonian. Her poetry focuses on the quiet details of the domestic, although a hint of underlying menace is sometimes discernible.

Wexford, that Danish and Norman town with old narrow winding streets, is the unlikely home of an internationally respected Opera Season in the autumn. It was the birthplace (in 1949) of Billy Roche and is the location of his *Wexford Trilogy*. Roche could not get an Irish theatre to produce his play *A Handful of Stars* in the early 1990s. At the Bush Theatre in London, however, it got rave notices. The three dramas capture the very pulse of a small town: *A Handful of Stars* is set in a pool hall, *Poor Beast in the Rain* in a bookmaker's and the third, *Belfry*, is about an adulterous affair conducted mainly in the church. They were all familiar places to young Roche as he was growing up and helping out in his father's pub. *Tumbling Down* (Wolfhound Press, 1994) is Roche's humorous account of his teenage years in Wexford town.

Wexford is also the birthplace of John Banville (b.1945). Medieval Europe, rather than Wexford, is the setting for three of his most distinguished novels, those about the great thinkers, Copernicus, Kepler and Newton. Another, *The Book of Evidence*, is based on a real-life Irish murder drama, the denouement of which, in a posh apartment in Dublin, gave rise to what has since become a cant phrase in Ireland, GUBU i.e. grotesque, unbelievable, bizarre, unprecedented.

Just up the coast is Enniscorthy. It is here that Colm Tóibín, author and journalist, was born in 1955. Some of his books, including *Homage to Barcelona*, reflect his years teaching in Spain, but *The Heather Blazing* is set in his home territory of Enniscorthy and the adjoining coast. In this prize-winning novel, a retiring High Court Judge remembers his family's involvement in the Rising of 1798, and watches as the sea gradually eats away at the land. A very different landscape is evoked in *Walking Along the Border* (republished as *Bad Blood*). This is Tóibín's account of the weeks in the mid-1980s when he walked the whole stretch of that invisible yet intensely real division between people and place, the border between the Republic and Northern Ireland.

Limerick brings us to Frank McCourt and *Angela's Ashes*. This must have been the publishing phenomenon of the decade. The first edition swept up a plethora of awards and became a world-wide bestseller. There can be few people in the English-speaking world who have not heard by now, even without having read the book, of the grotesquely deprived childhood of Frank and his siblings in the Limerick of the 1930s and 1940s. The memoir has had such a powerful impact that one can now avail of tours of 'Frank McCourt's Limerick'. Much imagination is required for this tour of a Limerick that no longer exists. The awful Roden Lane is gone, or rather has been subsumed into a row of modern houses. What was Leamy's School on Hartstonge Street is now a Business Centre. On the same street is Osnam House, local headquarters of the St Vincent de Paul Society, still dispensing charity but with more sensitivity and compassion than remembered by Frank in *Angela's Ashes*.

In 1998, the novel *Four Letters of Love* brought Niall Williams much acclaim. Set in Galway and the Aran Islands, it is about passion and destiny and the transformative power of love. Niall was born in Dublin in 1958, but he eventually settled in the town of Kiltumper near Kilmihil, Co. Clare. He and his partner have written several books about adjusting to life on a farm in Clare after many years spent in New York.

London and Broadway were taken by storm during the 1990s by the bizarre and cruel tragi-comedies of young Martin McDonagh (b. 1971). In *The Beauty Queen of Leenane*, middle-aged Maureen is cheated of the opportunity of happiness by her manipulative mother. In *The Cripple of Inishmaan*, the orphaned and crippled Billy attempts to make a film career for himself in Hollywood during the filming of *Man of Aran*, but the film company prefers an able-bodied man who can act as a cripple over a cripple with no acting talent. Leenane is a tiny village situated in the heart of the Connemara mountains, and Inishmaan is the least accessible of the three Aran Islands lying off the coast of Galway Bay. They are the kind of remote rural locations that early twentieth century playwrights wrote about, but none of these older dramas were quite as savage or earthy as McDonagh's.

An intriguing Irish dimension has emerged relating to Graham Greene's novel *The End of the Affair*, of which Neil Jordan has made a well-received film. It seems that the wealthy woman in the real-life drama on which the story is based, Catherine Walston, rented a cottage at Dooagh on Achill Island in Co. Mayo. Greene stayed there several times, and regarded the times he spent with her there as among his happiest: 'I long to have you lazily stretched on an Achill sofa with a book and a pencil and interrupt you every 10 minutes with something I want to talk about and every 12 minutes [with how] I was in love'. Walston brought some of her other lovers there as well, to Greene's intense jealousy. The cottage is unlikely to have survived until now, as its destruction was the price of Planning Permission for the building of a new house on a nearby site.

Neil Jordan was born in Sligo in 1950, but moved to Dublin at an early age to live, as he likes to explain, just up the road from the home of Bram Stoker (of Dracula fame) in Clontarf. Before becoming a film director, he had already gained attention as a writer with a collection of short stories, entitled *Night in Tunisia*. Jordan's stories have nothing at all to do with Tunisia, but are mostly set in Laytown and the adjoining seaside resorts north of County Dublin. Neil Jordan also directed the film of Patrick McCabe's *The Butcher Boy*, the disturbing tale of a youth's disintegrating personality. McCabe's home town of Clones, Co. Monaghan, became the setting for the film.

Sebastian Barry (b.1955) is another playwright who has achieved notable success in recent years. He was born in Dublin but his maternal family background is in Sligo. Several of his plays have been based on the lives of near or distant relatives. *Our Lady of Sligo* concerns Joan, who pictures her mother Mai as Our Lady of Sorrows having lost her little boy. In *The Only True History of Lizzie Fin*, Lizzie talks about her singing father who travelled the roads of Kerry: 'He was the very singing soul of Corkaguiney'. *The Steward of Christendom*, with the late lamented Donal McCann in the leading role, was the most-talked-of drama of 1995 in Dublin and London. Barry's first book, *Time out of Mind & Strappado Square* (now out of print), was published in 1985 by Wolfhound Press.

The North, its border and its borderlands, have given rise to a flood of writing throughout the years of conflict, much of it opportunistic nonsense or ritualistic polemicising, but some of it psychologically powerful and emotionally searing. Apart from those included in earlier chapters, we can list, in terms of Drama alone, Robin Glendinning's *Donny Boy*, Jennifer Johnston's *Twinkletoes*, Marie Jones's *A Night in November*, *Hubert Murray's Widow* by Michael Harding, *Hard to Believe* by Conall Morrison, *Pentecost* by Stewart Parker and *At the Black Pig's Dyke* by Vincent Woods.

As to novels, among the finest are Bernard MacLaverty's *Cal*, which has been made into a successful film (as has *Lamb*, another of McLaverty's novels), *The Smoke King* by Maurice Leitch, *Ripley Bogle* by Robert MacLiam Wilson and *Burning Your Own* by Glenn Patterson. Most acclaimed has been *Reading in the Dark*, Seamus Deane's autobiographical novel of childhood and adolescence in Derry. Deane (b.1940) was editor of the monumental and controversial *Field Day Anthology of Irish Writing*, published in 1991 in three volumes.

Although I have mentioned several of the established poets in earlier chapters, there are others who should not escape our attention. Amongst these is Belfastman Padraic Fiacc (b. 1924), whose poetry expresses so much of the pain of the angry years, the even-handed Tom Paulin, and Paul Muldoon whose seriousness is tempered by wit. Maedbh McGuckian, a unique voice, should also be included. She describes her own poems as 'very intricate ... a weaving of patterns of ins and outs and contradictions, one thing playing off another'.

James Simmons has moved to the glorious location of Falcarragh, at the foot of Muckish mountain in the Donegal Gaeltacht, where he has established 'The Poets' House'. This is a residential centre for literary workshops, lectures and music festivals. The centre's facilities include a library and performance area, and, in good weather work can sometimes move outside, hedge-school style.

Near Oldcastle, Co. Meath, several 5,000-year-old passage tombs lie scattered over the slopes of Sliabh na Caillighe, the hill of the hag or witch. Here, at Loughcrew, is where poet Peter Fallon (b.1951), founder of The Gallery Press, lives and runs his sheep farm. It is here that he writes so beautifully of the history and myth of the landscape, and of the age-old rituals and routines of the seasons, in a kind of pastoral poetry which is reminiscent of an older time.

Marina Carr (b.1964) is one of the rising young playwrights. *The Mai*, the play which first brought her to our attention, is set at 'Owl Lake' which we can take to be Lough Owel, just north of Carr's native Tullamore.

Not surprisingly, Dublin has incubated the lion's share of writers over the past couple of decades. Maeve Binchy (b.1940) must be one of the most popular novelists in Europe or North America today. Her stories are set in middle-class Dublin or against the deceptively cosy backdrop of small provincial towns. She grew up in Dalkey and attended the Holy Child School there. She now shares her time between London and her home in Dalkey.

Dermot Bolger (b.1959), novelist, poet and publisher, is a native of Finglas, a Dublin suburb which features in several of his novels. His are not sentimental stories; the themes are often injustice and loss of innocence, determinedly set in his own territory. The voice of Maureen, who is a heroin addict in *One Last White Horse* is typical. She describes a community bonfire and sing-song on 'the scuttery estate in Balbriggan' and how the only songs they could sing along to were the jingles from the television advertisements.

Peter Sheridan (b. 1944), by contrast, celebrates the city of Dublin: 'If Dublin was a woman, I'd marry her'. He has spent most of his adult life writing, directing and collaborating in the theatre, often with his brother Jim. His recollections of growing up at 44 Seville Place (the book is simply named *44 a Dublin Memoir*) is vivid with characters, talk, argument, mischief, fun and ingenuity. If Frank McCourt had you weeping at his portrait of the Limerick of his youth, Sheridan and his Dublin will have you laughing all the way to the last page.

The above are just some of the talented writers in Ireland today. It would take an entire volume to outline the literary landscape of the past few decades. Ireland has changed more than any other western country over the past two decades in social, economic, structural and psychological terms. The old, familiar rural Ireland has almost disappeared, and with it the themes that have been central to Irish writing for many generations. Irish cities have gone through an extraordinary growth, which has brought new problems and new perspectives. The essentials of human nature remain the same, however. The old human passions of love, grief, joy, hope, death and longing remain central themes and will surely continue to be explored as long as writers .are writing.

FURTHER READING

As a general reference to the works of individual writers and to the background and contexts of Irish literature, I recommend two books by Dr Maurice Harmon: *Modern Irish Literature, 1800–1967* (in good libraries) which lists Irish short stories, novels, plays and poetry; and his *Select Bibliography for the Study of Anglo-Irish Literature and its Backgrounds - An Irish Studies Handbook* (more accessible than its title might suggest). The standard biographical and literary histories include Brady and Cleeve, *A Biographical Dictionary of Irish Writers*, and Robert Hogan, *Dictionary of Irish Literature*.

The titles listed below will provide some further reading, and include biographies and a personal selection of works by individual authors.

Allingham, William *A Diary* (Macmillan 1907)

Behan, Brendan *Borstal Boy* (Corgi 1961)

Bidwell, Bruce & Linda Heffer *The Joycean Way: A Topographical Guide to Dubliners and A Portrait* (Wolfhound Press 1982)

Bowen, Elizabeth *Bowen's Court* (Longmans Green 1942)

Butler, Marilyn *Maria Edgeworth: A Literary Biography* (Clarendon 1972)

Carleton, William *Traits and Stories of the Irish Peasantry* (W.F. Wakeman 1833)

Collis, Maurice *Somerville & Ross* (Faber & Faber 1968)

Colum, Padraic *The Poet's Circuit: Collected Poems of Ireland* (Dolmen 1981)

Comerford, R.V. *Charles J. Kickham: A* Biography (Wolfhound Press 1979)

Corkery, Daniel *The Hidden Ireland* (Gill and Macmillan)

Cross, Eric *The Tailor & Ansty* (Mercier Press 1970)

Curtayne Alice, *Francis Ledwidge: A Life of the Poet* (Martin Brian & O'Keefe 1972)

Delaney, Frank *James Joyce's Odyssey: A Guide to the Dublin of Ulysses* (Hodder & Stoughton 1981)

Dunne, Sean (ed) *The Cork Anthology* (Cork University Press 1993)

Edgeworth, Maria *Tour in Connemara and the Martins of Ballynahinch* (Constable 1950)

Fitzmaurice, George *The Plays of George Fitzmaurice*

Flanagan, Thomas *The Year of the French* (Macmillan 1979)

Flower, Robin *The Western Island* (Oxford 1944)

Friel, Brian *The Freedom of the City* (Faber 1974)

Friel, Brian *Translations*

Glendenning, Victoria *Elizabeth Bowen* (Weidenfeld & Nicholson 1977)

Greene, David H (ed) *An Anthology of Irish Literature, 2 Vols* (New York University Press 1954)

Gregory, Anne *Me and Nu - Childhood at Coole* (Colin Smythe 1970)

Griffin, Gerald *The Collegians*

Harmon, Maurice *Sean O'Faolain* (Constable, 1994)

Healy, Elizabeth *The Book of the Liffey: from source to the sea* (Wolfhound Press 1988)

Heaney, Seamus *Door Into the Dark* (Faber 1969)

Heaney, Seamus *Sweeney Astray* (Field Day 1983)

Hone, Joseph *The Moores of Moore Hall* (Jonathan Cape 1939)

Hyde, Douglas *Love Songs of Connacht* (IUP 1969)

Hyde, Douglas *Songs Ascribed to Raftery* (IUP 1973)

Igoe, Vivien *A Literary Guide to Dublin* (Methuen 1994)

Joyce, James *Dubliners* (Grafton 1977)

Kavanagh, P.J. *Voices in Ireland - A Traveller's Literary Companion* (John Murray 1994)

Kavanagh, Patrick *Collected Poems of Patrick Kavanagh* (McGibbon & Kee 1964)

Kavanagh, Patrick *Tarry Flynn* (Pilot 1948)

Keane, John B. *The Field* (Mercier Press)

Kickham, Charles J. *Knocknagow* (Duffy 1879)

Kiely, Benedict *Drink to the Bird*

Kiely, Benedict *Poor Scholar* (a study of Carleton)(Sheed & Ward 1948)

Kiely, Benedict *Yeats' Ireland - An Illustrated Anthology* (Aurum 1989)

Kinsella, Thomas (trans) *The Táin from the Irish Táin Bó Cuailnge* (Dolmen 1969)

Kinsella, Thomas *Another September* (Dolmen 1958)

Kinsella, Thomas (ed) *The New Oxford Book of Irish Verse* (1986)

Kirby, Sheelah *The Yeats Country* (Dolmen 1977)

Lady Gregory *Gods and Fighting Men* (Colin Smythe 1970)

Lady Gregory *Lady Gregory's Journals 1916–1930* (Macmillan 1946)

Lavin, Mary *Tales from Bective Bridge* (Michael Joseph 1946)

Lord Dunsany *The Curse of the Wise Woman* (Collins 1972)

Lynam, Shevawn *Humanity Dick* (Hamish Hamilton 1975)

MacConghail, Muiris (ed) *The Blaskets: A Kerry Island Library* (Country House 1988)

MacGahern, John *Amongst Women*

MacGill Patrick *Children of the Dead End* (Herbert Jenkins 1914)

MacMahon, Bryan *The Master* (Poolbeg Press)

Maxwell, W.H. *Wild Sports of the West*

McGarry, James *Place Names in the Writings of William Butler Yeats* (Colin Smythe 1976)

McGuinness, Frank *Carthaginians*

Merriman, Bryan *The Midnight Court*

Montague, John (ed) *The Faber Book of Irish Verse* (Faber & Faber 1974)

Montague, John *Selected Poems* (Dolmen 1982)

Montague, John *The Rough Field* (Dolmen 1972)

Moore, George *The Lake*

Moore, George *The Untilled Field* (Colin Smythe 1976)

Murphy, Richard *High Island* (Harper & Row 1974)

Murphy, Seamus *Stone Mad*

Nicholson, Robert *The Ulysses Guide: Tours Through Joyce's Dublin* (Methuen 1988)

O Criomthain, Tomas *The Islandman* (Oxford 1951)

O hEithir, Breandan *An Aran Reader* (Lilliput)

O Suilleabhain, Muiris *Twenty Years a-Growing* (Oxford 1953)

O'Brien, Eoin *Beckett Country* (Black Cat Press/Faber & Faber)

O'Brien, Flann *The Dalkey Archive*

O'Brien, Kate *My Ireland* (Batsford 1962)

O'Brien, Kate *Without my Cloak* (Virago 1986)

O'Casey, Sean *I Knock at the Door & Pictures in the Hallway. Vols I and II of 6. Autobiography of Sean O'Casey*

O'Conaire, Padraic *Short Stories of Padraic O'Conaire* (Poolbeg 1982)

O'Connor, Frank (trans) *Kings Lords and Commons: An Anthology from the Irish* (Gill & Macmillan 1970)

O'Connor, Frank *An Only Child. Autobiography, Vol 1 of 6* (Macmillan 1961 and Pan Paperback 1970)

O'Connor, Frank *My Father's Son. Vol 2* (Pan Paperbacks 1971)

O'Donnell, Peadar *There Will Be Another Day* (Dolmen 1963)

O'Donnell, Peadar *Islanders* (Mercier 1963)

O'Faolain, Sean *Vive Moi. Autobiography* (Little, Brown and Co 1961)

O'Flaherty, Liam *Short Stories of Liam O'Flaherty* (Digit Books 1961)

O'Flaherty, Liam *Thy Neighbour's Wife* (Wolfhound 1992)

O'Meara, John J (trans) *The Voyage of Saint Brendan translated from the Latin* (Dolmen 1978)

O'Tuama, Seán and Kinsella, Thomas *An Duanaire 1600–1900: Poems of the Dispossessed* (Dolmen 1981)

Price, Alan (ed) *Autobiography of J.M. Synge* (Dolmen 1965)

Robinson, Tim *Stones of Aran: Labyrinth* (Lilliput 1995)

Robinson, Tim *Stones of Aran: Pilgrimage* (Lilliput/Wolfhound Press 1988)

Ryan, John *Remembering How We Stood* (Lilliput 1993)

Sells, A. Lytton *Oliver Goldsmith – His Life and Works* (Allen & Unwin 1974)

Severin, Tim *The Brendan Voyage* (Hutchinston 1978)

Shaw, George Bernard *John Bull's Other Island* (Constable 1907)

Shaw, George Bernard *Sixteen Self Sketches* (Constable 1950)

Skelton, Robin *J.M. Synge and his World* (Thames and Hudson 1971)

Somerville & Ross, *Experiences of an Irish R.M.* (Everyman 1969)

St John Gogarty, Oliver *As I Was Going Down Sackville Street* (Sphere 1980)

Stephens, James *The Crock of Gold* (Gill and Macmillan 1980)

Swift, Jonathan *Journals to Stella* (Clarendon 1948)

Synge, J.M. *Collected Works of J.M. Synge* (Oxford 1962–68)

Synge, J.M. *In Wicklow, West Kerry and Connemara* (O'Brien Press 1980)

Synge, J.M. *Riders to the Sea*

Synge, J.M. *The Playboy of the Western World*

Thomson, David *Woodbrook*

Trevor, William *A Writer's Ireland: Landscape in Literature* (Thames & Hudson 1984)

Warner, Alan *William Allingham* (Bucknell University Press 1975)

Wilde, Sir William *Lough Corrib, its Shores and Islands* (Three Candles 1936)

Wyse Jackson, Robert *The Best of Swift* (Mercier 1967)

Yeats W.B. *Collected Poems of William Butler Yeats* (Macmillan 1950)

Yeats, W.B. *Collected Plays of William Butler Yeats* (Macmillan 1934)

ACKNOWLEDGEMENTS

The publishers are grateful to the following for permission to reproduce illustrations in this book: **Elizabeth Healy:** pages 11 (bottom), 13 (right), 16, 60, 66 (top), 87, 88, 95 (top), 103, 104, 111 (top), 136, 162, 164, 175 (top) / **The Irish Times:** pages 68 (bottom), 99 (bottom), 134 (top), 156, 208, 211, 213, 216, 223. / **The Ulster Museum:** pages 146 (bottom), 160. / **The National Gallery of Ireland:** page 247 (top and bottom). / **The National Library of Ireland:** page 102 (top). / **Paul Caponigro:** pages 148, 185, 188, 192 (bottom). / **The Arts Council of Northern Ireland:** pages 152, 153. / **Giselle Freund:** page 250, 257. / **Bord Failte:** pages 18, 21 (bottom right), 40, 46, 49, 52, 57 (top), 58, 62, 64, 71, 78, 79 (top), 80 (bottom), 83, 85, 92, 94 (top), 95 (bottom), 109, 123 (bottom), 130, 131, 174 (top), 184 (left), 186, 190, 234 (bottom right), 241 (bottom), 245 (top left). / **Jan de Fouw:** pages 21 (top), 206, 209, 210, 214, 217, 218 (top and bottom), 222, 226, 231 (middle and bottom), 232, 233, 236 (top and bottom), 237 (top and bottom), 239, 241 (top), 242, 243 (bottom), 244 (top), 245 (top right and bottom right), 251. / **The O'Brien Press:** pages 68 (top), 56 and 57 (from *The Voyage of St. Brendan*), 79 (bottom), 80 (top), 135, 141 (top). / **The Office of Public Works:** pages 14, 20, 84, 86, 119, 120, 126 (bottom left), 137, 169, 192 (top), 199. / **Head of the Department of Irish Folklore, University College, Dublin:** pages 53, 54. / **Seamus Cashman:** page 100 (top and bottom). / **Richard Murphy:** pages 27, 111 (bottom). / **J.M. Dent & Sons Ltd.:** pages 28, 33, 38, 108, 105 (bottom), 244 (bottom). / **The Linen Hall Library:** page 157. / **The Goldsmith Press/Brian Bourke:** page 195. / **The Abbey Theatre:** page 224 (bottom). / **Bryan MacMahon:** page 67 (courtesy of the author). / *Ireland of the Welcomes:* page 74 (top), 94 (bottom). / **University College, Galway:** page 96. / **Navan Fort Assoc:** page 159. / **The Bronte Homeland:** page 166. / **The British Library:** page 207. / **The Percy French Society:** page 184. / *The Crock of Gold* by James Stephens, Ilustrated by Thomas MacKenzie, Gill & Macmillan: page 240 (right). / *Film Ireland:* p. 219. / **Hugh Lane Gallery:** p.101 (bottom left). / **Wolfhound Press:** p 154 (top), 156, 220. / **Jeanette Dunne and Wolfhound Press:** page 101 (bottom right). / **The Sligo Library:** page 124. / **The Royal Irish Academy:** page140. / **Benedict Kiely:** pages 146 (top), 151, 194. / **Hulton Deutsch:** pages 34, 191. / **Anne and Michael Yeats:** p 37. / **Rank/British Film Institute:** pp 96, 98. (Stills from the film *Man of Aran* by courtesy of the Rank Organisation Plc.) / **Dervla Murphy:** p 29 (right). / **University College, Cork:** p 39. / **The Irish Academic Press:** p 91. / **Trinity College, Dublin:** pp 19, 23 (bottom). / **Harriet Sheehy:** p 25 (top and bottom), 26 (top). / **Shevawn Lynam:** page 87. (Picture presented by S.C. Hall, *The Times* parliamentary reporter, to Humanity Dick's daughter. In the possession of Ms Florence Martin of Canada, his direct descendant. From Shevawn Lynam's biography of him, *Humanity Dick*.) / **Jonathan Cape Ltd.:** pp 121, 122. / **Peter Harbison:** p 23 (top). / **Lawrence, Dublin, c.1900:** p 47. / **Sir Toby Coghill:** p 63. / **Michael K. Barron (photographer):** p 99. / *Image* Magazine: p 143. / **Dublin Corporation:** p 25.

For COLOUR ILLUSTRATIONS: **Bord Failte:** pages i (top left), ii (bottom), iii, v (top), xi (top), xiii (top and bottom), xv (top right), xvii (top), xxv, xxvi, xxvii (bottom), xxx (top right and left), xxxi (top). / **Jan de Fouw:** pages i (top right and bottom), ii (top left), vi (top left), vii, ix, x, xiv(top), xx (bottom), xxviii (bottom), xxxiv (bottom). / **Peter Zoller:** page iv. / **The National Art Gallery:** pages v (bottom), xvi. / **Slide File:** pages ixx, xxvii (top), xix, xxix, xxxi (bottom). / **Office of Public Works:** page xi (bottom). / **The Northern Ireland Tourist Board:** page xx (top), xxiii (top). / **The Ulster Museum:** page xxiv. / **By courtesy of Nicola Gordon Bowe:** page vii (top). / **Lady Dunraven/Photo Brian Lynch:** page vi (bottom). / **By W.B. Yeats, from the cover of *A Guide to Coole Park* by Colin Smythe:** page xii (top). / **Tom Kelly:** page xvii (bottom). / **Ron Langenus:** page xviii (top). / **Elizabeth Healy:** pages ii (top right), xv (top and bottom left, and bottom right), xxi (top and bottom), xxii (left), xxiii (bottom), xxviii (top), xxxii. / **Michael Diggin (photographer):** page viii (bottom pics).

TEXT CREDITS: The publishers have made every reasonable effort to contact the copyright holders of material reproduced in this book. I any involuntary infringement of copyright has occurred, sincere apologies are offered and the owners of such copyright are requested to contact the publishers. For permission to reproduce copyright material, we gratefully acknowledge the following:

Eavan Boland, 'The Gorgon Child', courtesy of the author; / Willian Trevor, from *Excursions in the Real World*, Hutchinson; / Eilis Dillon from her translation of *Caoineadh Airt Ui Laoghaire*, courtesy of Cormac O Cuilleanain; / Proinsias MacCana, from his translation of *The Voyage of Bran*, courtesy of Jonathan Williams; / John Hewitt, from 'Once Alien Here', 'The Colony', and 'Planter's Gothic', Blackstaff Press; / Paul Durcan, from *A Snail in my Prime: New and Selected Poems*, courtesy of Blackstaff Press, Harvill and Paul Durcan; / Brendan Kennelly quotations by permission of Bloodaxe Books Ltd, from *A Time for Voices* (Bloodaxe Books 1990), and *Cromwell* (Bloodaxe Books, 1987); / Bishop Wyse-Jackson, 'The traditional poets of the Maigue', courtesy of Lois Wyse-Jackson; / Derek Mahon quotations from *Poems 1962-1978* (Oxford University Press, 1979), Oxford University Press; / Patrick Kavanagh, from 'Stony Grey Soil', 'A Christmas Childhood', 'Shancoduff', 'Epic', 'Lines Written on a Seat on the Grand Canal', and his novel, courtesy of Peter Fallon; / Frank O'Connor, from *The Little Monasteries, An Only Child*, 'The Majesty of the Law', *My Father's Son Leinster, Munster & Connacht*, and his translation of the poetry of O Rathaille, Eoghan Rua, Brian Merriman, Raftery, and 'Cill Cais', Peters Fraser & Dunlop Group Ltd; / Gabriel Fitzmaurice, from *Homecoming* courtesy of the author; / Sean O'Casey, from *I Knock at the Door* Macmillan; / Padraic Colum, translation of Ferriter's 'O Woman shapely as the swan,' Macmillan; / Peadar O'Donnell, from *There Will Be Another Day* and *The Big Windows*, The O'Brien Press; / Kate O'Brien from *Without My Cloak*, Virago Press; / Theo Dorgan, from 'Nocturne For Blackpool', courtesy of Theo Dorgan; / Amanda M'Kittrick Ros from *Helen Huddleson*, Chatto & Windus; / Bryan MacMahon, courtesy of the author; / John Betjeman, from 'Ireland with Emily', *Collected Poems*, John Murray (Publishers) Ltd.; / Dervla Murphy, from *Full Tilt*, John Murray (Publishers) Ltd.; / Paula Meehan, from *The Man Who Was Marked By Winter*, The Gallery Press; / Oliver St John Gogarty, from *As I Was Going Down Sackville Street* and 'Others To Adorn', The O'Brien Press; / Tim Robinson, from *Stones of Aran: Pilgrimage*, The Lilliput Press; / John Ryan, from *Remembering How We Stood*, The Lilliput Press; / Molly Keane, from *Ireland: An Anthology*, edited by Molly Keane and Sally Phipps, HarperCollins; / Edna O'Brien, from *Mother Ireland*, and Evelyn Waugh, from *The Diaries of Evelyn Waugh*, edited by Michael Davie, Weidenfeld & Nicolson; / Mary Lavin, 'Brother Boniface' and 'Lilacs', Constable Publishers; / Richard Murphy quotations, Faber & Faber; / Louis Macneice, from 'Malediction', 'Thalassa', and 'Carrickfergus', Faber & Faber; / Seamus Heaney, from 'Belberg', *Lough Neagh Sequence*, 'Kinship', 'Sweeney Astray', and *Seeing Things*, Faber & Faber; / Robert Graves, 'The Song of Amergin', from *The White Goddess*, Faber & Faber; / Heinrich Boll, from *Irish Journal*, Martin Secker & Warburg Ltd.; / Nuala Ni Dhomhnaill, from 'Pharoah's Daughter' and 'Stronghold', The Gallery Press; / John Montague, from 'The Lure', 'Mount Eagle', 'Home Again', 'A Slow Dance', 'Herbert Street Revisited', *The Rough Field,* and his translations of 'The Hag of Beara', 'Pharoah's Daughter', and 'Stronghold', The Gallery Press; / Ciaran Carson, from 'Belfast Confetti', The Gallery Press; / Michael Hartnett, from his translation of Haicead's 'I will sew up my lips...', The Gallery Press; / Austin Clarke, from 'Pilgrimage' and *Twice Round the Black Church*, courtesy of Dardis Clarke; / Patrick MacGill, from *Children of the Dead End*, Caliban Books; / Susan and Thomas Cahill, from a *Literary Guide to Ireland*, Wolfhound Press; / Benedict Kiely quotation, courtesy of the author; / Douglas Hyde quotations, courtesy of Douglas Sealy; / Elizabeth Bowen extracts, Curtis Brown.

INDEX

COLOUR SECTION

ERRATA

Page 31, fourth line from end page, for 'Farrahy' read 'Farahy'; Page 32, last line, for 'Farrahy' read 'Farahy'; Page 56, picture caption, for 'A fifteenth-century illustration' read 'Based on a fifteenth-century illustration'; Page 57, second picture caption, for 'Wood cut' read 'Based on a woodcut'; Page 111, final para, last line, for 'Interpretive' read 'Interpretative'; Page 134, caption, the general election mentioned was in 1994; Page 212, para 3, line 3, for 'Telenachus' read 'Telemachus'; Page 222, final para, line 2 from end page, for 'Square' read 'Place'; Page 238, para 6, line 2, for 'Mespil' read 'Court'